D0852663

CONFIRMATION

ITS PLACE IN THE BAPTISMAL MYSTERY

By the same Author

THE COMMON LIFE
IN THE BODY OF CHRIST

★

THE FORM OF THE SERVANT

PART I

REVELATION AND THE MODERN WORLD

PART II

THE DOMINION OF CHRIST

PART III

in preparation

★

DACRE PRESS : A. AND C. BLACK

CONFIRMATION

ITS PLACE IN THE BAPTISMAL MYSTERY

BY

L. S. THORNTON, C.R.

D.D. CAMBRIDGE, HON. D.D. DURHAM

dacre press
westminster

FIRST PUBLISHED 1954

DACRE PRESS : A. AND C. BLACK LTD
4, 5 AND 6 SOHO SQUARE LONDON W.1

PRINTED IN GREAT BRITAIN BY ROBERT MACLEHOSE AND CO. LTD
THE UNIVERSITY PRESS GLASGOW

In piam memoriam

Gregory Dix, O.S.B.

PREFACE

This volume does not form part of the series entitled 'The form of the Servant', although I hope that it may be regarded as further illustrating the principles of biblical interpretation there adopted. In the course of the past century there has been amongst Anglicans a periodic discussion of matters connected with baptism and confirmation. During the second half of this period, however, a number of new factors have been contributing to the development of a fresh situation. Amongst these are the growing recognition that both Jewish and more ancient backgrounds are all-important and secondly the recovery of early liturgical texts amongst which *The Apostolic Tradition* of Hippolytus stands out. My own interest was first aroused by F. Gavin's small, but learned, book on *The Jewish antecedents of the Christian Sacraments* (1928), which shewed a close continuity between Jewish and Christian forms of initiation and which, in that respect, is still highly relevant. For example, it makes clear the strongly Jewish background of the Hippolytan rites, and even a substantial identity of rubrics.

Next came a series of contributions from the late Dom Gregory Dix which adopted a standpoint closely similar to that of Gavin, but which proceeded to conclusions generally felt to be decidedly startling. Dix's flair for stating fresh problems in an attractively independent fashion compelled one to give close attention to whatever he wrote, and perhaps all the more so because his assessment of evidence did not always prove to be convincing. My debt to him has been made clear in the text of the present work which, notwithstanding points of difference, I have ventured to dedicate to his memory in token of a warm friendship tragically interrupted by his lamented death. My debt to the English Benedictines of Nashdom Abbey has been increased by the timely loan of a volume presented to Dom Gregory by the author. I refer to *Bible et Liturgie* (Paris, 1951) by Père Jean Daniélou, S.J., Professor at the Catholic Institut of Paris. His work reflects the current interest in a close relation between liturgy and scripture. In that respect it has an obvious connexion with the contributions of Gavin and Dix as well as with the present volume.

In the treatise of Bishop Jeremy Taylor bearing a significant Greek title, which he also called *A Discourse of Confirmation*, the opening section defends 'the Divine, Original, Warranty, and Institution of the holy Rite of Confirmation' against a current opinion of some Roman theologians that confirmation was 'so unnecessary, that a little excuse may justify the omission and almost neglect of it'. It seems that in the seventeenth century 'English Jesuits' were for a time in agreement with this opinion. 'But the Theological Faculty of Paris have condemned their doctrine as temerarious, and savouring of heresy.'[1] It is, therefore, a peculiar pleasure that, over and above my debt to a Catholic professor in Paris already mentioned, I have been able in the appendix to the present volume to cite a paper by a learned Jesuit domiciled in England in support of positions taken up by me in defence of Jeremy Taylor's thesis. For the rest it is, perhaps, enough to say that, as the present work is primarily an inquiry into the teaching of Holy Scripture, a survey of Christian thought and practice outside the New Testament has been limited to what seemed necessary for the purpose of setting that teaching within sufficiently wide horizons.

All Saints' Day, 1953 L. S. THORNTON, C.R.

[1] Jeremy Taylor, *Collected Works* (London, 1839), vol. xi, p. 233.

CONTENTS

BOOK I. A survey of facts

Chapter VI. THE MEANING OF CONFIRMATION

PAGE

Note: Abbreviations are generally as in my previous works, two of which are, as in *The Dominion of Christ*, referred to respectively as *The Common Life* and *Revelation*.

BOOK I

A SURVEY OF FACTS

CHAPTER I

BIBLICAL IDIOMS AND BAPTISMAL RITES

I

'CHRISTIAN INITIATION' IS A SUBJECT UPON WHICH FRESH LIGHT CAN BE THROWN BY ATTENDING TO THE BIBLICAL WAY OF THINKING. IN SCRIPTURE, AS IN THE BODY OF CHRIST, ALL THE PARTS ARE VITALLY RELATED TO THE WHOLE. THE PATTERN OF REVEALED TRUTH SHEWN IN MANY PICTURE-IMAGES. YET ONE IMAGE SOMETIMES REPRESENTS THE WHOLE INCLUSIVELY.

In a previous volume I wrote: 'Organic revelation means, amongst other things, an organic unity between scripture and church tradition on the one hand, as it also involves on the other side a massive interconnexion of scripture itself with the whole world of facts contained in the ancient cultures. This far-reaching continuity of revelation . . . sends us back from the patristic theology to primitive Hebrew psychology.'[1] If revelation is organic in the sense here indicated it is obvious that the modern study of Hebrew psychology must have an important bearing upon the whole range of Christian faith and practice. In particular it may be expected to throw fresh light upon difficulties and obscurities which have proved intractable to more traditional methods of investigation. The topic of 'Christian initiation' is pre-eminently one to which the preceding remarks are relevant. For example, Anglican discussions of this subject during the past century have revealed marked differences of opinion cutting right across those more traditional diversities of opinion and practice which have characterized the *ecclesia Anglicana* in recent centuries.

[1] *Revelation*, p. 149.

In the opinion of the present writer the most recent phases of this debate show no signs of producing an adequate solution of the problems investigated. From the more narrowly ecclesiastical point of view the subject as a whole is highly controversial for reasons which are rooted in history. Yet it is precisely over such controversial questions that some approach to agreed conclusions can be hoped for only through a radical return to the form of revelation. With regard to that form something further must be said. The bible is not a collection of infallible oracles. It is, strictly speaking, a record embodying a historical revelation. This embodiment, however, is organic after a fashion which corresponds to the cumulative character of the revelation. It moves to a fulfilment in the Christ in such wise that divine truth shines through the pattern of the whole in its relation to the Christ. In such a revelation there must needs be development from less to more, and further a great variety of modes in which the parts are relevant to the whole as that whole is fulfilled in the Christ.

Yet all the parts *are* relevant in some sense and in some degree; and the manner in which this statement can be seen to be true becomes apparent when we pay attention to the exposition of a parallel theme in scripture itself. I have in mind here St Paul's explanations of the principles operating in the Body of Christ, and especially the description contained in 1 Corinthians 12. The analogy between the bible and the church thus indicated can be applied more fully when regarded from the point of view which characterized the biblical world of thought. Here one may fitly call to mind something previously written concerning the Hebrew way of thinking and concerning the difference made when that mode of thought was transformed in Christ.[1] In that Semitic thought-world the various parts of a whole are so co-ordinated that the whole is implicit in them. Yet the fulfilment in Christ introduced inevitably a new emphasis upon the one mystery to which the many parts now belong. Here we come upon the arresting topic of 'the One and the Many', a subject which has many ramifications, as I have sought to explain elsewhere.[2]

[1] *Revelation*, p. 153.

[2] See especially *op. cit.*, ch. v.

Our primary purpose in the present volume is to examine that theme in its bearing upon the mystery of Christian initiation, the latter being regarded as a complex whole embracing a plurality of parts. It is precisely in this respect that we may find occasion to develop more fully the analogy between scripture and the Body of Christ referred to in the preceding paragraph. If that analogy is accepted as a guiding principle it may be expected that both sides of the parallel will be correspondingly illuminated. At present, however, let us confine our attention to the literary forms of this essentially biblical phenomenon, and let us return to a point already emphasized, namely that all the parts of scripture are relevant to the pattern of the whole. If this dictum be understood in the organic sense already indicated important consequences must follow for the whole technique of biblical interpretation. In particular, methods of exegesis which seem to carry the implication that any one of the New Testament writers was more deeply inspired than the others will be viewed with the deepest suspicion.

For if the revelation is given in the pattern of the whole, then no single part, however important it may be, can possibly convey that whole in all its wealth and diversity. Such a part would indeed be representative of the whole according to its own proper measure, since the whole is implicit in every part.[1] That fact, however, could not justify us in treating one particular part as though it were the whole, or even in regarding it as the master-key to the whole. Moreover, there is another factor which must be taken into account. The New Testament was written by members of the Christian community; and recently there has been a growing recognition of the important part played by that community as a whole in the formation of its corpus of inspired writings. The four evangelists for example, were not primarily 'biographers' composing their works in a predominantly individual fashion. They could be regarded more accurately as *servants of a gospel* in which there is 'proclamation' of the faith by which the church lives. Moreover this proclamation (*kêrygma*), as St Paul's use of the word

[1] This theme was more fully developed in *Revelation*, especially in ch. viii, § ii.

shews, was essentially one with that of the other apostolic writers. The gospels, like the epistles, were in the first instance addressed to the worshipping community of believers, and in turn reflect back from that community the intense orientation of its multiform life.[1]

The principles of interpretation enunciated in the preceding paragraphs will, as the argument proceeds, be applied in detail to various aspects of the problem with which this work is occupied. Certain points of procedure, however, are already explicit in what has just been said. If we set aside the notion that there are degrees of inspiration in the New Testament some practical considerations follow at once. Where one biblical writer is preferred to another, on the ground that he is more likely to be right, a conclusion in favour of the one author against the other may unduly simplify the evidence. If, for example, two witnesses in a law-court appear to disagree about the facts, it may very well be that their apparent disagreement throws further light upon those same facts. 'Disagreement' may, indeed, turn out to be largely a matter of surface impressions, in which case diversities of standpoint or of nomenclature might well prove to be compatible with mutual corroboration. The application of these considerations to our present problem is sufficiently obvious.

As between the writings attributed respectively to St Paul, St Luke, and St John there are great diversities both of language and of standpoint. Moreover, it might with some justification be said that these diversities are at their maximum in the way in which these three writers severally handle topics bearing upon Christian initiation. In such a situation the diversities in question must be examined with complete impartiality and objectivity. A technique of the 'either . . . or' type which seeks to explain away or to discount one author's contribution in favour of another's is only too likely to have a blinding effect upon the whole investigation. In accordance with these suggestions I have recently indicated

[1] The reader is referred to R. H. Lightfoot's *The Gospel Message of St Mark* (O.U.P.), with his comments upon the earlier work of C. H. Dodd there cited (pp. 6 ff.).

grounds for dismissing a supposed conflict between St Paul and St John in respect of 'new birth' imagery.[1] In that particular instance it was found that the divergent modes of expression adopted by the two apostolic writers were in fact complementary, each representing one aspect of a complex piece of imagery running through Hebrew prophecy.

Sometimes, however, the 'either . . . or' technique which we are criticizing takes a rather different form. It may have reference, not to the reliability of the inspired writers, but to the customs or habits of the first Christians. These, again, may be exhibited either in external practices or in mental processes. Simplifications are attempted which suggest either (1) a strict uniformity of practice in the primitive Christian community or (2) severely logical discriminations in the thought-processes of the early Christians. Reasons will be given for concluding that neither of these assumptions is justifiable. An example of the former would be the supposition that the rite now called 'confirmation' was always administered *either* by laying-on of hands *or* by an anointing of the head, with the implication that either the one method or the other must have been universal. In fact, however, there is evidence for both practices; and a supposition that evidence for the one must contribute to the elimination of the other opens the way to a more radical conclusion which reduces the universal rite of initiation to baptism with water only.

The second type of assumption mentioned above may be not unconnected with the first; but it has a more radical character about which there is much to be said. It is natural that we should attribute to persons of the ancient world thought-processes which are habitual amongst ourselves. Nevertheless, to do so argues an attitude of mind which has not sufficiently realized how greatly mental habits can be altered in the course of centuries. Modern habits of thought are analytical, making distinctions which tend to separate sharply the things so distinguished. On the other hand, the ancient world to which scripture and Christian origins belong lived much nearer to the vivid associations of the concrete whole

[1] *The Dominion of Christ*, pp. 145 ff.

where likeness and contiguity easily melt into all-embracing unities. Accordingly the Hebrew mind did not move primarily along logical lines, at least in the sense in which we understand logic. The pillars upon which the biblical chain of thought rests are not abstract propositions but concrete images, one image suggesting another, sometimes through purely verbal associations. Here 'the pattern of the whole', that is the form under which revelation is given, can be considered from a fresh point of view. The unity of the whole is presented to us in scripture through a succession of picture-images. The Revelation of St John is a dramatic representation which is wholly composed of such images moving across the pages of apocalyptic history.

In such a world of image-thinking it is a serious mistake to suppose that logical distinctions are consistently observed; for where logic might emphasize difference the imagination may emphasize likeness or close association. It is in this world of pictorial representation that a whole is implicit in a co-ordination of parts. Such parts present themselves as images. How then can the whole be represented without passing beyond the orbit of the picture-world? Here the limitations of that world become apparent. For any one image can have only a limited reference. It represents, at best, one aspect of the whole. Two alternative courses are available. The whole might be represented as a complex of images. But this is not easy; in practice it would often mean passing by rapid transition from one image to another. The second alternative, often employed by biblical writers, is one in which the whole is referred to in terms of *one* of the parts. When this idiom is employed it carries a consequence which deserves our attention. *Language appropriate to one element in the whole is stretched so that it begins to possess a more inclusive meaning*. The image which properly represents one aspect of the whole acquires a more representative character. Something of this kind appears in the New Testament wherever our Lord is referred to under the imagery of a single Old Testament type such as Adam or the Messiah.

II

TO A COMPLEX WHOLE OF IMAGE-THINKING THERE MIGHT CORRESPOND A CONCRETE WHOLE OF INITIATORY RITES. THUS A COMPLEX OF RITES COULD BE DEFINED IN TERMS PROPER TO ONE ASPECT OF THE WHOLE. PAULINE EXAMPLES, HOWEVER, ALSO INCLUDE A CONTRARY TENDENCY, AS IN GALATIANS 4^6 WHERE TWO STAGES OF INITIATION ARE INDICATED.

What bearing have such Hebrew idioms of picture-thinking upon the biblical way of referring to the facts of Christian initiation? It was hinted just now that a mistaken assumption about thought-processes might have some connexion with a corresponding misapprehension about external practice. Let us endeavour to see what might be the nature of such a connexion. In the early stages of any living development distinctions have not yet had time to emerge into the light of day. In primitive thought-processes distinctions certainly exist; but the predominance of picture-thinking retards the canalization of psychical image-entities into hard-and-fast logical grooves. Similarly institutions have not at first been departmentalized; and so an all-inclusive institution like that of the ancient priest-kingship corresponded in practice to a wide variety of image-associations. In this way the psychological wholeness which we have been scrutinizing could have its counterpart in the sphere of religious cultus, as that in turn reflected and corresponded to the whole of life.[1] We can see here the possibility that a complex of ritual ceremonies would be envisaged as a concrete whole. Moreover the idioms of psychological wholeness which we have been considering would largely determine the way in which such a concrete whole was described.

A complex rite of initiation might be referred to in terms of any one of its parts; and if that occurred then, in accordance with what was said at the end of §1, language which originally represented one element of the whole might come to be regarded as normal for describing the entire complex. Something of this kind

[1] For a good illustration of this last point see J. Pedersen's account of the religious taboos imposed upon Hebrew military service (in *Israel III–IV*, pp. 1–32).

can actually be discerned in the apostolic writings in their manner of referring to the procedure by which sinners become Christians. An example of this may be quoted from St Paul. In Romans 13^{11} the apostle writes: 'Now is our salvation nearer than when we believed.' This sentence registers St Paul's expectation concerning a near approach of Christ's Second Advent. We are here concerned only with the final phrase. The word there rendered: 'we believed' is in the *aorist* tense and represents a definite moment in the past. This is an example of what is sometimes called the 'baptismal *aorist*', because the word points back to the moment of baptism. Why then does not St Paul say: 'when we were baptized?' The answer to this question must be twofold. In the first place, in early days adult baptism was the normal practice (as now in the mission field). The convert's profession of faith, therefore, was a vitally important factor. This may be seen in the actual method by which baptism came to be administered. The threefold submersion was interlaced with a threefold question and answer concerning the candidate's faith in the Trinity.

But secondly such a ceremony had two sides, faith and baptism. We might, therefore, have expected the apostle to write: 'When we believed and were baptized.' The context, however, is an exhortation to high Christian living. So the baptismal *aorist* is couched in terms of the faith of the neophytes confessed so dramatically at the moment of baptism. The solemn moment of their incorporation into Christ is defined in terms of a single aspect of the whole mystery. Now we know from this same epistle how much importance the apostle attached to the baptismal plunge beneath the waters, which was the other side of the event now under consideration. He could emphasize either aspect without fear of misapprehension. Accordingly the graphic symbolism unfolded in Romans 6 could be implied in the single word with which in 13^{11} he recalled the baptismal confession of faith. The whole was implicit in the part actually expressed. This illustration is particularly clear, because the faith of the candidates cannot possibly be supposed to be the whole meaning of the sacrament which they then received. This instance then should put us on our guard against supposing that an apostolic reference to Christian initiation is likely to be stated in terms which give expression to every aspect of the mystery.

In the preceding example a single image stands for the whole complex. In what follows we will first take note of a similar instance with a contrasted emphasis and then pass on to some Pauline expressions in which a different tendency can be discerned. In Romans 5^5 we read that 'the love of God has been poured out in our hearts through the Holy Spirit which was given to us'. Elsewhere I have given reasons for holding that the word rendered 'was given' is another example of the baptismal aorist.[1] In the rites of initiation the neophyte became a sharer in that gift of the Spirit with which the church was endowed on the first Whitsunday, the pentecostal reference being present in the word rendered 'has been poured out'.[2] It would be hazardous to suppose, without more ado, that the apostle was here thinking analytically of this or that part of the baptismal mystery. For him it was *one* mystery which could be adequately described in terms of a Spirit-gift corresponding to the original bestowal at Pentecost. In the New Testament a Christian is pre-eminently one who has received the Holy Spirit. Yet in the chapter of Romans which follows this great utterance baptism is more exactly described in language which makes no mention of the Holy Spirit at all!

Shall we then say that the gift of the Spirit mentioned in Romans 5^5 is pre-supposed in the exposition which occupies chapter 6? To that question we shall return presently. But first of all let us go back to some earlier utterances of the apostle. In Galatians 3^{2-5} he asks a series of questions:

> Did ye receive the Spirit from works of the law? Or from hearing of faith? . . .
> Having begun in the Spirit are ye now being perfected in the flesh? . . .
> He then who supplies to you the Spirit . . . is it from works of the law or from hearing of faith?

'Did ye receive?' is most probably a baptismal aorist. If so, the expression 'hearing of faith' must refer to the catechetical instruc-

[1] *The Common Life*, pp. 88 f. [2] *Op. cit.*, pp. 85–87.

tion which preceded the sacrament and which led up to the baptismal confession of faith. Here, then, the two preceding examples are brought together. The gift of the Spirit is the divine answer to the neophyte's profession of faith at the moment of baptism (a faith in which 'works of the law', as such, have no place). The next line of the quotation contains a familiar Hebraic contrast between 'flesh' and 'Spirit', that is, between human frailty and divine power. The new life had its origin, not in feeble human efforts, but in the power of the divine Spirit; and as it began so it continues. For the Christian lives by a continuous supply of the Spirit, which is bestowed in response to faith.

It is noteworthy that in the passage now under consideration the expression 'hearing of faith' is introduced twice. It is repeated in verse 5 (the third line of our quotation above), where the question, couched as it is in the present tense, seems to be referring, not to the occasion of baptism, but more generally to the Christian life wherein the continuous supply of the Spirit 'effects mighty works'. The statements which follow also support this view. For here (vv. 6, 7) 'They that are of faith', being justified like Abraham, are accounted to be his spiritual children. Thus both baptism and the baptized life are defined in terms of 'faith' by contrast with 'works of the law'. It is this which makes intelligible the otherwise startling statement that reception of the Spirit proceeds from the 'hearing of faith'. Once more the faith of the candidate for baptism stands for the whole mystery by which the Spirit is given. But also (in the second line of our quotation) the contrast between faith and works is restated in the form of a contrast between Spirit and flesh. The new life of the believer has a divine origin. 'The hearing of faith' can stand for the whole mystery because faith is the way of entrance into the supply of the Spirit. That supply, moreover, 'began' to be bestowed at the font, but is also continuously bestowed for a process of 'perfecting' (verse 3b).

In the preceding analysis 'the hearing of faith', representing as it does the whole baptismal mystery, was also seen in the conclusion to be a permanent attitude of the Christian life, as though the believer always remained in that 'beginning' where life originates by the creative power of the Holy Spirit. It begins to look as though the whole life in the Spirit were thus included within the event of the baptismal crisis. That would be one way in which parts are included in a whole. But St Paul does not always write in this strain. We may profitably contrast another statement of his in the same epistle. In Galatians 4^{6} we read

> Because ye are sons, God sent forth the Spirit of his Son into your hearts, crying, Abba, Father.

As I have dealt with this passage exhaustively elsewhere,[1] we will confine our attention to a single point. The text quoted clearly indicates two stages in our entry into the status of Christians. The first stage is indicated in the phrase: 'because ye are sons.' Our adoption as sons took effect when we were incorporated into Christ; and this was undoubtedly due to the agency of the Spirit in accordance with the passage previously examined (3^{2-5}). The second stage is described in these words: 'God *sent forth* the Spirit of his Son into your hearts'; and the English phrase which I have placed in italics is deserving of attention.

The Greek word rendered 'sent forth' occurs in an utterance of the risen Lord as recorded in Luke 24^{49}: 'Behold *I send forth* the promise of my Father upon you.' The implications of this language in its bearing upon our subject will have to be considered more fully at a later stage. For the present let us be content to notice two things: (1) The fulfilment of our Lord's words concerning 'the promise of the Father', as recorded in St Luke's second volume (Acts 2^{33}), may be thought to give a pentecostal association to the phrase employed by St Paul in Galatians 4^{6}.[2] (2) The double use of the expression 'sent forth' in Galatians $4^{4,\,6}$ makes a remarkable parallel of which we must take note. 'God sent forth his Son' refers to the Incarnation. We might, therefore, have ex-

[1] See *The Common Life*, pp. 116–126, especially p. 125.

[2] In Ps. 103 $(104)^{30}$ the same Greek word is employed in the phrase: 'Thou shalt send forth thy Spirit.' Cp. also Wisd. 9^{10}: 'Send wisdom', and Gen. $8^{10,\,12}$: 'he sent forth the dove.'

pected the corresponding phrase to refer directly to Pentecost. If we have rightly understood the associations the parallel between the Incarnation and the pentecostal outpouring of the Spirit is certainly implicit in this passage. The main emphasis, however, is not upon two stages in the history of revelation as a whole, but upon the manner in which the individual is taken up into those two stages. The peculiarity of the parallel lies in the fact that, whereas in verses 4 and 5 we advance *seriatim* from the fact of the Incarnation to its individual consequences, in verse 6 the corresponding pentecostal theme of the Spirit 'sent forth' is stated exclusively in terms of its individual effects.

We have now reached a point where the contrasts in apostolic thought can be regarded from a particular point of view, namely the connexion between the baptismal mystery and the bestowal of the Spirit at Pentecost. The phraseology of two Pauline passages might suggest that such a connexion is being made in both instances, yet with what look like two sharply opposite tendencies. In Romans 5^5 the phrase: 'has been poured out' with its pentecostal echo describes an effect which is referred back to the 'baptismal' gift of the Spirit. The baptismal mystery as a whole, with its effects, is regarded as a renewal of the pentecostal outpouring in the individual neophyte. In Galatians 4^6 on the other hand the phrase which recalls Pentecost is connected definitely with a second stage of initiation. 'Because ye *are* sons, God sent forth the Spirit of his Son into your hearts.' In this statement, notwithstanding its duality, there is the closest possible connexion between the two parts of the sentence. We are sons in the Son. The filial relation to God which is proper to our humanity was re-established through our incorporation into the incarnate Son of God; and this took place in our baptism. Our sonship was renewed in his Sonship, wherein we were originally created. By that act of new creation, however, we were now fitted for a further stage of renewal, the indispensable corollary of that first beginning. The Spirit of the Son is the proper complement of that new sonship to which we have been admitted.

Our sonship is moulded upon that of the Christ; and it is therefore a sharing in his messianic sonship. Moreover the Messiah is God's 'first-born' who like David was anointed with the Spirit (Psalm 89[20, 27], Isaiah 11[1, 2]). It was then by virtue of his own previous anointing with the Spirit that, in reference to a gift of the Spirit foreshadowed in prophecy, the risen Lord could say: 'Behold I send the promise of my Father upon you.' When we connect this saying with its fulfilment at Pentecost and again with the baptismal implementation as indicated in Galatians 4[6], we can begin to see the deep inward congruity of St Paul's words. The two stages of Christian initiation are referred back to a corresponding two-foldness in the gospel story which must, in due course, receive fuller investigation. Meanwhile we have reached a point where certain characteristic idioms of thought stand out. The apostolic descriptions thus far examined show two alternating tendencies. In the baptismal whole there is profound unity, and yet also plurality. The mystery can be presented in terms of some one of its parts or aspects; and yet this phenomenon by itself is not adequate to the fulness of truth.

III

CONTRASTS IN ST PAUL'S TREATMENT OF BAPTISM TO BE FURTHER ILLUSTRATED. I CORINTHIANS 12[13] SHOWS A COMPLEX OF IMAGES WHEREIN ARE DISCLOSED TWO DIFFERENT FUNCTIONS OF THE HOLY SPIRIT IN RELATION TO THE BODY OF THE NEW ADAM. THE SPIRIT FIRST ACTS UPON THE NEOPHYTE AND THEN ENTERS INTO HIM. THIS PATTERN FULLY DEVELOPED IN ROMANS 5–8.

It is a well-recognized fact that in the Pauline epistles the sacramental entry into the Christian life and its consequences are regarded from two points of view. Sometimes the change effected through baptism is described as something once for all completed in that sacrament. Sometimes, again, the change is regarded as a process, begun indeed at the baptismal font, but only gradually completed in the course of the Christian life. The writer oscillates between these two points of view because, although both are true, yet neither the one nor the other conveys the whole truth of the mystery. Such oscillation is characteristic of biblical thinking precisely because no one picture can convey the fulness of the given reality. In the preceding section we have been examining another example of this same class of phenomena. Not only can several different aspects of the Whole represent that whole successively in the apostle's thought, but also that whole can on different occasions be presented in two different relations to the sequence of time. In regard to this question of time-sequence the duality of Galatians 4^{6} has a certain measure of correspondence with the duality mentioned in the opening sentences of the present paragraph. The correspondence, however, is only partial inasmuch as the text in Galatians seems to be referring, not to the Christian life as a whole, but rather to a particular event following upon, and comparable to, the original event of baptism.

Of the Pauline texts so far surveyed two (Gal. 3^{2-5}, Rom. 5^{5}) speak of a baptismal reception of the Spirit as though it were the source from which the new life proceeds, whereas the second Galatian passage as clearly indicates a gift of the Spirit which follows upon the new Christian status and crowns it. We will examine next a passage from the First Epistle to the Corinthians which might be supposed to represent a point of view mediating between these two positions:

> For by one Spirit were we all baptized into one body. . . .
> And were all imbued with one Spirit
> (1 Cor. 12^{13}).

In this rendering the two verbs are taken to be baptismal aorists. Secondly, the word here rendered 'imbued' is used in the Septuagint most commonly for 'giving drink' either to men or to animals; but it sometimes means to moisten or saturate the ground. The latter image is implied in Moffat's 'new translation' of our text here followed. In its favour are the following facts: The word is twice used in this sense in the Greek version of the second creation-story (Genesis $2^{6, 10}$). Moreover there may well be another literary echo of that story in the Corinthian passage.

The phrase 'God *set*' (the members, etc. in the body), occurring twice in 1 Cor. $12^{18, 28}$ corresponds verbally to 'The Lord God *set* the man' (in the garden of Eden), occurring twice in Gen. $2^{8, 15}$. It looks as if St Paul is continuing the Adam typology already elaborated in the preceding chapter (11^{3-12}), to which he will also recur again in chapter 15.[1] If the apostle was thinking along these lines then the fashioning of Adam from many particles of dust would, for him, prefigure the act of new creation by which many members are united in the Body of Christ. The imagery of Genesis 2, however, does not seem to enter into the Corinthian passage until the last clause of verse 13 where the Spirit is likened to water binding together the many dust particles into a single plastic substance. The correspondence of this image to that of the bodily organism (verse 12) is not of course exact. The sole point in common is provided by the opening clause of verse 13. The Spirit is the unifying agency by which the many enter into the One. Even so, there is difficulty. For the literal meaning of that opening clause is that we were all 'dipped into one body', and 'dipping' does not fit the biological image. At this point, then, the author shifts his ground. The 'one body' is that of the new Adam fashioned from many moist particles of earth.

At first sight the change of imagery might seem to result in a simple example of Hebrew parallelism of the type called 'synonymous'.[2] If that were a satisfactory account of the matter the two lines of our quotation would be saying the same thing under two different figures of speech. Actually, however, such a conclusion would not cover all the facts. The difficulty which we encountered in the first line of our quotation was occasioned by the awkward circumstance that the apostle was here attempting to describe a sacramental event in terms of a biological image. If it were not for the fact that he has just identified the 'body' with 'the Christ' (verse 12) the language of verse 13 (apart from the last clause) would present a picture suggestive of the worshipping community. The writer is thinking of a baptismal service in which

[1] For fuller details of the creationist background in 1 Cor. see *Revelation*, pp. 135, 139–141, 160 f. and notes.

[2] For the various forms of Hebrew parallelism see Briggs' commentary on the Psalms in ICC, pp. xxxiv ff.

Jews and Greeks, slaves and free persons are all made to be one. But secondly this mysterious effect is represented as being brought about by the agency of the 'one Spirit'. To that agency various operations in the Church of God have been attributed in the preceding section (vv. 1–11); and this description concludes with an emphatic affirmation that the divine agent so acting is fully personal; 'one and the same Spirit dividing to every man severally as he will.'

It seems, then, that in 1 Corinthians 12[13] the Holy Spirit is thought of in two quite different ways. In the earlier statement the Spirit is a divine Person *acting upon and through the water of baptism* to bring about a certain result, namely the incorporation of a new member into the body of Christ. On the other hand, in the final clause of the verse the Spirit is *identified with water*. So far we have been content to think of that identification in terms of the imagery derived from Genesis 2. At this point, however, we must recognize the possibility of something like a double meaning. In saying that I am not suggesting a deliberate play upon words, but rather something which happens to be implicit in the actual language used. Of the Hebrew people it has been said: 'all things appear to them to live.'[1] Moreover, the various *strata* of creation from stones up to men are, by virtue of their creatureliness, very near together. The dry soil 'thirsts' like animals and men; and so men may be compared to dry particles of earth which drink in water like living beings. All of this, it appears, is reflected in the apostle's brief statement: 'we were all imbued with one Spirit.'

That statement, then, can be considered from two points of view: (1) If we stress the associations of the creation-story the redeemed community of the new creation is here envisaged as the body of the second Adam being moulded into shape by the hands of the Creator-artist. From this point of view there comes to light a further contrast between the two parts of our quotation. The incorporation of an individual into the body of Christ in

[1] For the saying and its implications see *Revelation*, p. 239 and notes. For what follows in the text above cp. *The Dominion of Christ*, p. 40.

baptism is an act which is completed once for all in a few moments of time. It is quite otherwise with the operation referred to in our second clause. The moulding of the new Adam-figure is a complex process which takes time. Moreover, we are concerned, here, not with the adding of a single new part to the whole, however mysterious that may be, but with a process whereby all the several parts are bound together into the unity of that whole. The imagery implies that the particles of earth are amenable to that process precisely because they have been drenched with that moisture which is the Spirit of God. It is only so that they become unifiable; and it is only by virtue of their retaining that spiritual moisture that they continue to be firmly united in the plastic substance of the whole.

In further development of the same point of view the distinctions which we have been considering may also be differentiated by reference to the image of body and members with which the passage as a whole is occupied. In the world of thought to which St Paul belonged the analogy between the individual (the body corporal) and the social organism (the body corporate) was strongly emphasized. In the present context, therefore, baptism bears a certain likeness to the formal admission of a new member to any voluntary society of persons. Such an event is normally followed by a process in which the new member is gradually assimilated to the social ethos which he has entered. The assimilation will be successful just so far as the individual in question proves to be adaptable to the process. In this illustration 'adaptability' will depend upon the natural disposition of the person concerned. In the Pauline context, to which we now return, the assimilation is possible because the neophyte has been 'imbued' with the Spirit, precisely in order that he may find his true place in the unity of the whole. Thus in 1 Corinthians 12[13] two distinct aspects of initiation seem to be envisaged, namely (*a*) inclusion in the body corporate by an act of the Holy Spirit, and (*b*) endowment with the Spirit for due assimilation to the distinctive life of the Christ-organism.

(2) The two aspects of initiation just mentioned will have to be

considered more fully as the argument of this book unfolds. Let us now turn to the second point of view from which we may regard the statement that 'we were all imbued with one Spirit'. In the biblical world of thought, we said, men may be compared to earth-particles which drink in water like living beings; and the word rendered 'imbued' in our translation means literally 'caused to drink'. The Spirit who acts as the divine agent in the rite of water-baptism is also able to enter into the newly-baptized neophyte as water enters into the body of a thirsty person. The latter relationship is clearly more intimate than the former. For the Spirit is now not simply *acting upon* our human nature, however wondrously; he is actually *entering into* the recesses of our personality. It is as though the new status of membership in Christ demanded completion in a more intimate relation with the divine Spirit by whom that new status was inaugurated. This interpretation of the Corinthian text has the advantage that it corresponds very closely to the earlier teaching of the apostle in Galatians, as described in the preceding section of this chapter. Moreover that teaching in Galatians is expanded more fully in Romans. We are now in a position, therefore, to trace a continuity of apostolic thought through three epistles.

We 'began with the Spirit' (Galatians 3^{4}); and by that new beginning we became the adopted children of God. So then, because by the Spirit's agency we had been granted this filial status 'God sent forth the Spirit of his Son into our hearts crying, Abba, Father' (4^{6}). Here again the initiatory act of the Spirit is implemented at a second stage by an entry of that same divine Person into the interior recesses of our being. The parallel with this comes out most clearly in the middle of Romans 8 where the repeated affirmation of the Spirit's indwelling ($8^{9, 11}$) is followed by a statement which completes the sequence traced in Galatians 4^{6}: 'Ye received the Spirit of adoption whereby we cry, Abba, Father' (8^{15}). The wealth of teaching about the Spirit in this chapter is in marked contrast with chapters 6 and 7 where the Holy Spirit is not mentioned. But perhaps there is an explanation In Romans 5–8 the earlier hints of a sequence have been brought into more systematic form.[1] Membership in the body of the new Adam effected by the Spirit (5^{5}–6^{11}) has set us free from the old order (6^{12}–8^{8}); and the indwelling Spirit will bring our adopted sonship to its fulfilment ($8^{9-\text{end}}$). Here, as before, an initiatory gift of the Spirit (5^{5}) inaugurates in us that identification with the Christ which is eventually consummated by the Spirit's indwelling. The pattern of thought corresponds broadly to what we have previously traced.

IV

A JOHANNINE PARALLEL TO THE DUALITY OF PAULINE INITIATION. THE TEACHING OF I JOHN 2^{20-27} REFLECTS BIBLICAL IDIOMS OF IDENTIFICATION. THE CHRISM WITH WHICH CHRISTIAN NEOPHYTES WERE ANOINTED IS IDENTIFIED WITH THE HOLY SPIRIT. AS SUCH IT IS A SAFEGUARD AGAINST HERESY, LINKING THE INTERIOR DIVINE INDWELLING WITH THE PUBLIC APOSTOLIC TRADITION. THE SCRIPTURAL ASSOCIATIONS OF BAPTISMAL ANOINTING AN ORTHODOX DEFENCE AGAINST FREE-LANCE PROGRESSIVIST ILLUMINISM.

In St John's Gospel there appears a sequence of images not unlike that which we have found in the Pauline epistles. Here also the symbolism of water is prominent, and its development deserves attention. John baptized with water only; but Jesus upon whom the Spirit descended is 'he who baptizes with Holy Spirit' (John 1^{33}).[2] The contrast between 'water' and 'Spirit' in this passage amounts to an antithesis comparable to that of the first 'beginning' when the Spirit supervened to bring order out of watery chaos. Yet when the Word incarnate had stood in the waters of earth, water and Spirit were conjoined in the baptismal

[1] In Galatians the hints of a sequence are fragmentary. Thus, in $2^{19\text{ ff.}}$ identification with Christ, crucified and risen, is followed by a first statement about the Spirit, just as in 4^{4-6} our participation in the incarnate Sonship is followed by the Spirit's indwelling. On the other hand in 5^{24} identity with Christ's sufferings is inserted into the theme of 'life in the Spirit'; moreover in between these fragments are sandwiched arguments which nullify 'the old order'.

[2] The preposition rendered 'with' could have various meanings. The parallel here implies that it is instrumental (cp. M), whereas in 1 Cor. 12^{13} the context suggests personal agency.

font; so that to be born of 'water and Spirit' is to be born 'of the Spirit' (John 3^{5-8}). In this passage, however, Spirit is associated with water, but not identified with it. In the Old Testament, as here in verse 8, the Holy Spirit is likened to wind and not infrequently identified with the divine breath in its creative function. But in the fourth gospel the creative inbreathing of Genesis 2^{7} is the exclusive function of the risen Lord (20^{22}). Nevertheless the divine breath is likened in scripture to 'an overflowing stream' (Isaiah 30^{28}).[1] Accordingly the verbal identification of wind and Spirit (John 3^{8}) might point to a further identification between water and Spirit, as elsewhere in scripture.

This duly occurs in the next chapter where, at the well of Sychar, the Spirit is clearly referred to in our Lord's words concerning a 'fountain' of 'living water' (4^{10-14}). The identification becomes explicit in the evangelist's comment at 7^{39}. Moreover the 'fountain' in 4^{14} may be an echo of the Greek phrase in Genesis 2^{6}. This Johannine sequence corresponds to that of the baptismal rites as known to us a century later. The Spirit, conjoined with water, first renews the whole man. Then, entering like water to the thirsty soul, the Spirit becomes a fountain of life within. Similarly, in Revelation 7^{14-17} those who 'washed their robes and whitened them in the blood of the Lamb' are afterwards led by him to slake their thirst at the fountain of waters. In what follows the Johannine sayings about the Paraclete will be linked up with a peculiar idiom of speech occurring in the first Johannine epistle. For at this initial stage of the argument we are occupied with no more than a preliminary survey of biblical thought-forms and modes of presentation. A further preliminary investigation will be undertaken in our second chapter; and we shall then be in a position to move forward into the development of our main thesis concerning Christian initiation.

So we pass on to a markedly different Johannine illustration, in which we are confronted with the familiar biblical practice of 'anointing'. In Acts 10^{38} St Peter tells Cornelius how, after John's baptism, 'God anointed Jesus of Nazareth with Holy Spirit and

[1] Cp. the 'moist whistling wind' of Dan. 3^{50}.

power.' This saying provides the necessary background to the 'chrism' doctrine of 1 John 2^{20-27}. The statement that 'Ye have a chrism (unction) from the Holy One' (2^{20}) points us back to the figure of him whom the Father anointed. For the title: 'Holy One' is a synonym for the Christ, as we see from the Johannine version of St. Peter's confession: 'Thou art the Holy One of God' (John 6^{69}). 'Christians' are those who receive the anointing from the Anointed One (*ho Christos*). As the Father anointed his Son, so the Son repeats the same act in his church through his chosen representative. The parallel continues. As the Spirit 'abode upon him' (John 1^{32}), so now 'the chrism which ye received from him abideth in you' (1 John 2^{27}). It is as though the Epistle were showing the sacramental fulfilment of the promise given in the Gospel. For as (in the Gospel) the Paraclete 'will teach you all things' (14^{26}) so the Epistle continues: 'his chrism teacheth you concerning all things.'

The 'chrism' here referred to is clearly a concrete object (as in the Greek version of Exodus 30^{25}). Moreover, in typical Hebrew fashion, this holy oil is personified and actually identified in function with the Holy Spirit. That would be all the more natural inasmuch as in the picture-language of the bible the Spirit is frequently represented as a fluid substance. But further, the identification in question exemplifies an idiom of thought which is characteristic of scripture. God is present in his words and acts, and again, by further extension, in the instruments of those words and acts. The first stage of this process is represented in the classic utterance of Isaiah 55^{11}:

> So shall my word be that goeth forth out of my mouth: it shall not return unto me void, but it shall accomplish that which I please, and it shall prosper in the thing whereto I sent it.

Here the word is an objective reality which is actively instrumental to the divine purpose, like the rain to which it is compared. Its objectivity is living and effectual. But further the word itself has its instruments, as we see in one of Zechariah's prophetic visions. The prophet saw a flying roll which embodied a divine curse, and so consumed the houses which it entered (Zechariah 5^{1-4}).

A similar instance occurs in the story of the sacred ark which fell into the hands of the Philistine army. The ark, embodying the divine presence, did not remain passive, but took vengeance upon its captors for their presumption. In the despairing cry of the Ekronites the deadly plague is attributed to the ark, and, in the narrator's comment, to 'the hand of God' (1 Sam. $5^{10, 11}$). Clearly the ark, like the flying roll, is an instrument of divine wrath. But further the ark, as seat of the divine presence, is identified with deity. It is regarded as God himself in action, just as in 1 John the chrism is identified with the Holy Spirit in action towards the neophyte. Here we need to bear in mind two other features of the biblical background: (1) All material objects are conceived to have a life of their own, which enables them to co-operate with the Creator.[1] (2) The assimilation of chrism to the Spirit is assisted by the fact that in biblical thought Spirit is never contrasted with matter as such, being itself conceived to be simply a higher, more ethereal kind of substance. When 'Spirit' is contrasted with 'flesh', the contrast is between divine power and creaturely weakness, as appears in Isaiah 31^3. This is quite a different conception from that of hellenistic dualism, and is still further removed from the modern, Cartesian, opposition between mind and matter.

It is also worth while to point out that 'chrism' appears to belong to that class of Greek words which might mean an action (in this case 'the act of anointing'). The concreteness of Hebrew thought, however, tended in some such instances to transfer the meaning to the object in which the action was embodied. A notable example of this is the word *paradosis* which originally meant 'an act of delivery', but which in the New Testament means 'that which is delivered', that is to say 'tradition'. Thus there is good reason for holding that the statements in 1 John $2^{20, 27}$ refer to the chrism with which Christians were anointed at the time of their baptism. We may, therefore, next ask why the author concentrates his remarks upon this particular ceremony rather than upon the administration of water-baptism. The con-

[1] On this see *Revelation*, p. 239 and notes.

text provides the answer to this question. The readers of the Epistle were confronted with a subtle heresy which claimed to be the true apostolic tradition. But the heretics were denying cardinal points of that tradition concerning the Incarnation and concerning the Christian way of life. In such circumstances those to whom the writer addresses himself needed guidance; and for this they were appropriately directed to two factors, both of which belonged to the form and order of their baptismal initiation.

In the first place they were reminded of the teaching given to them in their preparation for baptism. 'Let that which ye heard from the beginning abide in you' (verse 24). This is an appeal to the tradition of the church unto which (in Pauline phrase) they had been 'delivered up' or 'handed over' (Romans 6^{17}) when they were christened. But, secondly, they had something else even more intimately their own. They had received the Spirit and had been illuminated by his grace, as is indicated in a parallel passage by another apostolic writer (Hebrews 6^{4}). This illumination of the mind is, in the passage under examination, connected with the fact that, like their Lord and Saviour, they had been anointed with the Spirit. According to the most probable text of verse 20 the readers are told: 'Ye have a chrism from the Holy One; *ye all know*.' In the endowments of grace all Christians are on the same footing. They are all alike equipped by the Spirit's gifts to grasp the truth and to eschew error; for

> The chrism which ye received from him abideth in you,
> and ye have no need that anyone teach you;
> but as his chrism teacheth you concerning all things
> and is true and is no lie—even as it taught you,
> abide in him. (1 John 2^{27})

It will be noticed that this citation begins and ends with the familiar Johannine language about 'abiding'. Actually the word occurs no less than six times in five verses (24–28); and it is instructive to note the three distinct ways in which this peculiar terminology is used. In verse 24 two modes of abiding are linked together. The commentary on the Gospel is again in evidence. Jesus had said: 'If ye abide in my word, ye are truly my disciples'

(John 8[31]). So here, those in whom the apostolic teaching abides will themselves 'abide in the Son and in the Father'. But when error raises its head, how shall they hold fast to the tradition? The answer lies in their sacramental endowment with the Spirit. If need be, they can stand firm without a human teacher. For they have an indwelling of the Spirit. Our quotation above makes it clear that the chrism which they 'received' serves a double purpose. It is (*a*) their continuous teacher because (*b*) it abides in them. In both aspects it is identified with the Spirit, as surely as the ark in Philistia was identified with the hand of God. This third form of 'abiding' is clearly the link between the other two; that is to say, the 'abiding' of the chrism in anointed Christians is the means whereby the apostolic tradition 'abiding' in their minds is conducive to their continued 'abiding' in the Son and in the Father.

The indwelling of Christ's word in his people is mediated through the teaching office of the church. But the true discipleship promised in the Gospel (8[31]) comes to fulfilment through the divine indwelling which Jesus also promised. For the author of the Epistle this indwelling depends ultimately upon something more than teaching, however faithfully given. In the practice of the church as he knew it the Word was implemented through a sacramental act of anointing which gave individual illumination. Teaching may prepare the mind for the understanding of divine mysteries. But a fuller depth of enlightenment is reached only in and through a personal relationship with deity. It is this to which the author refers when he speaks of abiding 'in the Son and in the Father'. Moreover, in the tradition for which he stands this interior relationship became actual through sacramental rites when those whom he is addressing became Christians, and in particular through the rite of anointing. There are several further questions arising from his way of referring to 'chrism' which we shall hope to elucidate by stages in the course of this enquiry. But a preliminary statement here may serve to open up what I have in mind.

We have already noticed a parallel between what is said here about the chrism which 'teacheth you concerning all things' and again the promise in the Gospel with regard to the teaching of the Paraclete. But if we compare Epistle and Gospel more exactly we can detect another point of similarity between them. Whereas they both speak of an indwelling of Father and Son, neither document speaks *explicitly* of a personal indwelling by the Spirit. At the most this truth is obscurely hinted at in John 14^{17}, whereas the Epistle substitutes an indwelling of the chrism! What are we to make of this apparently deliberate silence which is in such obvious contrast to the usage of St Paul? In a matter of this sort there are too many unknown factors for explanations to be other than speculative. But with that proviso we may surmise that this Johannine peculiarity of language was decided, at least in part, by apologetic considerations. Both the Gospel and the Epistle were written in full view of incipient gnostic heresies; and if the heretics were claiming to possess the Spirit such a claim could not be rebutted directly.

Such a claim in heretical quarters, however, might lead the champion of orthodoxy to avoid using similar language. The author of the Epistle does, indeed, in one passage claim the witness of the Spirit to the reality of Christ's abiding 'in us' (3^{24}). But he proceeds at once to give a warning against spirits which are not of God, and to furnish his readers with objective tests of orthodoxy (4^{1-6}). Similarly he avoids altogether the language of spirit-possession. In place of this he seeks to draw out for his readers the implications of their sacramental initiation. One advantage of this method was that it would recall to their minds the vital link between their interior illumination and the authority of church tradition through which that illumination had originally been mediated. Moreover, there was another aspect of the mediatorial factor. The parallel between their anointing and that of the Christ would connect their spiritual illumination with the historical fact of the Incarnation in its scriptural setting. Here we return to our starting-point.[1] The anointing of the baptized signified their identification with the messianic mission of him who, after *his*

[1] See above, p. 21.

baptism, was anointed as King and Servant in fulfilment of prophecy.

With respect to this last point it is not difficult to see how the church, as represented in this epistle, was forearming herself against the withering blasts of heresy which were destined to assail the apostolic tradition in the following century. That attack had already begun with a theory which dissolved the incarnate Lord into two parts, implicitly denying that Jesus was the Christ of prophetic expectation, and separating the divine and the human into two, so that God and man were after all not united in a divine-human Saviour. At the next stage the false Christ was to be forcibly detached from the historical revelation to Israel; and eventually, in Montanism, the finality of the gospel revelation was to be repudiated. In this way, if heresy had won, the organic unity between scripture and church tradition would have been shattered and the way prepared for a free-lance progressivist illuminism unchecked by church or bible. The whole of this impending danger was crisply defined and judged by the author of 2 John. After recapitulating the relevant teaching of the former epistle he wrote: 'Everyone who *goeth forward* and doth not abide in the teaching of the Christ hath not God' (verse 9). For the progressivism of heresy the Johannine Epistles find an antidote in a return to 'that which was from the beginning'. Moreover, at the heart of that return is set no abstract metaphor concerning 'anointing', but the reminder of a ritual symbolism, scriptural in its origin, Christological in its significance, and divinely instrumental to a continuous spiritual endowment.

CHAPTER II

FOREGROUND AND BACKGROUND—JUSTIN MARTYR AND ST PAUL

I

SOME FACTORS RELEVANT TO THE CENTRAL PROBLEM OF THIS BOOK (i) JEWISH ADMISSION OF PROSELYTES AND THE *ORDER* OF CHRISTIAN INITIATION; (2) THE RELIGIOUS SIGNIFICANCE OF BODILY MARKINGS IN SCRIPTURE; (3) THE 'SEAL' IMAGERY AND ITS APPLICATION TO CIRCUMCISION. 'SEALING' SIGNIFIES THE COMPLETION OF A PROCESS. ST PAUL'S USE OF THIS IMAGE POINTS TO A RITE WHICH *FOLLOWS* BAPTISM.

In the course of modern investigations concerning the subject of Christian initiation a number of problems have emerged, each of which still awaits satisfactory solution. Of these the most fundamental is the problem as to how we ought to conceive the relation between baptism and confirmation in respect of their theological significance. This is the all-embracing topic with which we are primarily concerned in the present work. In dependence upon this central question, however, a number of ancillary questions have been raised at the present time; and in our approach to the major problem, these secondary issues cannot be ignored. For upon their correct solution will depend an adequate treatment of the more fundamental matters at issue in sacramental theology. It will be well, therefore, to open this chapter with an enumeration of some of the factors which will have to be taken into account. This is all the more necessary as we shall find at certain points some very close interconnexions between the various secondary problems which surround the principal issue.

(1) The first of the factors to be enumerated arises from the modern study of Jewish background to early Christian practices. Attention to the Jewish rites for receiving a Gentile proselyte has suggested a connexion between that procedure and early Christian

rites of initiation as practised in Syria. According to the Jewish custom which synchronized with the writing of the New Testament a male convert was first circumcised and then baptized. In the Christian Syrian rite of initiation there were two ceremonies in a corresponding order. Baptism in water came last; but circumcision was replaced by an act of anointing, oil being poured upon the neophyte's head by the bishop. In the New Testament we have a record of one notable incident which corresponds closely to this particular procedure. It is the story of a blind man whom our Lord healed of his blindness. First the Lord spat upon the ground and made clay which he applied to the man's eyes. Then he bade him go and wash in a pool with a significant name; and the man 'washed and came seeing' (John 9$^{6, 7}$). In the early liturgical practice of the Church this incident was connected with the preparation of candidates for baptism.[1]

It is obvious that the relevance of a connexion thus made between two different liturgical practices and a gospel story is open to dispute. Its justification would depend upon the elucidation of many pieces of evidence; and that, in turn, must await a more developed stage of the argument upon which we are now engaged. There are, however, certain points upon which immediate comment will be appropriate. First of all the relevance of Jewish background to early Christian liturgical practice is becoming increasingly recognized. But secondly, wherever this factor is present it has to be remembered that the new creation in Christ transforms the material upon which it works. In the present instance Jewish precedent may suggest a double rite of initiation in a certain order. Circumcision, however, has been abrogated in Christ; yet his title, 'the anointed One', furnishes a new symbolism for Christian *praxis*. So in a region where Jewish influence is strong, the Christian proselyte is first anointed and then washed. Further, when this parallel is coupled with the afore-mentioned gospel incident the background is correspondingly enlarged and deepened with far-reaching associations of biblical imagery.[2]

[1] For fuller details see *Revelation*, pp. 177–181 with notes.
[2] See last note.

(2) In the last two paragraphs we were concerned with the *order* of Jewish rites for the admission of a proselyte. This, however, is not the only aspect of circumcision which must be taken into account in the present context. For the practice in question falls within a class of customs wide-spread in ancient times whereby a living body, human or animal, was marked with a view to the indication of some specific status or relationship. Thus slaves and cattle were branded by their owners to show whose property they were; and a parallel custom obtained in religion. In the latter case a distinctive mark upon the body of a devotee was believed to place him under the protection of a particular deity.[1] Israel, indeed, was forbidden to make certain bodily markings which were associated with idolatrous practices.[2] But the notion in itself has important biblical applications which are highly relevant to our argument. In particular there are in Scripture three notable 'markings' of which we must take account. The first of these is, of course, circumcision. A second is the blood-mark which preserved Israelite houses from the destroying angel on the original paschal night in Egypt. A third is the mark placed, under divine direction, upon the foreheads of the faithful Israelites in Jerusalem that they might escape impending judgment (Ezekiel 9$^{4, 6}$).

(3) Of the three instances last mentioned the second falls outside the class of bodily markings, although in other respects it is closely parallel to the third. Of this we shall have to take account later. There is, however, another kind of mark placed upon inanimate objects which covers a very wide group of scriptural images. I refer to the 'seal'. The traditional language about 'the seal of the Spirit', which begins in certain Pauline phrases,[3] has its roots in at least two biblical images; and each of these in turn may have various applications. A seal may be used to attest a document, or again to secure the safety of valuables. A document may be sealed to give it validity or sealed up to keep it secret. The two uses, in fact, have something in common. In ancient times the royal seal gave authority to a proclamation, and it might also mark particu-

[1] A similar practice persists to this day, in India for example.

[2] Lev. 19^{28}, 21^{5}; Deut. 14^{1}.

[3] 2 Cor. 1^{22}; Eph. 1^{13}, 4^{30}.

lar objects as property of 'the Crown'. In both cases it transmitted the aura of majesty to that to which it was affixed. At this point we must take note of one particular application of the 'seal' imagery which brings it into connexion with the first of the 'three notable markings' referred to at the end of the last paragraph, namely circumcision.

In Romans 4^{11} St Paul refers to the circumcision of Abraham (Genesis 17) as a 'seal'. He has been recalling the fact that the patriarch 'believed God, and it was reckoned to him for righteousness'. The father of the faithful was, therefore, justified by faith because he embraced the promises of God. God's covenant with him was thus established upon a basis of faith; but it was afterwards confirmed by a formal, ceremonial act: 'He received the sign of circumcision, as a seal of the righteousness of the faith which he had in uncircumcision.' It is clear that the apostle is thinking in semi-legal terms. The covenant with Abraham was personal (like a contract). But its substance was simply a divine promise believed by a man; and a marking on the man's body was made to serve as evidence of the fact. In this way of speaking a symbolic cutting of human flesh is understood to have the significance of a seal attached to a document. Thus a parallel is made between two sorts of markings; and it is important to see what exactly is implied. We may put it this way: the relation of the circumcision-seal to the covenant-status of 'righteousness by faith', previously inaugurated, bears a certain analogy to the relation of a signature-seal to the substance of the document which it validates.

For reasons already indicated a biblical link between the Jewish rite of initiation and the Christian conception of 'sealing' a convert might have an important bearing upon our central problem. But at this point a preliminary question may be raised concerning the Christian relevance of that Jewish rite. Is not a depreciation of circumcision implied in St Paul's appeal to the fact that Abraham was justified by faith apart from circumcision? Yes, certainly. But let us recall a governing principle of interpretation already stated. The new creation transforms the significance of the old material upon which it works. How, then, does it do so? For an answer we may turn to the very next section of Romans ($5^{12 \text{ ff.}}$). Adam was 'a type of him that was to come', in part because he was in certain respects the very opposite of his antitype. Similarly, in the preceding chapter circumcision is indeed depreciated, but in such a way as to remind us that, although it is a symbol of all that we have left behind, it is also a type of what the apostle elsewhere calls the 'circumcision not made with hands' (Colossians 2^{11}). The seal of the old covenant proved to be of transitory significance by contrast with the substance of the document. Yet when that substance—'the righteousness of faith' fulfilled in Christ (Romans 10^{4-11})—was re-written by the Spirit of God upon human hearts it received a new 'seal of the Spirit' of which Jewish circumcision was a foreshadowing type.

A further problem now presents itself. Earlier in this section we considered the possibility of Jewish influence upon the *order* of Christian rites of initiation. The analogy of the seal, as handled in Romans 4, also implies a certain order of events. A document is first written and then sealed. So the covenant with Abraham was first made on a basis of justifying faith and then sealed in his flesh. In the following chapters of Romans justification by faith is closely connected with baptism; and this might suggest that the Christian seal of the Spirit *follows after baptism*. Such an interpretation would be entirely consistent with the teaching of Galatians 3^{23}–4^{7}. For there justification by faith is clearly synchronized with baptism (3^{24-27}), whereas the sending forth of the Spirit into our hearts follows afterwards (4^{6}). If this diagnosis is correct the teachings of Galatians and Romans corroborate one another along lines already indicated in Chapter I. Moreover, that again would imply that for St Paul and the Gentile churches the Jewish order of initiation was already reversed. In the first age of the Church, while the great transformation was still in process, considerable diversity of ritual practice may well have existed. At present we are content to recognize the evidences of such a change, leaving to a later stage in the argument the consideration of its causes and *rationale*.

There is one more aspect of 'seal' imagery in Romans of which it will be well to take account. This may conveniently be introduced by recalling the alternative form of the image as it appears at a later point of the epistle. In Romans 15[28] St Paul describes the completion of his mission to Jerusalem with the collection for the poor saints as 'having sealed up this fruit for them'. Here 'sealing' is simply a necessary precaution for securing valuable property. But the figure of speech as employed by the apostle serves to emphasize the conclusion of a process. For in the business of a fruit-farm the sealing up of the fruit in bags for despatch and sale was the last of a whole series of operations which began, may-be, as far back as the planting of the trees. In the documentary form of the seal-image which we were considering previously the nuance of *completion* is even more pronounced. For the sealing of a legal document, as here understood, is not merely the conclusion of a process. It is that which gives to the document its effective character. In this connexion there is one biblical passage which is particularly pertinent to the thought of St Paul. He might well have had in his mind the great scene where the covenant was renewed by Israel after the Exile.

In the ninth chapter of Nehemiah a solemn recital of the covenant history begins with its inauguration in the story of Abraham and ends with the renewed sealing of the covenant by the heads of the post-exilic community. As the covenant was originally sealed in the flesh of Abraham by circumcision, so its renewal was sealed once more in a written document. This line of thought was already present in the apostle's mind when he wrote a slightly earlier epistle, now known to us under the title: '2 Corinthians.' There he likened the Christian covenant to a writing upon human hearts in accordance with Jeremiah's prophecy.[1] If then we put together the teachings of the two epistles we may trace out the following series: The divine signature to the covenant was originally signed and sealed upon Abraham's flesh. The second edition of the covenant, under Moses, was written by the finger of God upon tables of stone (and its renewal

[1] 2 Cor. 3[3]; Jer. 31[33].

was sealed in a written document in a later age).[1] Finally the new covenant was once more written upon human flesh after a new fashion 'by the Spirit of the living God' in those who became Christians. The baptismal covenant was engraved in 'tables that are hearts of flesh'; and in every case this process also was 'sealed' with a gift of the Spirit.[2]

II

'THE CIRCUMCISION OF THE CHRIST' IN COLOSSIANS 2^{8-15}. LIGHT IS SHED UPON THIS STATEMENT IN ST JUSTIN'S *DIALOGUE WITH TRYPHO* WHICH CONNECTS THE BAPTISM OF JESUS IN JORDAN WITH THE 'SECOND CIRCUMCISION' IN JOSHUA 5^{2-12}. FOR EARLY CHRISTIAN TYPOLOGY THIS STORY WOULD FORESHADOW THREE STAGES OF CHRISTIAN INITIATION (BAPTISM, CHRISM, EUCHARIST) IN DETAILED CONTRAST WITH THE CORRESPONDING JEWISH ORDINANCES

In the writings of St Paul there is one passage in which the apostle refers to Christian initiation in language which might seem to suggest that what he is describing is to be regarded as nothing less than a new rite of circumcision. The passage in question is Colossians 2^{8-15}; and the deliberate use of language drawn from the Jewish rite is to be found in verse 11. Here, after a profoundly significant statement concerning the person of Christ and concerning his functions in the status of incarnate deity, the apostle proceeds to identify his readers with their Saviour in the following words:

> In whom also ye were circumcised with a circumcision not made with hands, in the putting off of the body of the flesh, in the circumcision of the Christ.

The clauses which follow repeat the teaching of Romans 6 concerning baptism, and culminate in a difficult statement about the Cross of Christ (verses 14, 15). In this obscure conclusion we shall hope to find a principal clue to the meaning of the passage as a

[1] Exod. 31^{18}. Neh. $9^{38 \text{ ff.}}$ According to Exod. 24^{7} the Mosaic covenant also was written in a book.

[2] 2 Cor. 3^{3}, 1^{22}.

whole. Nevertheless the elucidation will not be easy, and cannot be brief, for the simple reason that within the few sentences of this apostolic utterance there is compressed a whole pattern of biblical thought and tradition.

A most illuminating commentary upon the substance of what St Paul is here saying can be found in *The Dialogue with Trypho* written by St Justin Martyr, most probably about a century after the apostolic statement which we are now considering. Justin's treatment is illuminating because his interpretation of Old Testament types and prophecies has the effect of associating both our Lord's own baptism and ours with the entire scriptural theme of a new or 'second circumcision' of God's people. Thus he brings together baptism, circumcision and the sign of the cross precisely as St Paul does in our key passage from Colossians. In fact, if we follow his guidance we shall be able to trace a great part of the biblical pattern of images which in all probability lies behind St Paul's statement. There is, indeed, one important prophetic incident, of crucial importance for the interpretation of Colossians 2^{14} and of other New Testament passages, to which Justin does not, as might have been expected, explicitly refer. In the opinion of important authorities, however, it is implicit in the tradition which he is following; and this can be illustrated from rabbinical sources as well as from Justin's patristic successors.[1]

There would perhaps be general agreement to-day that continuity is to be sought between Christian baptismal rites and the descent of Jesus himself into the river Jordan to be baptized by John.[2] We have now, however, to trace a connexion between this

[1] The 'prophetic incident' referred to in the text is that of the *Tau* mark in Ezek. $9^{4, 6}$. The authorities cited above are: (1) J. C. T. Otto's edition of Justin's Works, Vol. II, p. 374, note 9: (2) A. Lukyn Williams' edition of *The Dialogue* in English (SPCK, 1930), p. 229, note 3; (3) *Greek in Jewish Palestine*, studies in the life and manners of Jewish Palestine in the II–IV centuries C. E. (New York, 1942), by Professor Saul Lieberman, of the Jewish Theological Seminary of America—Appendix on 'X and Θ' (pp. 185 ff.). To these authorities I owe a great debt. It is much to be hoped that Prof. Lieberman's book will pass into a 2nd edition.

[2] See, e.g., the valuable treatment of this subject in *The New Testament doctrine of Baptism* by W. F. Flemington (1948).

same event and the idea of a new circumcision. For this purpose a major clue is provided by Justin in *The Dialogue*, a clue, moreover, which could scarcely have become evident until the recent elucidation of the Jewish background had taken place. We may recall at this point the suggested analogy between the pre-baptismal unction of Syrian Christian initiates and the pre-baptismal circumcision of Jewish proselytes.[1] In Justin, however, there is clearly assumed to have taken place that reversal of order in Christian initiatory rites of which we have found traces in St Paul. As Jesus passed from the waters of Jordan to the descent of the Spirit,[2] so must it be for his disciples. In *The Dialogue* the connexion of a new circumcision with Jordan's waters emerges with the introduction of Joshua's story. Every Christian reader of the Septuagint knew Joshua, the conqueror of Canaan, under the Greek version of his name—Jesus;[3] and the story of Jesus-Joshua, the successor of Moses, would from the first be read as shewing how Jesus Christ, the all-sufficient successor of Moses, had become 'the mediator of a better covenant' (cp. Acts 7^{45}, Hebrews 7^{22}).

Justin is apparently the earliest Christian writer known to us who fastens upon the incident of the 'second circumcision' recorded in Joshua 5^{2-12} (*Dialogue*, chs. 12, 24, 113, 114), and gives it a new Christian meaning. Let us consider the details. The scriptural narrative explains that the older generation of Israelites had been circumcised in Egypt. But all these had died, save only Joshua and Caleb; and their children were as yet uncircumcised. These were 'the little ones' who, unlike their rebellious parents, were to inherit the land (Numbers 14^{31}). So immediately after the miraculous crossing of the Jordan Joshua was directed to make 'knives of flint, and circumcise the children of Israel again the second time'; and Joshua did so. As we now know, this circumcision of an entire

[1] See above, § i, par. 2.

[2] The united testimony of the first three gospels on this point stands unshaken by a recent attempt to divide them. See further below, ch. IV, § ii, last par. but one, and the Appendix.

[3] In Hebrews 4^{8} he is referred to as the 'Jesus' who fell short of his antitype in failing to give permanent rest to Israel. Cp. the contrast between the two Adams in St Paul, and see above § i, par. 7.

army before entering upon a war of conquest was a solemn religious act comparable with all the other religious taboos which surrounded the military organism and preserved its sanctity.[1] It is not difficult, then, to see how the story would look when read through Christian eyes. 'The little ones' who were embarking upon this crusade were types of new-born Christians, as I have elsewhere shewn.[2]

So first they passed through Jordan with 'Jesus' leading the way, and then they were circumcised by 'Jesus'. In this fashion they entered the land 'flowing with milk and honey' (verse 6). It would seem that in Justin's time the attention given to this Hebrew story was already providing a biblical background for the liturgical custom of feeding 'milk and honey' to Christian initiates at their first communion. Next, according to the Septuagint, 'they had rest, sitting there in the camp until they became whole' (verse 8). The language used would carry on the suggestion. For the final verb is used by St Luke twice to indicate the 'wholeness' which the Good Physician brought (Luke 5^{31}, 7^{10}). Moreover, the word which I have rendered 'rest' is a synonym for the messianic 'peace' promised to David for Solomon (1 Chronicles 22^{9}; cp. 4^{40}). Thus we get a glimpse of the Christian neophytes, who had passed through Jordan's waters in baptism, and who had received from the bishop the seal of the new circumcision upon their foreheads and the kiss of peace, taking their places in the congregation of the new Israel, where, cured of sin's sickness, they entered upon the way of health and wholeness in which salvation consists. In this description we have partly anticipated the direction which the argument will take; but before going further we must pay attention to some implications of the story as seen through Christian eyes.[3]

[1] Cp. again the section of Pedersen's book referred to above, ch. I, § ii, par. 1, note.

[2] See *The Apostolic Ministry*, notes on pp. 56 and 59 f., and *The Dominion of Christ*, ch. III.

[3] In the above account I have assumed that Justin's text of Joshua 5^{4-6} stood nearer to the Hebrew than to the text of LXX as printed by Swete; and that on the ground of Justin's own statement in *Dial.*, ch. 113, that Joshua, 'the only one

In the text of Joshua the next verse (9) is important: 'The Lord said unto Joshua, This day have I rolled away the reproach of Egypt from off you.' If we follow the Hebrew text (for which see the last note), this must refer to the fact that the circumcision of the rebels who died in the wilderness had taken place in Egypt, 'the house of bondage', whereas the new circumcision was that of free men entering the promised land. There was also a difference of order. For *after* circumcision in Egypt Israel passed through the Red sea; and this event was in Christian eyes Israel's baptism (1 Corinthians 10[1, 2]).[1] Finally there would be a third and culminating point in the analogy with its contrasts. The passage of the Red sea led to Sinai, 'which corresponds to Jerusalem which now is, for she is in bondage with her children' (Galatians 4[25]). Circumcision followed by baptism led the Jewish proselyte to nothing but the cult-privileges of the Mosaic Law. By contrast with this the story of Joshua-Jesus tells how the newly circumcised host of Israel 'kept the passover' (verse 10); and in the new Israel the paschal liturgy of Easter followed upon the admission of new members to the Church. Moreover the eucharistic reference might be carried further. For 'the manna ceased on the morrow'. Wilderness food was replaced by corn-bread proper to the land of promise (verses 11, 12).

The typology, however, gains in significance if in Justin's time the new circumcision of the Spirit followed upon the baptism of water, as we have been assuming. *The Dialogue* contains evidence that this was actually the case. In chapter 18 he quotes the words of Isaiah 1[16]: 'Wash therefore, and now become clean ...' and continues: 'God bids you to wash yourselves with this laver and to be

of his contemporaries who had come forth from Egypt, led the people that survived into the Holy Land' (as rendered in E.T. by Lukyn Williams). Caleb is ignored; but otherwise this agrees closely with H against the confused statement of LXX. See also the Introduction by Lukyn Williams, p. xxxiv, with ref. to Swete's *Introduction to the O.T. in Greek*.

[1] I do not accept the argument that 'the cloud' before 'the sea' indicates 'confirmation' before 'baptism'. For the cloud could signify the activity of the Spirit in baptism. Moreover St Paul is not giving an exact parallel to Christian sacraments, but rather a general warning on the misuse of sacramental privileges.

circumcised with the true circumcision.' In chapter 19 he repeats the injunction, perhaps even more significantly. For he first repudiates Jewish circumcision and baptism *in that order*, referring to the latter in terms of Jeremiah's broken cisterns (Jer. 2^{13}); and by contrast upholds in turn 'this baptism of ours, which belongs to life' and then 'our circumcision'. Thus he refers, in the second passage, to the two rites of Christian initiation *in the same order as in chapter* 18 by contrast with the reverse order used in reference to the Jewish ordinances. It is also worthy of notice that in this second statement he refers to the ordinances of the two religions in such a way as to make it impossible to suppose that he is identifying 'the true circumcision' with Christian baptism. For he makes a precise contrast, first between the two baptisms and then between the two other rites: 'You indeed, who are circumcised in your flesh have need of our circumcision, but we possessing this have no need of that.'

The points made in the last paragraph arise out of Justin's controversial method in dealing with Jews. There is much more of the same sort in the *Dialogue* which throws light upon current Christian presuppositions concerning the rites of initiation. For example, if we work through chapters 11 to 29 we find the following: Justin twice treats of circumcision by itself in the context of a general contrast between the two covenants; and in each case this leads to a pronouncement concerning the necessity and superiority of the 'second circumcision' (chapters 12, 24). But in 13–16 we have an earlier version of the argument which we have just traced out in 18 and 19. Here also the contrast between the two circumcisions (12) leads to Isaiah's laver which points to Christian baptism in contrast to 'broken cisterns' (an earlier reference to Jeremiah 2^{13}), and eventually to the true completion of baptism which he now defines as a 'circumcision of the heart' with an extended quotation from Deuteronomy $10^{16\,f.}$ Here once more the Christian rites of initiation are placed in their final order, whereas in 29 he repudiates the Jewish rites in that order in which proselytes received them, namely first circumcision and then baptism.[1]

[1] The analogy and contrast between Jewish and Christian stages of initiation has been defined above from the Christian point of view. In a rabbinic analogy

III

JUSTIN CONNECTS THE JOSHUA TYPOLOGY WITH 'CIRCUMCISION OF THE HEART' AND SUGGESTS PROPHETIC PARALLELS WITH ST PAUL. TWO DISTINCT FORMS OF INITIATION IN JOSHUA AND IN EZEKIEL ARE PARALLELED IN JUSTIN. THIS YIELDS A FOUR-FOLD SCHEME OF CHRISTIAN INITIATION, IN JUSTIN AS IN TERTULLIAN, IN WHICH THE 'NEW CIRCUMCISION' IS REPRESENTED BY AN ANOINTING OF THE NEOPHYTE'S HEAD WITH OIL AFTER BAPTISM.

In the course of his argument Justin connects Joshua's 'second circumcision' with other parts of scripture. Thus, in his final and most detailed treatment of the Joshua story (chapters 113, 114) he expands a reference already made, as we have just seen, in chapter 16. Here he explains that the knives of flint[1] with which 'the circumcision of the Christ' is effected are the words of Jesus which effect 'the circumcision of the heart'. The phrase takes us back once more to the teaching of Deuteronomy with which, in this respect, so much in the prophetic teaching of Jeremiah and Ezekiel appears to be closely connected. Moreover, the whole of Justin's treatment of this subject starts from an appeal to the well-known passage in Jeremiah 31^{31-33}:

> I will make a new covenant with the house of Israel, and with the house of Judah: not according to the covenant that I made with their fathers in the day that I took them by the hand to bring them out of the land of Egypt . . . this is the covenant that I will make . . . I will put my law in their inward parts, and in their heart will I write it.

In chapter 11 of the *Dialogue* Justin quotes part of this prophetic

between the admission of a proselyte and 'the experience of Israel' the three stages of this experience are defined as follows: (1) circumcised in Egypt; (2) baptized in the desert (Exod. 19^{10}, 'Sanctify yourselves'); (3) after pledging obedience to God's commandments 'they were sprinkled with the blood of the covenant sacrifice' (Exod, 24^{3-8})—Judah the Patriarch, as summarized by G. F. Moore in *Judaism in the First Centuries*, etc. Vol. I, p. 334 (see the whole Chapter).

[1] In LXX they are 'swords of *petra*' (cp. Matt. 16^{18}), and Justin uses the same Greek phrase. This he connects with the biblical texts which Christians applied to Jesus as 'the Stone'. On this see also the valuable note by Lukyn Williams (*op. cit.*, p. 234) covering rabbinical and patristic interpretations of Josh. 5^2.

oracle, and in chapter 12, after referring to Jeremiah's 'cry', he declares that 'a second circumcision is now necessary'. Thus he connects the Joshua typology with this key utterance of prophecy as well as with the Deuteronomic teaching.

The Hebrew idiom of '*cutting* a covenant' might suggest a surgical operation such as is implied in the literal meaning of the Deuteronomic texts. Thus a prophetic interpretation of Deuteronomy 30^6 would take very seriously both halves of its statement: 'The Lord thy God will circumcise thine heart ... to love the Lord thy God with all thine heart.' Nothing short of an act of God would produce such a result. If Jeremiah had such teaching in mind, it might well explain how it was that he looked forward to a covenant quite different in character from that of Sinai-Horeb. A like difference between the two covenants is expressed by St Paul, partly in a contrast between tablets of stone and hearts of flesh (2 Corinthians 3^3), and partly in a contrast between two circumcisions, the one outward 'in the flesh', the other 'of the heart in the Spirit' (Romans $2^{28, 29}$). At the conclusion of this latter passage he seems to be blending the two figures of speech by adding 'not in the letter' to the phrase last quoted. If we combine the teachings of these two epistles we get the following contrast: as the Jewish boy became subject to the letter of the Law through his circumcision, so for the Christian there is an act of new circumcision by which the sword of the Spirit cuts into the heart, and, like a pen, writes upon it the new law of Christ.

In the *Dialogue* Justin's use of the prophet Jeremiah appears to correspond closely with St Paul's; it may therefore serve as a pointer to the apostle's movement of thought. There is a common starting point in the 'new covenant' prophecy; and then Justin takes us back to earlier statements of the prophet about circumcision which are appropriate to the apostle's argument (*Dialogue*, 28).[1] In the first of these (Jeremiah $4^{3, 4}$) the circumcision of the heart is compared to the breaking up of fallow ground. The Greek rendering here, both in the Septuagint and in the *Dialogue*, might carry for Christians a suggestion of the 'new creation'

[1] Ch. 23 appears to have a definite echo of Rom. 4^{11}.

doctrine,[1] all the more so as the Jews have just been urged to become Christian proselytes, that is 'new-born children', before it is too late.[2] There is affinity here with the apostolic thought unfolded in 2 Corinthians 3–6. The second passage (Jeremiah $9^{24, 25}$)[3] refers to those who are 'circumcised in their uncircumcision' and contains in germ the argument developed by St Paul at the end of Romans 2. Justin here follows the Hebrew text closely, whereas the apostle may have had the Greek text also in mind (as elsewhere).[4] For the Septuagint alters the argument of the prophet by introducing in the concluding verse the contrast between 'flesh' and 'heart' which we have already noticed in Romans $2^{28, 29}$.

Ezekiel 44^{7-9} has a similar combination of phrases, but without the contrast. Now, however, we must notice other striking developments of Jeremiah's thought in utterances attributed to his younger contemporary. For example, in Ezekiel 11^{19} there is an elaboration of Jeremiah's blending of agricultural and surgical images. The fallow ground contains stones which must be dug up. So the promise of the Spirit carries with it a removal of the stony heart out of the flesh that the heart may be all flesh. This contrast corresponds to 2 Corinthians rather than to Romans; for 'heart' and 'flesh' are not contrasted but identified. But further, as we read on in Ezekiel's book we come to a much fuller statement concerning a spiritual regeneration of Israel which is connected with a promise of their return to the holy land. This theme involves an elaborate parallel between the return from Babylon and the original journey from Egypt to Palestine under Moses and Joshua.[5] From details actually given it seems certain that the prophet had in mind the story of Israel's first entry and some of its

[1] *νεώσατε. . . νεώματα.*

[2] And in the very next chapter Justin repudiates the *Jewish* form of proselyte initiation in its correct order as indicated above at the end of § ii. Thus, in these two chapters he appears to have rites of initiation and their significance very much in mind.

[3] H. ($9^{25, 26}$ in LXX and EVV).

[4] In Rom. 4^{25} he first quotes Isa. 53^{12} from LXX; and then 53^{11} (Hebrew text) is echoed.

[5] Ch. 20. For fuller details see *The Dominion of Christ*, pp. 45 f.

circumstances. In place of the carcases of rebellious Israel in the wilderness he sets the hordes of the uncircumcised dead of Israel's enemies who 'bear their shame with them that go down to the pit', even as Israel had once lapsed into the idolatry of Egypt and shared its shame. But as the reproach was once 'rolled away', so it would be now (chapters 31^{18}–32).

In chapter 36 we have a final statement of the Return of the 'remnant' with initiatory features corresponding in some measure to those of the original Entry. By contrast with the shamed hordes in the wilderness returning Israel is sprinkled with water, receives a new heart of flesh in exchange for the stony heart, and finally is dowered with the indwelling Spirit of God (36^{24-28}). If we now place this oracle in parallel columns with Pauline utterances the comparison is sufficiently instructive:

Ezekiel 36^{25-27}.	*St Paul*
(1) I will sprinkle clean water upon you, and ye shall be clean: from all your filthiness . . . will I cleanse you	In one Spirit were we all baptized into one body . . . and we were all imbued with one Spirit[1] (1 Corinthians 12^{13}).
(2) (*a*) A new heart also will I give you, and a new Spirit will I put within you;	Ye are an epistle of Christ, written not with ink but with the Spirit of the living God,
(*b*) and I will take away the stony heart out of your flesh, and I will give you an heart of flesh	not in tables of stone, but in tables that are hearts of flesh (2 Corinthians 3^{3}).
(3) And I will put my Spirit within you, and cause you to walk in my statutes, and ye shall keep my judgements and do them.	. . . that the righteous ordinance of the law might be fulfilled in us. . . .[2] So Surely as the Spirit of God dwelleth in you (Romans $8^{4, 9}$).

[1] This imagery, explained above in ch. I, § iii, can now be seen to draw together the two parts of initiation through the fact that 'water' is a common factor in both phases of the Spirit's action. Also St Paul, in the texts here quoted, applies to the Spirit three sorts of imagery, whereas Ezekiel (in the other column) uses solely the image to which Rom. 8^{9} corresponds.

[2] The intervening clauses (8^{4b-9a}) continue the antithesis between flesh and spirit which began in Rom. $2^{28f.}$ In contrast to the imagery of 2 Cor. 3 Romans gives to 'flesh' a derogatory nuance.

In view of what was said previously[1] as to a blending of two figures of speech in Romans 2[29] it may be suggested that Ezekiel 36 would naturally be understood to foreshadow a threefold pattern of initiation consisting of water-baptism, circumcision of the heart, and an indwelling of the Spirit.

At this point let us recall the trend of the argument which we have been pursuing with Justin's help. Under his guidance we found in the Book of Joshua a foreshadowing type of Christian initiation which made the neophytes one with Jesus in three stages, that is, through baptism, 'second circumcision' and the first communions which occurred at the paschal eucharist of Easter. Secondly, Justin's interpretation of the second stage in this triad in terms of prophetic teachings led us eventually to the Book of Ezekiel where we found something like a repetition of Joshua's initiatory rites on the occasion of a second entry into the holy land as anticipated by the prophet. In the repetition, moreover, initiation is also in three stages; but at the third stage a new factor is introduced. Here we seem to move from the outward to the inward, from cleansing water through a transformed heart to the indwelling of God's Spirit. Has Justin any teaching which corresponds to the second triad? And further, has he given any indication as to what he understands by the biblical language about 'circumcision', the term which occupies the second place in both the above-mentioned patterns of initiation? Upon both of these two questions new light has recently been thrown.

In an article in *Theology*[2] entitled *Justin Martyr and Confirmation* the Reverend A. H. Couratin has examined two sections of *The Dialogue with Trypho*, namely chapters 41 and 86, 87. He draws attention to the significance of this father's allusion to Leviticus 14, where the offering of fine flour 'on behalf of those who are being purified from leprosy' is treated as a type of the eucharist. It is then suggested that Justin's selection of this passage ('apparently alone of Christian writers') is due to the fact that 'the sequence described in Lev. 14 sufficiently resembled the Baptism-Eucharist

[1] In the second par. of the present section.
[2] Vol. LV, No. 390 (Dec. 1952).

sequence with which he was familiar', that is to say the sequence of baptismal rites which reached its climax in the paschal eucharist of Easter-Day. Details of this parallel are worked out in an impressive analysis of *Dialogue* 41, and a corresponding sequence is deduced from the later chapters. In the former section the third item is the paschal eucharist, whereas in chapters 86, 87 baptism and anointing are followed by 'the Descent of the Messianic Spirit'. Thus we may infer that 'the initiatory rite known to Justin consisted of Baptism with Water, Anointing with Oil, Prayer for the Descent of the Messianic Spirit and Baptismal Eucharist, and is identical with that known to Tertullian'.

The argument which we have just summarized offers timely corroboration to the conclusions towards which the present chapter has been moving. In the four-fold sequence of initiation which Justin is found to share with Tertullian the second item, namely anointing with oil, occupies precisely that place in the sequence which, in the present work, we have found assigned to a new circumcision in Joshua 5 and in Ezekiel 36. Moreover the four-fold sequence deduced from Justin's two sections was drawn from two triadic sequences; and these correspond exactly to the two which, in the present chapter, we have found to be respectively implicit or explicit in those two biblical passages. Finally we can add to the above observations an additional point concerning *Dialogue* 41 which did not fall within the compass of the Article in *Theology*. After Justin has completed his argument concerning the leper's offering as a type of the eucharist, he suddenly switches over in a final paragraph to a statement concerning 'the true circumcision' of which Jewish circumcision is allowed to be a type. When this isolated statement is connected with Justin's repeated references to Joshua's 'second circumcision' in the same treatise we can see at once that this final paragraph of chapter 41 convincingly proves the case that Leviticus 14 is cited because it provides an exact parallel to Christian initiation.

IV

CONNEXION OF THE PRECEDING ARGUMENT WITH ESCHATOLOGICAL 'SEALING' OF THE FOREHEAD IN NT, AND OF THE LATTER WITH ITS BACKGROUND IN EZEKIEL 9^{4-6}. SYMBOLISM OF THIS PROPHETIC 'MARK' IN JEWISH AND CHRISTIAN THOUGHT. ITS IDENTIFICATION WITH THE SIGN OF THE CROSS IN A NEW EXODUS ILLUMINATES A BIBLICAL PATTERN OF MANIFOLD TYPOLOGY IN JUSTIN'S *DIALOGUE*. WOVEN INTO UNITY UPON THE UNDERLYING MOTIF OF CHRISTIAN INITIATORY RITES, THIS FORMS AN EVIDENTIAL BRIDGE JOINING NT TO THE THIRD CENTURY.

The operation which effects a writing upon the heart is an invisible act of God. For that reason it is appropriately called a 'circumcision not made with hands' (Colossians 2^{11}). Nevertheless we have found this divine act mediated visibly through human agency by the pouring of oil upon the head of the newly-baptized Christian. This rite was, it seems, customary in the Church about the middle of the second century in places known to St Justin such as Rome and Ephesus. Moreover we have also found good reason for thinking that a similar rite was in use at Ephesus half a century earlier according to the testimony of St John's First Epistle.[1] Such facts as these cannot be eliminated by deductions from the use of the word 'seal' in the second and later centuries. Within the compass of the present inquiry, however, all uses of that word originate in scripture; and this brings us to a further point of importance relevant to the stage which the present investigation has now reached. In the New Testament the only *Christian* use of the 'seal' terminology which is unmistakeably clear is that which is to be found in the Revelation of St John (7^{2-4}), where the servants of God are sealed by an angel upon their foreheads. This evidence provides an important link between the liturgical practice of 'sealing' the Christian neophyte with chrism upon the forehead and a corresponding incident in the Old Testament.

The biblical background of 'anointing' is, as we have already noticed, particularly rich, and ultimately Christological in its

[1] See above, ch. I, § iv.

significance.[1] But there is another aspect of the 'seal' terminology in the New Testament which points back to a different source, namely its eschatological reference. In Revelation 7^{2-4} the faithful Israelites are sealed with a mark which is to preserve them from impending judgement,[2] whereas the followers of Antichrist are doomed precisely because they have upon them the mark of God's earthly arch-enemy (13^{16}, 14^{9} ff.). In Ephesians 4^{30} a corresponding note is struck when Christians are told that they were once 'sealed' by the Holy Spirit 'unto the day of redemption'. The incident in the Old Testament with which eschatological sealing can most obviously be connected is that which is described in Ezekiel 9, where the prophet sees an angel, under divine direction, place a mark upon the foreheads of the faithful Israelites, in order that they may escape from the threatened destruction which is then executed by other agents of the deity upon the idolaters in the holy city, that is upon all who have not received the mark, including young and old alike. There are also points of similarity between this prophetic vision and the story of the blood-marks placed on Israelite houses in Egypt to preserve them from the destroying angel on the paschal night (Exodus 12).

It will be noticed that these are the two other 'notable markings' in scripture, besides circumcision, of which it was previously remarked that they must be taken into account.[3] Their close connexion will emerge as we proceed. For the present we must concentrate our attention upon the incident described in Ezekiel. In the English versions Ezekiel 9^{4} reads as follows:

> Go through the midst of the city . . . and set a *mark* upon the foreheads of the men that sigh and that cry for all the abominations that be done in the midst thereof.

The word rendered 'mark' here, and again in verse 6, is the Hebrew word which we pronounce: TAW, and is the name given

[1] See last note.

[2] This corresponds to the contrasted effects of the sinister 'beast' seal as implied in $14^{9\,\text{ff.}}$, but need not prejudge issues discussed by Charles at this point in his IC Comm., Vol. I, pp. 194 ff.

[3] Above, § i, par. 4.

to the last letter of the Hebrew alphabet. In the old script it corresponded in shape to the Greek letter *Chi*, or the English X. On the other hand it was pronounced like the Greek *Theta* (Θ) which corresponds in sound to the English TH. Under Roman imperial custom a Θ marked on a criminal's forehead indicated that he had been sentenced to death (*thanatos*). On the other hand in Ezekiel's vision the mark preserved from death those who received it; and this again corresponded to one possible meaning of the Greek X with which the Taw was in appearance identical.[1]

With these facts in mind we are not surprised to learn that for some Jewish authorities the Taw mark had a double meaning—'either life (for the righteous) or death (for the wicked)'. In a sense this corresponds to the details in Ezekiel's story; for the mark separated those who were to live from those sentenced to death. In one Jewish version both classes were marked by the angel, those for life in ink and those for death in blood. But this has the appearance of a rationalization which was due to the exigencies of controversy with Christians. It seems likely that originally 'the inkmark had served as a sign of death, whereas the blood-mark (reminiscent of the blood of the Paschal lamb) had served as a sign of salvation'.[2] This agrees with the evidence of contemporary custom which gave to the 'black theta' (Θ) such sinister associations.[3] If Lieberman's conclusions are justified, Jews as well as Christians originally connected the Taw mark with the paschal blood; and we shall find that fact important as we turn now to the Christian interpretation of Ezekiel's vision of judgement.

The original shape of the Taw was well known in the early Church. For Christians, moreover, the appearance of the mark which Ezekiel saw was the appearance of the Cross. To ourselves the shape of the *Chi* (X) is commonly known by the name of the 'St Andrew's Cross' which forms one element in the flag universally called the Union Jack. We will now cite two authori-

[1] See below, § v, p. 53.

[2] So Prof. Lieberman concludes in his survey of the relevant Jewish material (*op. cit.*, pp. 190, 191).

[3] Lieberman quotes from the Epigrams of Martial a reference to 'the quaestor's death-bringing mark'.

ties from the early part of the third century who together represent the two main theological traditions of that time. Tertullian identifies the Taw with the sign of the cross prophetically foreshadowed, which would be 'upon our foreheads in the true and catholic Jerusalem'.[1] Origen, again, consulted a Jewish Christian who replied that 'the form of the Taw in the old script resembles the cross, and it predicts the mark which is to be placed on the foreheads of the Christians'.[2] Such complete unanimity between the widely different traditions of Christian outlook which obtained respectively in Latin North Africa and in the school of Alexandria suggests a practice which goes much further back. Concerning Tertullian's explanation of the Taw in terms of the Cross the distinguished Jewish scholar whom we have been quoting remarks: 'He probably was not the inventor of this idea but found it in the various "books of testimonies" current among the Christians.'[3]

Another possibility, however, presents itself. In all the great religions ideas are commonly embedded in practice. Identification of the Taw mark with the cross, then, might indicate that Christians were familiar with the rite in which the bishop made the sign of the Cross upon the foreheads of all newly-made Christians in the chrism with which they had just been anointed. Moreover, where we have reason to believe that the application of oil to the head was a basic ceremony of initiation, there we should not be surprised to find scriptural exegesis concerning the Cross closely connected with a parallel exegesis concerning the forms of Christian initiation. This, I believe, corresponds precisely to what we do actually find in Justin's *Dialogue*, to which accordingly we now return. For this the reader is referred to what has been said already concerning a parallel between Justin and St Paul at the beginning of our treatment of the *Dialogue*,[4] and further concerning the contents of *Dialogue*, ch. 41, as analyzed in A. H. Couratin's Article with the further comments on chapters 86 and

[1] *Adv. Marcionem*, Lib. III, 22.

[2] Quoted by Lieberman (*op. cit.* pp. 187 f.) from *Selecta in Ezekielem*, Migne PG xiii, 800d.

[3] *Op. cit.*, p. 187.

[4] Above, § ii, par. 2.

87.[1] In the light of what has been said previously we shall find it worth while to examine the context of these two passages more extensively.

We turn first to chapter 40 which immediately precedes the levitical counterpart of the baptismal sequence with its concluding reference to the true circumcision. The passage begins with a reference to the paschal lamb as a type of Christ, and continues:

> With whose blood they who believe on him anoint their own houses, that is themselves, in accordance with their faith in him. For that the plasm of which God moulded Adam became a house of the inbreathing which was from God you can all understand.

This cryptic utterance contains a double reference to scripture, first to the blood of Exodus 12 and then to the creation story in Genesis 2. In Job 4^{19} human bodies are called 'houses of clay'; and the implicit reference to Genesis 2^{7} there is accentuated in the Septuagint.[2] This characteristic biblical idiom would doubtless enable Justin, a man of Palestinian origins, to see in the Israelite houses of Exodus 12 the bodies of the Christian neophytes who 'anoint themselves'. Self-baptism was the original Jewish conception of what happened to the proselyte after his circumcision; and it is possible that this idea is present in 1 Corinthians 6^{11}, where 'you washed yourselves' seems to be intended in contrast to the passive verbs which follow. Moreover self-anointing in our quotation above, natural in reference to 'blood', may imply a reminiscence of a pre-baptismal anointing as we find it later in Hippolytus.

But a surprising feature in this statement of Justin's is the abrupt transition from the Exodus story to the creation of Adam. This, however, might become intelligible to 'all' those addressed (actually the Christian readers for whom the *Dialogue* was written) if their minds passed from the preliminary self-baptism to the plasmic act of the bishop's thumb upon the chrism and to the

[1] § iii, last two pars.

[2] Where in the context (4^{21}) the divine breath destroys, as in Genesis it created life.

ensuing event whereby the Creator once more breathed the divine Spirit-breath into our newly-created nature. That would imply a repetition of Adam's creation in the initiation of Christians. Every chrismation would be also a plasmation; and this in turn corresponds to our Lord's method of healing the blind man in John 9 with its clearly creationist significance as well as its liturgical relevance to the rites of Christian initiation, concerning which I have written elsewhere.[1] It is noticeable that this reference to initiatory rites in terms of biblical types begins with the blood of the paschal lamb and leads on next into an explanation by which the method of roasting the lamb upon two spits is made to symbolize Christ on the Cross.[2] We shall see presently that there is ground for thinking that Justin associated the sign of the cross (i.e. the Taw mark) with the blood-marks of the Exodus story. Thus in chapters 40, 41 we have a double baptismal sequence, in the first part of which there is reference to baptismal anointing, chrismation, the descent of the Spirit and the sign of the cross.

A special feature of the *Dialogue* which has just received illustration is the way in which the biblical pattern of creation and redemption is presented in terms suggestive of the ritual sequence which we have in mind. There is more of this in succeeding chapters. But we pass on now to a more extensive example of the same kind of thing which gives an almost unbroken unity to the series of chapters 86–114. After the sequence: 'Water, oil, Spirit' in 86, 87 we pass on to gifts of the Spirit, the baptism of Jesus and the descent of the Dove (88). Next come types of the cross in which Joshua is twice introduced, followed by a reference to 'circumcision of the heart' (90–92). In 94 the brazen serpent uplifted is identified with the 'sign' of the cross, and this is to be connected with the Septuagint rendering of Numbers 21^{8}: 'make for thyself a serpent, and set it upon a *sign*'. The same Greek word is used for the Taw mark in Ezekiel $9^{4,\,6}$; and once more it occurs in Exodus 12^{13}, where we read the blood shall be to you 'in a *sign*'

[1] Cp. above, § i, par. 2 with note.

[2] Lukyn Williams in a note (p. 80) refers to the Samaritan custom by which the paschal lambs, when slain, 'are crucified on rough wooden crosses.'

upon the houses wherein ye are. These two Pentateuchal 'sign' texts are evidently associated in Justin's mind; for in chapters 111, 112 he mentions them in close connexion in such a way as to suggest that in both contexts 'the sign' is the cross.

So in a note upon 111 Lukyn Williams remarks that Justin's treatment of the Exodus story implies a belief that 'the blood was sprinkled in the form of a cross, like the old form of Taw'.[1] This comment throws light also upon the previous treatment of the sprinkled houses as signifying the bodies of the Christian neophytes (40). In view of these cross-connexions it is reasonable to conclude that 'the sign' of the Taw was for Justin the cross imprinted after baptism upon the foreheads of Christian initiates. The chapters between 94 and 111 are largely occupied with an exegesis of Psalm 22 in terms of Christ's passion together with other biblical types of the same order such as the sign of Jonah. One of Justin's favourite types in these chapters is obtained by combining the cruciform figure of Moses at prayer (arms outstretched) with Joshua victorious in battle (Exodus 17). This combination of the cross with associations of victorious conflict is true to St Paul's deepest thought; and we shall find it present in the key-passage from Colossians 2. Finally let us notice that the sign of the cross, as typified in chapters 111, 112, leads straight into Justin's fullest exposition of the 'second circumcision' by 'Jesus' in 113, 114. Thus the typology of the Cross and the typology of Joshua's story are woven onto the theme of the baptismal sequence and its paschal associations.

V

THE SEAL UPON THE FOREHEAD, (*a*) AS THE SIGNATURE-MARK OF THE LAMB IN A NEW EXODUS, (*b*) AS THE 'CROSS-LETTER' [X] WHICH CANCELS SIN'S DEBT—CALVARY AND CHRISMATION—ANALYSIS OF COLOSSIANS 2^{8-15}. IT EXHIBITS A THREEFOLD INTEGRATION: (1) OF BIBLICAL TYPES IN ITS SCRIPTURAL BACKGROUND (JOSHUA, EZEKIEL, 2 CORINTHIANS); (2) OF CHARACTERISTIC NT TEACHING, INTERWEAVING THE THEMES OF

[1] *Op. cit.*, p. 229, note 3. Otto agrees; and adds other patristic comments in support. See above § ii, note to par. 2.

REDEMPTION AND INITIATION; (3) OF THE PARTS OF CHRISTIAN INITIATION IN RECIPROCITY WITHIN THE BAPTISMAL WHOLE.

We have seen grounds for thinking that in the second century there was a definite tendency, both Jewish and Christian, to connect the Taw mark in Ezekiel 9 with the paschal blood in Exodus 12. The conjunction of these two types as early as the Revelation of St John, if accepted, should have relieved modern commentators of some at least of their perplexities with regard to the sealing of the 144,000 'servants of God upon their foreheads'. For the sealing in chapter 7 takes place between two groups of plagues (recorded in chapters 6 and 8). So also in Exodus the blood is placed on the lintels after nine plagues and before the final plague with its hazardous sequel. Thus, in the Apocalypse, the sealed persons are the new Israel; and their sealing upon the forehead secures to each and all of them their participation in the new Exodus. To the symbolism of Ezekiel and Exodus, however, we must add that of Numbers. For there the numbering of the tribes concludes with the Aaronic blessing and the words: 'So shall they put my Name upon the children of Israel' (Numbers $6^{22\text{ ff.}}$). Likewise in the Christian apocalypse the seal takes the form of the divine name written upon the forehead. Moreover in Exodus 28^{9-12} the high-priest is bidden to bear on his shoulders the names of the tribes 'like the engravings of a signet'. Under the new covenant, by contrast, there is also an engraving like that of a signet-seal. But here the 'seal' is like a signature-mark of the Paschal Lamb upon the forehead of each Christian (Revelation 14^{1}; cp. 3^{12}, $22^{3,4}$).[1]

This Christian variation upon the 'signet-seal' imagery of Exodus would, perhaps, blend the more easily with the picture in Ezekiel since the mark like a cross which the prophet saw placed upon the foreheads of the faithful was also familiar as a signature-mark, used like a signet-seal to attest a document (cp.

[1] Thus three injunctions of Deut. 6^{6-9} receive fulfilment. The words of the new Law are upon the 'circumcised heart', the sealed head, and the door-posts of the new Israel which is the temple of deity (1 Cor. 3^{16}; and cp. Exod. 12^{7} with the quotation from *Dialogue* 40 above, § iv, par. 7).

Job 31[35]).[1] This use of the symbol X is not unfamiliar to ourselves (witness the ballot-paper). But in ancient times this sign had yet another significance which bears upon the correct interpretation of Colossians 2[14]. In our discussion of the 'mark' in Ezekiel 9, which is in appearance similar to the Greek *Chi*, attention was drawn to the fact that this mark preserved from death those who received it and that 'this again corresponded to one possible meaning of the Greek X'.[2] The explanation has been given by Deissmann;[3] who 'called attention to the X found in documents of the first century, which served as a mark for cancelling a debt'. Deissmann's exact words are as follows: 'We have learned from the new texts that it was generally customary to cancel a bond (or other document) by crossing it out with the Greek cross-letter Chi (X).' Lieberman, in turn, offers evidence that 'this practice is thus much earlier than' the first century of the Christian era.

The relevance of this practice for the exegesis of the passage in Colossians must now be made clear. In Colossians 2[13, 14] St Paul says:

> You, who were dead in trespasses and in the uncircumcision of your flesh, you he quickened together with him, having forgiven us all our trespasses, having blotted out the bond written against us in ordinances, which was contrary to us: and he hath taken it out of the way, having nailed it to the cross.

In the Lord's Prayer we are taught to pray for forgiveness in the words: 'remit to us our debts' (Matthew 6[12]); and elsewhere our Lord declared in a parable that sin is like a debt too vast to be payable (*ib.* 18[23 ff.]). St Paul's picture of a bond or promissory note being cancelled corresponds precisely to our Lord's picture of the debt remitted to the slave by his lord. Moreover, although the apostle's readers were Gentiles, as is shown by the reference to uncircumcision in verse 13, they were being subjected to pressure

[1] See Driver-Gray's comment in ICC *ad loc.*, p. 274, and G. A. Cooke's in his comment on Ezek. 9[4], p. 106 in his ICC. Cp. also Soncino Comm. on Job, p. 163.

[2] Above, § iv, par. 3.

[3] *Light from the Ancient East*, pp. 332 ff. (ET 1927, from 4th German ed.). See also Lieberman's comments (*op. cit.*, pp. 188, 193).

by a Jewish Gnostic heresy, which made much of the law and its angelic mediators. In certain respects the situation was parallel to that which called forth the earlier Epistle to the Galatians. In both cases circumcision was being pressed upon Christians; and, as the apostle had said before, everyone who has been circumcised 'is a debtor to keep the whole law' (Galatians 5^3).

Elsewhere the apostle had taught that 'ye died to the law through the body of Christ' (Romans 7^4); and the context shows that this release from the Jewish Law and all that it symbolized was effected in the 'death unto sin' which took place in baptism (cp. *ib.* 6^7). In Colossians $2^{12, 13}$ this teaching given in Romans 6, 7 is very exactly summed up. But we remember that the argument of Romans concerning Christian initiation is completed in chapter 8; and so also the summary of baptismal teaching in Colossians $2^{12, 13}$ is completed in what follows. There we are told that the cancelled debt has been taken out of the way and 'nailed to the cross'; and this statement is capable of interpretation in two senses, both of which are true. Jesus took the burden of our sins up on to the Cross, where 'him who knew no sin' God 'made to be sin for us, that we might become the righteousness of God in him' (2 Corinthians 5^{21}). When Jesus was nailed to the Cross our sins were also nailed up there; for he had identified himself with those sins. But how then did 'we become the righteousness of God in him'? Surely, by our identification with him, which was effected in the rites of initiation. At this point we come upon the second possible sense of the words: 'he nailed it to the cross.'

When sin was nailed to the Cross in the flesh of Jesus, the wood of the Cross formed 'the Greek cross-letter *Chi*' which cancelled the debt; and this event is sacramentally repeated when the same cross-letter (X) is applied to the forehead of the newly baptized Christian. If this explanation of the apostle's language be accepted, it will be found, I believe, to throw new light upon the passage as a whole, and that in three respects. We shall, therefore, now attempt to re-think the argument of Colossians 2^{8-15} (1) in relation to St Paul's use of the Old Testament, (2) in relation to his characteristic teaching about redemption, (3) in relation to his way of handling the rites of Christian initiation. We cannot, indeed, hope to clear up every obscurity. For the background of this epistle is a form of Jewish gnosticism based upon ancient views about cosmology, concerning which we know all too little. Some of the difficulties usually discussed in the commentaries are here relegated to an additional note. Moreover, the three points mentioned above cannot be kept separate for reasons which will appear as we proceed.

The section which we are examining begins in verse 8 with a religious contrast. 'The elements of the world' here mentioned are the 'weak and beggarly elements' referred to in Galatians 4^9. They are the angel-rulers of the heavenly bodies, some of whom were believed to have been instrumental in giving the Law to Israel. To worship these weak mediators is of no avail to deliver from the bondage of the flesh.[1] At best they rank amongst the rulers and powers, for all of whom Christ, incarnate and risen, is 'head' in his all-sufficing deity.[2] The difference of religion thus indicated (vv. 8–10) is now further defined by a contrast drawn between the old circumcision and the new (verse 11). The old Jewish form was merely a symbolic cutting of the flesh, whereas 'the circumcision of the Christ' which Christians undergo is that complete removal of 'flesh' which no human hands can effect. It is this which our Lord himself underwent in his death upon the cross. In order to make his point the apostle coins a new noun, with a double prefix, to signify the total stripping off of the old-Adam-flesh which takes place at every Christian initiation because it once took place on Calvary. At the end of the passage which we are examining he coins the corresponding verb, and applies it to the death of Christ (2^{15}); in the next chapter (3^9) he re-applies it to our 'putting off' of the old Adam in baptism.

It appears, then, that St Paul here describes, first the death of Christ, and then the baptismal rites of the church, in terms of a *second circumcision*. Moreover, as we shall see, this is regarded as the indispensable means through which Jesus, with his people, has

[1] Cp. vv. 20–23.

[2] For 'head' see my remarks on OT usage in *The Apostolic Ministry*, pp. 68 f.

conquered the powers of darkness and taken possession of his kingdom. So we are back again in Joshua's camp. The first circumcision was in Egypt, the house of bondage to which the Judaizing theosophists of Colossae wished their Christian neighbours to return. The second, however, the circumcision of Jesus, follows upon our entry into the promised land through Jordan's waters; and it is *this* which is indispensable for those who wish to share in the triumph of Jesus over the hostile powers. It is worth noting at this point that Colossians 2^{15} is actually quoted by Justin in his 41st chapter at the conclusion of the levitical analogy to the baptismal sequence,[1] and shortly before his reference to 'the true circumcision with which we were circumcised from error and wickedness by him who rose from the dead on the first day of the week, Jesus Christ our Lord'.[2] It would seem that Justin, in fusing Joshua's second circumcision with our Lord's Easter victory over the hostile powers, believed himself to be drawing out the meaning of Colossians 2^{11-15}.

The probability that Joshua's story lies behind the Colossian passage is increased by what seems the most satisfying explanation of verse 15. The complex imagery of this final sentence rests upon a double nuance in the coined word. With the phrase: 'having stripped off the rulers and powers' St Paul implies two things. For first he is saying that our Lord carried to the cross our load of sin, to wear it in the garment of flesh which he had made his own. But secondly, the imagery suggests that 'the world-rulers of this darkness' (Ephesians 6^{12}) were clustered about him in his dying moments. There on the cross they 'crucified the Lord of the glory' (1 Corinthians 2^{8}). But in so doing they lost all that they hoped to gain. For Jesus was no longer in that garment of flesh about which they thronged. In stripping it off he stripped them off, thus spoiling the spoilers of their prey. So at the moment when he died upon a gibbet he was in reality a conqueror leading his

[1] Cp. Lukyn Williams' note (*op. cit.*, p. 82) with the text in Otto's edition, Vol. II, p. 134 (the ninth line of ch. 41).

[2] Circumcision on the eighth day is thus made to symbolize the resurrection of Jesus on the first day which 'is further called the eighth'.

enemies captive in a triumphal procession. That was the glorious reality hidden under the grim story of Calvary; and when we connect this picture of conflict and triumph with the preceding picture of a debt wiped out on the cross we have before us a complex of images which corresponds broadly to the apostle's teaching elsewhere.[1]

The story of the cross combines a victorious conflict with a consequent liberation of slaves from a debtors' prison. This was the Word of the Cross which in the ages to follow was written by the hand of the apostolic ministry upon the forehead of the baptized. Moreover, for the apostolic church this reality would seem to be clearly foreshadowed as the sequel to Joshua's story was read from the Greek bible.[2] For after his great victory this captain of new Israel led out the five defeated kings of the Canaanites from a cave and hanged them upon wooden gibbets until the sun went down (Joshua 10^{21-27}). If, in the light of our interpretation of St Paul, the seven verses of this Hebrew story be compared with the last twenty verses or so in St Matthew's version of our Saviour's passion,[3] the correspondence is sufficiently striking, the type unfolding the hidden meaning of the antitype. At the very hour when the body of our Saviour was being sealed into the rock-sepulchre, his enemies were cowering in the pit of hell awaiting the dread summons of the Victor: 'And Jesus slew them, and they hung them upon five gibbets . . . until the evening. And it came to pass at sunset Jesus commanded, and they took them down . . . and cast them into the cave where they had fled, and they rolled stones against the cave unto this day.'

As in Justin, so in the New Testament the themes of redemption by Christ and initiation into Christ are inevitably interwoven. In 1 John 'the anointing', identified with the Spirit as teacher and guide, anchors the Christian community to the apostolic tradition of faith and life in face of advancing heresy and the approach of

[1] Cp. Justin's use of Exodus 17, and my comments in the concluding paragraph of § iv. See further, the Additional Note which follows below.

[2] It must be remembered that in Joshua 5 the second circumcision was both a rolling away of shame and a prelude to victorious conflict.

[3] Matt. 27^{45-66}.

antichrist. Moreover, as we move back into the apostolic age the eschatological note becomes more marked. So in the Apocalypse sealing upon the forehead prepares for conflict and for the paschal victory of the Lamb; and those who bear his name will pass safely through the Armageddon which repeats the Exodus. In the Pauline corpus there is a diversity of images which makes for variety of interpretation. Yet here too we are 'sealed unto the day of redemption', and in Colossians the language of 'putting off the flesh' in a new circumcision is applied alike to Jesus and to his people who thus share with him in his cosmic victory. The diversity of images is baffling; yet perhaps we can see the types in process of merging together as the apostle writes. Joshua and Ezekiel are primary sources, the one a plain record of history, the other visionary and eschatological in its expectations; the one outward and even fleshly, the other inward in its talk of a new heart and a new spirit.

Yet, as Ezekiel's fullest statement starts from a baptismal flow of sprinkled water (36^{25}), so the Colossian statement begins with a circumcision more completely external than Joshua's in so far as it involves the spectacle of flesh wholly crucified on Calvary. To the Pauline parallel with Ezekiel previously noted[1] we can now with some probability add yet another. If we read through 2 Corinthians, say, from 1^{18} to 5^{10}, we find at 1^{22} anointing, sealing and 'the earnest' or 'first instalment of the Spirit'. Passing on to $3^{3\,ff.}$ we have the Pauline version of the circumcised heart upon which the Spirit writes. Finally in 5^{5} 'the earnest of the Spirit', which points forward to 'the day of redemption' (cp. Romans 8^{23} and Ephesians 4^{30}), reappears in a highly eschatological setting.[2] Thus we have a triad: seal-heart-Spirit. In Ezekiel the seal appears in an eschatological setting at $9^{4\,ff.}$ and a heart-spirit combination at 11^{19}. To this the Pauline sequence broadly corresponds, but with a difference. In the prophecy the Spirit does not become prominent until chapter 36. It is not mentioned in $9^{4\,ff.}$, and is subordinate to a

[1] See above, § iii, par. 5.

[2] Cp. the baptismal sequence in Ezek. 36 leading to a general resurrection in 37.

changed heart in 11^{19}. This difference corresponds to the richer reality of the fulfilment.

There is one aspect of Colossians 2^{11-15} to which attention must now be briefly drawn, inasmuch as it will occupy us more fully at a later stage. What I have in mind here exemplifies still further the principles of interpretation laid down in the second section of chapter I. It was there suggested 'that a complex of ritual ceremonies would be envisaged as a concrete whole', and further that description of such a concrete whole would be dominated by such 'idioms of psychological wholeness' as were considered in the course of that chapter. The passage which we have been examining provides an admirable illustration of these phenomena in which a profound unity of the whole is consistent with a plurality of parts. Moreover, as we there saw, the mystery as a whole can be presented in terms of some one of its aspects. Let us now trace the details. Colossians 2^{11-15} begins and ends with a single piece of imagery; and this is marked by the coined noun in verse 11 and its corresponding verb in verse 15. 'The circumcision of the Christ' is defined in terms of a 'total stripping off' of flesh. But secondly this definition, which covers and enfolds all that lies between (verses 12–14), includes within itself both baptism as defined in Romans 6 and the cross-symbol of the *Chi* (X) which is identical with the mark on the forehead in Ezekiel. Thus baptism with water and the cross sealing the forehead are included within the concept of the new circumcision.

But further, between the two parts of initiation there is here described yet another relationship which can best be designated as an 'interchange of properties'. For, whereas the two coined words start from a definition of the new circumcision and then undergo a graphic extension to Calvary, in 3^{9} the verb is used to describe the 'putting off of the old man' which we associate with baptism. Moreover there is a corresponding interchange on the other side. For in verse 14 the application of the cross-symbol to the written bond cancels the debt of sin. Thus the *Chi*, which is the form of Ezekiel's mark on the forehead, is the instrument of that forgiveness of sins which, in accordance with apostolic teaching, we associate with baptism in the Creed. This mutual interpenetration of effects as between the two parts of initiation aptly corresponds to the illustration of the sealed document which is familiar in scripture and reflected, as we have seen, in St Paul's writings.[1] For the document and the seal are interdependent. Together they form an adequate and integral whole. The seal gives validity to the written statement, whereas the latter gives precise significance to the seal.

Additional Note A—Colossians 2^{8-15}.

In this note I have in mind certain difficulties which first emerged clearly in the Critical Commentary by T. K. Abbott (3rd printing, 1909). The principal one concerns angelology. On the interpretation of 2^{15} offered in the text above, which follows J. B. Lightfoot, the question may be raised: Are the hostile powers, defeated on the Cross, to be regarded as including the angelic law-givers referred to in verses 8–10? If so, that would make the Law an evil legacy, whereas in Rom. 7^{12} it is declared to be holy. The context of that text, however, seems to provide a provisional answer to the question. For sin is there personified as a wicked agent who works 'through the good'. In this way the Law is conceived to have become an unwitting instrument of Sin's evil design. In 1 Cor. 15^{55-57} we get further light. There death, sin and the law are three hostile powers, amongst which death is the most prominent. Its sting, however, is furnished by sin, which in turns draws its strength from the law. Accordingly, the real antagonist is sin which manipulates the functions of the other two powers for its own ends. So also in Romans 8^{1-4} the law, in its weakness, can do no other than to hand over the sinner, as a legal defaulter, into the clutches of sin to become a convict in a debtors' prison.

In all of this there is a continuous interweaving of two sorts of imagery referring respectively to debt and to conflict. The two concepts meet in a gloomy picture of the sinner as a captive slave who needs to be ransomed (Gal. 4^5). This was effected by 'one man's act of redress' which 'issued in acquittal and life for all'

[1] Above, ch. II, § i, par. 5 to end.

(Rom. 5^{18} M), bringing sin's 'reign' to an end. The earlier of these two statements presupposes an enslavement to the angel-mediators of the law for a debt which can never be paid (cp. Gal. 4^3 with 5^3). In Romans, however, sin stands out as the enemy; and the sinner's debt is finally discharged by his baptismal death in Christ (Rom. 6^7). That is a typically Pauline application of a rabbinical notion—that physical death completes the sinner's acquittal (for which see Moore, *op. cit.*, Vol. I, pp. 546 f.; and on Rom. 6^7 see KTW, Vol. 2, p. 222). At this juncture it is necessary to point out, as against Abbott (*ib.*, p. 254, par. 3), that the two words used in Col. 2^{13} to express forgiveness of sins are employed elsewhere in NT with the imagery of release from debt. So Matt. 6^{12-15}, Mark 11^{25}, Luke $7^{42, 48}$. These references show that the commonest verb for 'forgive' in NT (*ἀφίημι*) also carries the idea of 'remitting' a debt (On which see also MM, p. 97, and their ref. to Brooke's ICC on 1 John, p. 20).

Returning to Colossians we can now take note of the significant combination of ideas in 1^{12-14}. This passage speaks of 'the redemption' which we have in Christ as a 'remission of sins'. The 'ransom' paid remits the debt, for which cp. 1 Cor. $6^{19, 20}$: 'ye are not your own; for ye were bought with a price', and again Gal. 4^5. It is clear that St Paul had no inhibitions against the notion that sin is a debt. But in Col. 1 this concept is combined with that of deliverance 'from the power of darkness'. This is precisely the combination of ideas which recurs in 2^{13-15}, that is to say, remission of a debt through victorious conflict with evil agencies. Are we, then, any nearer to a solution of our original problem about the angel-mediators of the Law? It has already been pointed out that in passing from Galatians to Romans emphasis shifts from conflict with the Law to the greater conflict with Sin. This comes out in Rom. 8^{1-4} where '*the* Law' appears to be referred to under the grim phrase: 'the law of sin and death.' Moreover, in the picture which follows (verse 3) the Law functions like a judge in a totalitarian state. It must obey the dictates of the ruling power which is Sin. So in the transformation which follows the Law is swept aside by the incarnate Saviour, who takes the sinner's place in the dock and thereby reverses the court's decision with a condemnation of the arch-enemy.

The condemnation of sin, however, was effected only by an 'offering for sin in the flesh'. Here the LXX phrase for a sin-offering is all-important. To it corresponds the picture in Col. 2^{14} of the bond cancelled by the cross-mark of Calvary. The cross cancels because upon it hangs the world's sin-offering. It is the blood of the Lamb which wipes out the debt and preserves from the destroying angel (Exod. 12). Here is another twist in the complex of biblical imagery. The destroying angel, like the angelic law-givers, is an agent of deity. Yet the true Israel must be protected from his sword by the sign of the cross as in Ezekiel's Taw-vision. Thus the destroying sword is enabled to fulfil its proper function; and so it is with the Law and its ministers. For 'Christ is the end of the law unto righteousness' (Rom. 10^{4}), a text which must be understood in terms of fulfilment. For such a fulfilment there was required 'the circumcision of the Christ' with its total stripping off of 'flesh' and the deadly conflict which that involved, a conflict, not with agents of deity, but with the powers of hell. We have now dealt with all the problems except one. I refer to the apparent change of subject from God the Father in verse 12 to Christ in verses 14, 15. With this we will conclude.

In verse 15 the coined verb which signifies a total stripping off of those hostile powers is in the middle voice; and this favours the view that the subject here is the crucified Saviour. On the other hand it is clear that in verse 13 the subject is God the Father. Accordingly we must suppose that somewhere in verse 14 a transition is made from Father to Son. There is a possible parallel to this peculiarity in $1^{19, 20}$; and it seems likely that the best explanation lies in the well-known Hebrew idiom by which the deity is identified with his representative, as is also the case with human principals and their deputies in OT. A. R. Johnson has given a number of examples in his small monograph on *The One and the Many in the Hebrew Conception of God*. In such instances language shows an oscillation between the two opposite tendencies to identification and distinction. But also, as in the present instance, it may equally pass insensibly from one subject to the other. On Christian presuppositions the Son is the one perfect representative of the Father. Accordingly Prof. Johnson is surely right in his suggestion that this idiom provided a bridge from the Jewish to the Christian doctrine of God (see *op. cit.*, p. 41; and cp. my note on p. 292 of *Revelation*).

The Patripassian heresy was a later symptom of clash between this Semitic idiom and other ways of thinking. But its presence in the passage of Colossians at present under examination, if rightly concluded, is certainly not the only instance of the idiom's occurrence in these few verses. Such insensible passing from one personal subject to another corresponds to two other examples of like phenomena which have come under our scrutiny. The interconnexion between the three sets of phenomena is worthy of notice, and may fitly conclude this short study. The second instance would be the complex of soteriological images which binds together into one the two contrasted pictures of deliverance or 'release' which are drawn respectively in terms of a debt to be paid and a victory to be won. The third instance is that with which we are most immediately concerned, but which becomes more intelligible when seen in the context of parallel groups of facts exhibiting like mental processes. I refer, of course, to that 'interchange of properties' as between the two parts of initiation, namely baptism and the cross signed upon the forehead, to which reference was made in the final paragraph of chapter II. These facts are so much material for further discussion.

CHAPTER III

CONCLUSIONS AND FURTHER PROBLEMS

I

THE TWO FOCI OF THE BAPTISMAL MYSTERY IN NT. IS THERE CONTINUITY OF BIBLICAL TRADITION IN THE SECOND CENTURY? BARNABAS A LINK BETWEEN NT AND JUSTIN. BUT THE DEVELOPMENT OF 'SEAL' IMAGERY CALLS FOR SCRUTINY OF LITERARY PHENOMENA. BIBLICAL IDIOMS IN 2 CLEMENT AND HERMAS. IN THE LATTER FLUCTUATING TERMINOLOGY AND PICTURE-THINKING FORM A BACKGROUND TO TEACHING WHICH IS HEBRAIC, BUT NOT APOSTOLIC. BEARING OF THE INCARNATION UPON THE PAULINE CONCEPT OF A BAPTISMAL WHOLE PERVADING ITS PARTS.

We have been pursuing an argument which has shewn itself to be cumulative in character. That is to say, various groups of facts have emerged, which, in their combined effect, point steadily in one direction. The conclusion indicated is that in the period covered by the New Testament Christian initiation was effected by a series of rites which contained two focal points. The evidence so far surveyed would suggest that the two crucial moments were represented respectively by baptism in water and by a ceremony of anointing the head or the forehead and marking the latter with the sign of the cross. It must be clear, however, that in the nature of the case such an argument could not be demonstrative. For all the available evidence presupposes a background of accepted custom and familiar habits which are no longer directly accessible to us. That background has to be slowly and tentatively reconstructed through careful attention to ancient methods of thinking and behaving which are no longer necessarily ours.

One of the greatest obstacles to such reconstruction lies in the scanty character of the literary evidence during the half-century which follows upon the completion of the New Testament writings. For this reason amongst others we are peculiarly fortunate in being able to point to so much evidential material as we have found to be present in a single writing of St Justin Martyr. Many of the surviving literary products of the second Christian century are tinged in one degree or another with heretical tendencies. All the more welcome, therefore, are the few orthodox stalwarts who stand out prominently in that period. As I have shewn elsewhere in reference to St Irenaeus, so also is it here; the *Dialogue* of St Justin exhibits a solid continuity of tradition with the New Testament writings in regard to the author's method of handling scripture. There is still no break in the lines along which the revelation of the Christ was being apprehended from the earliest days. For an absence of 'break' the chain of evidence is inevitably slender, yet sufficient to justify our assertion of genuine continuity.

This conclusion can be supported by a glance at one of the intermediate documents, namely the so-called Epistle of Barnabas.[1] In his ninth chapter the author gives a Christian interpretation of circumcision which has associations corresponding both to Justin's *Dialogue* and to writings of the New Testament. The details are as follows. In this chapter Barnabas anticipates Justin's use of texts in Jeremiah 4 and 9, where the prophet seems to foreshadow St Paul's method of expounding the true 'circumcision of the heart'.[2] Moreover Barnabas clearly has in mind the argument of Romans 4. For, like the apostle, he treats Jewish circumcision as 'a seal', and then proceeds to argue that 'Abraham, who first appointed circumcision, looked forward in the spirit unto Jesus' when he circumcised his entire household of three hundred and eighteen men. This number yields the first two letters of our Lord's name together with the letter T which signifies the cross. Here we have an early intimation that the seal of the new circumcision is connected with the sign of the cross. Similarly St Paul first treats the old circumcision as a seal annexed to a covenant document (Romans 4), and then finds the completion of the new circumcision in the sign of the cross (Colossians 2).

[1] If written within the first century, it still mediates between the inspired writers and later ecclesiastical tradition.

[2] Cp. above, ch. II, § iii, par. 3.

We remember that Justin reproduces some of these connexions. In particular, for both of these writers the new circumcision suggests the name of Jesus (Joshua); and this in turn reminds us of the cross. The latter association in both documents depends upon the typology of Exodus 17, where the outstretched arms of Moses form the cross whilst 'Jesus' wins the battle below. In this and in other ways *Barnabas*, chapters 11–13, anticipates Justin's typology in some detail. For example he underlines the connexion of the cross with baptismal water and its foreshadowing in the 'sign' of the uplifted serpent. Concerning the last of these types he once more precedes Justin in drawing attention to the fact that the image of the brazen serpent is a deliberate exception to the decree which forbad image-making. Probably both writers believed the cross on Calvary to be T-shaped, corresponding in this particular to the serpent-sign.[1] Lastly, the emphasis of these two authors upon the name of Jesus in connexion both with the new circumcision and with the sign of the cross might suggest that the new 'seal' of circumcision was to be identified with the Name as well as with the saving sign. This detail, although doubtless not overlooked by the author of Philippians 2^{5-11}, had been amply emphasized in the Apocalypse of St John (cp. $7^{2\text{ ff.}}$ with 14^{1} and 22^{4}).

At this stage of our inquiry it has become clear that in the New Testament the terminology of the 'seal' takes the two main forms which have just been indicated, the *explicit* references being either to circumcision or to a symbolic marking of the forehead. From the second century onwards, however, there is considerable variation in the application of this particular imagery in the context of Christian initiation. For that reason it is desirable that we should pay close attention to the manner in which such a development took place. This consideration makes it also advisable to say something, at this juncture, concerning the general character of two other documents belonging to the sub-apostolic period, namely, the so-called *Second Epistle of Clement* and the *Shepherd of Hermas*. In both documents the use made of the 'seal' terminology

[1] Cp. above, ch. II, § iv, last par. but one.

is very slight; and it is only in the latter that a new application of the word itself is explicit. 2 Clement refers to baptism once and to the seal twice in three consecutive chapters (6–8), employing in each instance the same semi-technical phrase for 'keeping' pure and undefiled that to which he is referring. 'Baptism' and 'the seal' are thus apparently synonyms for Christian initiation. Hermas, however, actually identifies the seal with the baptismal water.[1]

Now there is in the New Testament no statement which is even approximately equivalent to such an unqualified identification of 'the seal' with 'the water'. In fact the whole history of the terminology in question might seem to have rendered such language impossible. Moreover, there is nothing suggestive of water in a signet-seal, or again in the materials upon which it is commonly imprinted. On the other hand in its application to circumcision by St Paul the employment of this imagery could still suggest the setting of a mark upon a material object. It must, however, be observed that the apostle himself appears to have been largely responsible for a wider application of such language with Christian connotations, if we may judge by some of his actual statements. Thus he told the Corinthians that they were the seal of his apostleship in the Lord; and again he referred to the completion of his mission to the church in Jerusalem with a collection of alms from other churches as 'having sealed to them this fruit'.[2] Such examples suggest that this particular nomenclature might in course of time be made to cover a very wide range of meanings. This, indeed, proved to be the case even within the limited range of associations which we are now examining.

That being so, however, it is all the more desirable to look for some thread of connexion between the variations. As we pass beyond the New Testament into new applications of this imagery have we still grounds for presuming the existence of anything that could be called continuity? It is at this point that we may find it advantageous to examine closely the literary character of the

[1] *Sim.* 9, xvi, 4. This has no counterpart in 2 Clement.

[2] 1 Cor. 9^{2}; Rom. 15^{28}.

documents in which a new phase of development seems to begin. This is a procedure which we have already applied in detail to some parts of the New Testament and also to Justin's *Dialogue*. In the course of the preceding argument we have found ourselves constantly obliged to examine characteristically biblical idioms of thought in both of these literary areas. Let us then follow the same course with the intervening period, taking 2 Clement and Hermas as representative specimens. Can it be said of these two authors, as I have said concerning Justin, that here also there is 'no break in the lines along which the revelation of the Christ was being apprehended from the earliest days'?[1] We shall find that, with some qualifications, the answer may still be in the affirmative.

In 2 Clement 14 there is a rich crop of biblical idioms. For first of all Genesis 1^{27}: 'God made the man male and female' is cited as referring to Christ and the Church. This identification corresponds exactly to that which we find in Ephesians 5^{21-33}, the only difference being that the Pauline version is based upon Genesis 2.[2] Secondly, throughout this chapter 'spirit' and 'flesh' are treated in true biblical fashion; that is, they are not opposed, but complementary. The flesh is the counterpart (*antitupos*) of the spirit. It can partake of immortality if the Holy Spirit is joined to it. So too the Church is 'spiritual'; and as such was manifested 'in the flesh of Christ'. For Christians a precept is given (apparently as Christ's): 'Guard the flesh that ye may partake of the spirit.' Here a third idiom becomes discernible, namely that characteristic oscillation which hovers between identification and distinction. In the precept just now quoted 'spirit' is clearly the Holy Spirit, whereas 'flesh' seems to refer to our mortal nature, as frequently in scripture. Yet in the very next sentence 'the flesh' is identified with the Church and 'the spirit' with Christ. In the chapter as a whole flesh and spirit each have three meanings; for example the Church as flesh is 'in the flesh' of the incarnate Saviour, but also in

[1] See above, end of par. 2.

[2] For details see *Revelation*, pp. 163 f. and 164 n, ch. VI, § v, and pp. 241 ff. What is explicit in Eph. 5 is implicit in 1 Cor. $11^{3\,\text{ff}}$.

our flesh. In each case the thought moves to and fro in exact accord with the biblical phenomena of identification.

This fluctuation in the application of terms, in so far as it is a question of 'spirit', appears in Hermas in a form which has received noticeable development. For example, in *Similitude* 9.i the Holy Spirit is identified with the Son of God. Yet in 9.xxiv they are as clearly distinguished; for the blessed ones are told: 'Of his Spirit ye received.' This fluctuation receives its fullest expression in *Similitude* 5.ii–vii, where the parable of the vineyard (ii) is explained in terms of a Spirit-Christology (v, vi). Here 'the pre-existent Holy Spirit, which created the whole creation, God made to dwell in flesh that he desired'. In this paragraph (vi) 'the servant' of the parable is first identified with the Son of God, and then sharply distinguished from him. From that point we pass to the sentence quoted above; and the human 'flesh' (personified) through faithful co-operation with the indwelling Spirit is, in reward, made to be the Spirit's 'partner'. This reward, however, is at once extended to all flesh which follows the same course. In the next paragraph we are told that the Holy Spirit can be defiled by union with sinful flesh; and in the conclusion 'the spirit' is identified with the believer. For the flesh and the spirit 'share in common, and the one cannot be defiled without the other'.[1]

It would seem then that in this phase of Christian understanding identifications are never absolute, because they belong rather to the realm of imagination than of logic. Moreover, this has a direct bearing upon our inquiry with regard to the language of Christian initiation. In *Similitude* 9.xvi 'the seal' is identified with the water of baptism; and this meaning of the term continues apparently to the end of 9.xvii. Yet in an earlier passage (8.vi) there is a variation. Hermas pleads for certain defaulting Christians who 'believed and received the seal and have broken it

[1] Cp. the concluding image in *Mand.* 10.iii of the same work, where the indwelling Spirit is compared to wine mixed with vinegar. So, in a private communication to me, Dr Carrington, Archbishop of Quebec, writes of Hermas: 'The Spirit in the heart of the believer is at one moment *his* spirit and at another moment the Spirit of God.' On the 'Semitic' background of these phenomena cp. *Revelation*, p. 292, note.

and did not keep it sound' that they may 'repent, receiving from thee a seal, and may glorify the Lord, that he had compassion upon them and sent thee to renew their spirits'. The speaker is evidently feeling after some form of penitential discipline which will give to the lapsed a second chance for return to the communion of the Church. In such restoration he sees 'a seal' comparable to the original seal of their first beginning. Clearly the terminology is not fixed, since there is no question of repeating their baptism. Here we are not in the realm of definitions, but rather of symbolic picture-language concerning the securities of Christian salvation.

Similarly the vineyard parable is so far removed from the exactitude of an allegory that even Hermas himself is completely puzzled.[1] His very natural suggestion that the parable presents the Son of God 'in the guise of a servant' is violently repudiated by his instructor (5.v.5, vi.i). Is he here unconsciously re-acting against the Jewish mentality of the original apostolic circle at Rome? And is his Spirit-Christology the result of a failure to grip the realities of apostolic teaching through the medium of unfamiliar idioms? Be that as it may, the idioms which he manipulates in his own fashion have a distinctly Hebraic affinity. His treatment of 'spirit' has points of similarity with St Paul's teaching in the first part of Romans 8 and possibly with the difficult saying in 2 Corinthians 3^{17}. Behind both lies the picture in Genesis 2^{7} where 'the breath of life' in man is identified with the Breath of deity. In Hermas, however, the Hebrew idioms are no longer mastered by apostolic insight into the transforming effects of the Gospel revelation. The fluid Hebrew concept of divine Spirit as a substance which can clothe or be clothed in mortal flesh is not subordinated to the apostolic *kerygma*. His acceptance of a Hebrew tendency to pluralism in conceptions of deity has not been sufficiently moulded to the trinitarian pattern of apostolic teaching.

[1] Perhaps the best defence of Hermas would be to suggest that the nearest analogy to this sort of parable in NT might possibly be found in the story about the unjust steward (Luke 16^{1-13}). But see also the discussion of Marcan parables in Dr Carrington's *The Primitive Christian Calendar* (pp. 8–11) with its suggestion of different levels of meaning.

What bearing, then, will these considerations have upon our scrutiny of the terminology employed in second century references to Christian initiation? Let us recall two characteristics of Pauline thought concerning the theology of the baptismal mystery. The first of these was summarized in chapter I, at the conclusion of § ii as follows: 'In the baptismal whole there is a profound unity, and yet also plurality. The mystery can be presented in terms of some one of its parts or aspects; and yet this phenomenon by itself is not adequate to the fulness of truth.' The second characteristic is referred to in the final paragraph of chapter II where I suggested that in Colossians 2 the two parts of initiation are related to one another after a fashion which could be designated by the phrase: 'interchange of properties.' That expression is of course technical in its patristic use, where it refers to the mystery of union between the two natures in Christ. Elsewhere I have suggested that this 'interchange' between the divine and human in the Christ has a wider relevance, in that the same principle operates as between the two Testaments, and again as between the orders of nature and grace in Christ.[1]

Ultimately the 'interchange' noted in Colossians runs back to the Hebrew conception of a whole pervading all its parts, which comes to its fulfilment in Christ and the Church. For this reason I purposely introduced the Christological phrase into a description of Pauline thought concerning the inter-relation of parts within the baptismal whole. The defective Christology of Hermas has a bearing upon his restricted use of the 'seal' terminology. There is a sense in which the baptismal water of the new covenant corresponds to circumcision under the old covenant.[2] The analogy of the sealed letter is at this point illuminating. The seal gives validity to the document. But also the document so sealed may have a validity and authority of its own. It has the character conveyed by the seal. So baptism sealed in confirmation has the

[1] *Revelation*, pp. 318 f., where the reference is primarily to the complementary mystery of 'coinherence', which involves 'interchange of properties'.

[2] Aspects of this subject are well handled by O. Cullmann in his treatise: *Die Tauflehre des NT Erwachsenen und Kindetaufe.*

character of a document which gives security. It has the quality of the seal, whereby we are 'sealed unto the day of redemption'. The part represents the whole, because it is integrally related to the other part of the whole.

II

THE CONCLUSIONS REACHED BY K. LAKE AND H. J. CADBURY CONCERNING THE LAYING ON OF HANDS IN ACTS 8 AND 19 CORROBORATE AND ILLUSTRATE OUR ESTIMATE OF THE BIBLICAL IDIOMS WHICH ARE OPERATIVE. BUT THESE INCIDENTS OPEN UP FRESH PROBLEMS WHICH CONCERN BOTH THE SIGNIFICANCE OF THE OUTWARD RITE AND THE NATURE OF THE GIFT CONVEYED.

We return once more to the examination of facts as recorded in the New Testament. Until recently the incidents reported in Acts $8^{14\,ff.}$ and 19^{1-7} were regarded as being almost the only scriptural evidence for the rite of Confirmation. In the latest phases of the discussion, however, their relevance as evidence has been altogether denied. As late as the year 1933 the following opinions were expressed by K. Lake and H. J. Cadbury in their commentary upon the Acts of the Apostles (*The Beginnings of Christianity. I.* Vol. iv with Additional Notes in Vol. v):

On Acts 8^{14-25}: 'The meaning of this short story clearly is that the Apostles in Jerusalem wished to give the Samaritans the gift of the Spirit which they knew that Philip's baptism could not confer' (iv, p. 92).

On Acts 8^{16}: 'The implication of this verse is quite clear. Baptism in the name of the Lord Jesus does not confer the Spirit: the laying on of Apostolic hands does' (iv, p. 93).

On Acts $19^{5,\,6}$: 'Is a distinction made between the baptism and the laying of hands? . . . it seems probable that here at least the laying on of hands is regarded as the climax of baptism' (iv, p. 238).

In Note xi: 'In viii. 16f. the laying on of the hands of the Apostles is regarded as the cause of the gift of the Spirit to the Samaritans, and in xix. 1 ff. is apparently the direct cause of the reception of the Spirit by the Ephesian Christians, but here it is closely related to instead of being distinguished from baptism in the Name of the Lord Jesus' (v, p. 138).

At the conclusion of this last passage the authors observe that 'the Catholic association of Baptism and Confirmation, so closely combined yet never quite identified', is 'obviously the direct descendant' of the practice indicated in these passages from Acts. Moreover the difficulty which has been found in 'distinguishing between the gift of the Spirit in Baptism and in Confirmation' is for these authors analogous to their own difficulty in interpreting the passages in Acts. They are clearly right in noting a difference of emphasis in Acts 8 and 19. In the former the two rites are sharply contrasted, whereas in the latter they are so closely associated that in this second story we seem to have an anticipation of the teaching of Primasius who speaks of 'the gift of the Holy Spirit which is given in Baptism through the Imposition of the Hand of the bishops'.[1] For, whereas in verses 2–4 the apostle connects the Holy Spirit with baptism, in the conclusion the gift of the Spirit is actually conveyed through the imposition of the apostle's hands after baptism. From this story taken by itself it would be natural to conclude that St Paul is here represented as believing that the laying on of hands is an essential condition or ingredient in a baptism which conveys the Spirit.

The contrast between the stories in Acts 8 and 19 thus begins to become clear. In the former baptism is the first step only in the rites of initiation. Lake and Cadbury, indeed, go so far as to say (in view of Acts 8) that 'baptism in the Name of Jesus is the preliminary to the recognition of a proselyte; the gift of the Spirit (usually given by the laying on of hands) is a separate thing'. They feel obliged to add, however (in view of chapter 19), that the two 'are so closely associated that they are often merely two parts of one ceremony' (v, p. 136). Their phrase: 'usually given', etc. is thoroughly justified by the story in Acts 19. For, as we have seen, the language used by the apostle in that incident becomes intelligible in the light of the sequel only if baptism is understood to be a name for the whole complex of initiatory rites. Clearly in St Luke's use of the term there is *oscillation* between two

[1] Quoted by Mason in *The Relation of Confirmation to Baptism*, pp. 109 f. The Latin text of this sentence appears as a motto on the title page of Mason's book.

meanings. Sometimes baptism means the first part of initiation; sometimes, however, it stands for the whole baptismal mystery and includes the laying on of hands. This second meaning, moreover, carries the further implication that in the Lucan view the laying on of hands was the normal method of conveying the gift of the Spirit, at least in churches with which the author of Acts was acquainted.

On the evidence collected in preceding pages of the present work the reader should find no cause for surprise in the phenomenon of oscillation between two meanings of 'baptism'. We are here once more in the presence of a characteristic biblical idiom. It is to the credit of the two authors from whose work we have been making citations in this section that, although they are puzzled by some of the facts which they record, yet they handle them on the whole with admirable objectivity.[1] This quality of their work makes their estimates of the evidence more valuable than they themselves seem to realize. For example, in the additional note from which we have already quoted, their discussion of baptism in the Acts includes the following significant passage:

> Belief in Jesus (or in his Name), baptism, the remission of sins, the laying on of Apostolic hands, and the reception of the Spirit seem to have formed a single complex of associated ideas, any one of which might in any single narrative be either omitted or emphasized (v, p. 134).

This statement is introduced with a question concerning the 'powers or privileges' conferred by baptism and a comment to the effect that 'the evidence is definite but curiously inconsistent'. So it would be by our modern standards of verbal and logical exactitude. Our standards, however, are so widely different from those of the biblical writers. I have called the passage just quoted 'significant' because it corresponds so exactly to the conclusions reached in the present work concerning the way in which biblical writers handle a complex whole in relation to its parts. When 'the whole' is identified with one of its parts for the sake of emphasis, then there may be complete silence about other parts which

[1] This tribute cannot be extended to their *theological* judgements. But with those we are not here concerned.

are equally integral to the whole. Conversely, distinction between the parts may be the point to be emphasized. When this occurs, the contrast may be stated in an absolute form (as in Acts 8^{14-17}) which cannot cover all aspects of the mystery, witness the difference of tone and implication between the two baptismal incidents which we have been examining. A close parallel to these phenomena in Acts can be found in two sayings of Jesus reported by St Matthew. In 9^{13} Jesus quotes from Hosea: 'I will have mercy and not sacrifice', where mercy rules out sacrifice altogether. Yet in 23^{23}, rebuking the Pharisees' practice of neglecting mercy for ceremonial minutiæ, Jesus says: 'these ought ye to have done, and not to have left the other undone.'

So far, in this section, we have been occupied with an elucidation of certain facts recorded in the Acts of the Apostles concerning the laying on of hands in those passages where it is closely related to baptism. We have found reason for thinking that the facts examined show the now familiar phenomena of a complex whole comprising two parts,—a complex of initiatory rites corresponding to two stages of initiation, within which there is perceptible a fluctuation of emphasis as between unity of the whole and differentiation of the parts. The phenomena in question, however—familiar as they will be to those who have followed the course of this investigation—recur in an altogether new setting which opens up fresh problems. These problems, broadly speaking, are two in number, namely (1) what precisely is signified by the laying on of hands as a sequel to baptism? and (2) what is the distinctive character of the gift conveyed in this rite? These two questions cannot be altogether kept apart. Yet each has its own context and background which must be examined separately. The context in Acts is all-important; and there is also a wider background which cannot be ignored.

The former problem arises from the fact that there is no precise parallel in scripture to such a gift of the Spirit through the laying on of hands. This is not surprising, since that gift is normally connected in the Old Testament with anointing (e.g. 1 Samuel 10^{1-13}, 16^{13}). Moreover in the New Testament the promised messianic gift is fully bestowed upon the messianic community only at Pentecost; and after that event there is no certain parallel to the incidents in Acts 8 and 19.[1] Elsewhere in scripture the laying on of hands appears as a means of blessing, appointment to office or healing. Recently there has been a tendency to connect the rite described in Acts 8 and 19 with appointment to office, rather than with the completion of Christian initiation. It is regarded as the 'layman's ordination' or as corresponding to Isaiah's alleged ordination of prophets or the like. Secondly, the gift of the Spirit in Acts 19 is manifested in an outbreak of *glossolalia* and prophecy. In Acts 8 there is no corresponding statement. But it would seem that something similar is implied; for Simon's knowledge of the interior gift must have been by way of inference from sensible effects (8^{18}). At this point we can see clearly an interconnexion between the two problems. Neither can be fully clarified apart from the other. Yet it will be convenient to examine first some facts concerning the outward sign.

III

THE LAYING ON OF HANDS IN SCRIPTURE. 'ORDINATION' ANALOGIES. THE BLESSING OF CHILDREN BY JESUS 'REPEATED' IN THE APOSTOLIC BENEDICTION OF NEOPHYTES. BUT THE GOSPEL HEALINGS ARE ALSO RELEVANT, ESPECIALLY MARK 8^{22-26}. THE GOOD PHYSICIAN RESTORES AND ENLIGHTENS SICK HUMANITY THROUGH SYMBOLIC ACTS. RESTORATION IS 'REPEATED' IN ACTS; AND THE SYMBOLIC ACTIONS RECUR IN THE EARLY CHURCH, AT FIRST PERHAPS AS ALTERNATIVES. TRANSITION TO THE GIFTS OF THE SPIRIT.

In the Old Testament the laying on of hands appears in four types of action which are summarized by the late Bishop Chase in

[1] A *charisma* is bestowed upon Timothy through the laying on of hands in 1 Tim. 4^{14} and 2 Tim. $1^{6, 7}$. Only in the latter case is there a possible reference to the Holy Spirit. If Chase was right in identifying the latter incident as T's confirmation, the author is presumably in agreement with St Luke. But the gift is not exactly defined. See F. H. Chase, *Confirmation in the Apostolic Age*, pp. 35 ff.

his book.[1] In all four groups the idea expressed is 'the transference of character or of endowment'. Here we need notice only two of the four. In Genesis $48^{14\text{ ff.}}$ Jacob blesses his grandsons. In Numbers 27^{18-23}, under divine direction, Moses lays his hands upon Joshua, thus transferring to him his own authority as leader. In the latter instance it is noticeable that *before* the ceremony Joshua is described as 'a man in whom is the Spirit', whereas no mention is made of endowment with the Spirit through the actual rite. In Deuteronomy 34^9, however, we learn that Joshua 'was full of the spirit of wisdom; for Moses had laid his hands upon him'. The gift which was thus bestowed was not, then, the first bestowal of the Spirit upon the man who now received the laying on of hands. The incident, therefore, was not comparable to those recorded in Acts 8 and 19. There is, however, another passage in Acts which presents a remarkable parallel to the incident in Numbers. It occurs in chapter 6 which records the election and ordination of the Seven.

Here the Christian community is directed to choose seven men who are 'full of the Spirit and wisdom'; moreover one of those selected is 'Stephen, a man full of faith and the Holy Ghost'. There follows a brief statement of their ordination with prayer and imposition of the apostles' hands. But, as in Numbers, no mention is made of endowment with the Spirit at ordination. Nevertheless, just as Deuteronomy records such a gift after the event, so also Acts 6^8 records the fact that Stephen, newly ordained, was 'full of grace and power'. It certainly looks as if St Luke, when recording the facts concerning an ordination followed carefully the model set for him in the scriptural statements about Joshua. It is to that extent all the more unlikely that he has anything of the sort in mind in the incidents of Acts 8 and 19 where the laying on of hands is in two different ways made to be the complement of baptism and the appointed means of receiving a *first* gift of the Spirit. We are thus left with one possible precedent in the Old Testament, namely Jacob blessing two children.

[1] *Op. cit.*, pp. 61 ff. But Num. $8^{10\text{ ff.}}$ should be connected with sacrificial offerings rather than appointment to office, as RV. ref. margin, *ad loc.*, rightly indicates.

To this there is a definite counterpart in the Gospel, namely the story of Jesus blessing little children by laying his hands upon them. Is not that incident the most obvious background to the action of the apostles in laying their hands upon the newly-baptized? The story is told in Mark 10^{13-16}. The children are brought 'that he might touch them'. The disciples object; but their objection is set aside in unforgettable words. Then the Lord 'took them in his arms, laid his hands upon them and blessed them'. Matthew (19^{13-15}) has 'that he might lay his hands on them, and pray', shortens the incident as a whole, and concludes with 'he laid his hands on them'. These are, perhaps, typical simplifications, which call for no comment. On the other hand St Luke's handling of the incident is decidedly mysterious. So far as it goes it is almost verbally identical with the Marcan narrative.[1] But it entirely omits to mention the actual laying on of hands. Mark 10^{16} is ignored! What is the explanation? I suggest that here once more the authors of *Beginnings I*, Vol. iv, have given the correct clue. At various points in their commentary on Acts they draw attention to a Lucan peculiarity. In a number of instances words, phrases, sentences or incidents in St Mark's Gospel, which are absent from Luke's first volume, recur in Acts; and this appears to be part of a deliberate technique whereby the gospel story is shewn to undergo repetition in the story of the church.[2]

If we are right in supposing that St Luke omits the laying on of hands in his version of Mark 10^{13-16} for a reason corresponding to that which operates in the other instances referred to above, this will mean that St Mark's story of Jesus laying his hands in blessing upon the heads of children is 'repeated', in this peculiarly biblical sense, in St Luke's account of the apostles laying their hands upon the newly-baptized Christians. For clearly there is no other event recorded in Acts which would suitably symbolize such a repeti-

[1] Luke 18^{15-17} = Mark 10^{13-15}, except that he alters the word for 'children', perhaps in order not to anticipate the significant dominical use of the other word, especially in our Lord's concluding sentence.

[2] See further, *The Dominion of Christ*, p. 24 and note 1, where references are given.

tion. But further, by this means Gospel and Acts are made to throw light upon one another. Christian initiation is foreshadowed in our Lord's own act. But also the words used by our Lord on that occasion, so carefully recorded in St Luke's version, may be understood to throw light upon the meaning of the apostolic imposition of hands on Christian neophytes. The words of Christ emphasize the childlike character of the kingdom of God and its congruity with childhood. They indicate also that membership in the kingdom has for its pre-condition possession of an attitude or quality which may be called childlike. If the incidents in Acts are regarded as 'repeating' the gospel story, St Luke is here viewing new-born Christians in the light of such teaching.[1]

When the apostles laid their hands on the newly-baptized they could scarcely have failed to remember the corresponding action of their Lord in blessing little children. But they might also have remembered other incidents in our Lord's earthly ministry, when he laid hands upon the sick and those with physical defects with a view to their recovery. This further consideration becomes important for the present inquiry in view of the clearly symbolical character of the whole ministry of healing as treated in the Gospels and also in the Acts. As I have dealt with this matter fully elsewhere[2] a brief reminder of the facts will perhaps be sufficient. In a few instances we are told that Jesus 'took hold of the hand' of a person in restoring health or life,[3] or again that he 'touched' such individuals.[4] But on two occasions he was asked to lay his hands upon someone for restoration (Mark 5^{23}, 7^{32}); and two evangelists record occasions on which our Lord performed this act for a number of sick folk (Mark 6^{5}, Luke 4^{40}). The Lucan instance of this is noticeable because the evangelist there inserts the laying on of hands into a Marcan incident which does not contain it (Mark 1^{34}). There is, however, one incident in St Mark of a peculiar

[1] For fuller details concerning the gospel material see further, *The Dominion of Christ*, ch. III.

[2] *Op. cit.*, pp. 14–56.

[3] Mark 1^{31}, 5^{41} and Matt. 8^{15}, 9^{25}.

[4] Mark 1^{41} = Luke 5^{13}; cp. Matt. 8^{3}, 9^{27}, 20^{34}.

character to which, for reasons which will appear, we must now give special attention.[1]

As I have explained in a previous volume, the healing of the blind man recorded in Mark 8^{22-26} has the character of a key incident in that Gospel because of its symbolical relation to the context in which it is set, that is to say, the story of the enlightenment which the Twelve are undergoing in that part of the narrative. The symbolism is heightened by the language of *restoration* introduced in verse 25, as well as by the gradual nature of the 'restoration' process. But further, the incident is omitted by St Luke together with the sequence to which it belongs (7^{31}–8^{26}). Yet the restoration motif is introduced in full force again in Acts 1–4, notably in the healing of a cripple and the ensuing speech of St Peter. If there is for St Luke a repetition of the gospel in the story of the church there is no point at which this is more conspicuously evident than in the re-introduction of the restoration theme from St Mark's Gospel into the early chapters of Acts, especially when we take into account their common background in the Old Testament.[2] All of this must now be taken for granted. Its relevance to our present inquiry, however, has yet to be made clear. Briefly, it hinges upon the fact that the healing of the blind man in St Mark's story is effected through the laying on of hands, and the further fact that in the healing process this remedy is applied not once but twice.

The repetition of the symbolic act on this occasion helps to set the incident apart, giving it a character of its own to which other features of the story contribute. On the other hand, for our present purpose it is equally important to see those special features in the widest possible context. The symbolical character of the gospel healings is now widely recognized. They are enacted proclamations of the good news that Jesus offers to our fallen humanity salvation through restoration to wholeness of life—that wholeness and integrity for which our divided nature craves,

[1] For my earlier treatment of this incident and its relation to Acts see *op. cit.*, pp. 21–30.

[2] For which see the diagram, *op. cit.*, p. 30, footnote.

and to the recovery of which through God's saving grace the whole bible points. This is the theme of the Old Testament as well as of the New, and no one was more keenly aware of it than the evangelists themselves. All the synoptic gospels record the saying of Jesus in which he likens his mission to that of a physician who restores bodily health (Mark 2^{17} and parallels). Like a physician too the Lord uses his hands for healing purposes. At this point it will be well to bear in mind the Hebrew habit of regarding human nature as a unity. The dualism of the Greek contrast between body and soul hardly ever comes to the surface even in the New Testament. Healing and wholeness concern the whole man.

It is this fact which makes the healing of the blind man in Mark 8^{22-26} such a typically scriptural symbol of all that is signified by Christian initiation, and indeed of the whole nature of Christian sacraments, wherein the Hebrew tendency to 'identify' the inward and the outward comes to its fulfilment. Moreover, the details of the story are so remarkably like the liturgical practice of later times, as described for example by Tertullian, that the question naturally arises whether the one has not actually influenced the other. In the *De Baptismo* (chapters 7, 8) Tertullian first describes the anointing of newly-baptized Christians, quoting Acts 4^{27} for the anointing of Jesus by the Father, He then describes the imposition of the bishop's hand, invoking the Holy Spirit by this act of benediction. So in the gospel story anointing precedes the laying on of hands. For Jesus first anoints the blind eyes with his own saliva before the first imposition of his hands. There is no indication that the two practices were thus combined in the apostolic church, apart from the fact that St Paul is represented as associating Christian initiation both with anointing (2 Corinthians 1^{22}) and with laying on of hands (Acts 19^{6}). On the other hand in Hebrews 6^{1-6} it appears that baptism and the laying on of hands are regarded as the appointed means through which the neophyte undergoes a once-for-all 'enlightenment'.

It seems probable, therefore, that the two modes of restoring the wholeness of our nature practised by our Lord in healing the blind man were not at first conjoined in primitive Christian practice. They were, in fact, alternative modes of completing baptismal initiation. St Luke and the author of Hebrews who are thought to have belonged to the same literary circles were also, it seems, familiar with the same ritual customs as regards the forms of Christian initiation. Both emphasize the laying on of hands which is so prominent in the gospel story concerning the blind man. Both also have further points of contact with the story in respect of its symbolism. The physical illumination of the blind man has its counterpart in the language of the epistle concerning 'enlightenment' as a characteristic of the newly made Christian. Similarly the 'restoration' of the blind man so that 'he saw all things clearly' has its counterpart in the 'perfect soundness' granted to the cripple at the Beautiful Gate of the temple, 'saved' by faith in the Name of Jesus in token of the coming 'restoration of all things' (Acts 3^{1}–4^{12}). When St Luke re-introduces the laying on of hands a few chapters later, after characteristically omitting St Mark's striking story, we can recognize his familiar technique. The Lord Jesus is continuing his great work of restoration to wholeness through the hands of his apostles which are verily his own hands.

The theological implications of these contributions in Acts and the Epistle to the Hebrews will be matter for further consideration later, when we are concerned with the theology of Christian initiation. At present we are occupied with an elucidation of facts. It is, however, precisely at this point that there is urgent necessity to consider another set of facts which belong to the whole setting of the laying on of hands in St Luke's story concerning the early days of church history. The author of Hebrews urges his readers to press on from their present immaturity to the perfection which is their proper goal. St Paul found himself under a like necessity in dealing with his Corinthian converts. The latter set store by showy gifts of the Spirit which the apostle did not regard as the highest. Now it is precisely such gifts of the Spirit as the apostle thought to be of lesser importance which are most in evidence in the Acts of the Apostles. In Acts 19^{6}, moreover, 'speaking with tongues' is stated to have been a consequence of the apostolic imposition of hands upon the Ephesian group of neophytes. Something similar is clearly implied in the corresponding story of Acts 8. At this early stage the bestowal of the Spirit is recognized in external manifestations. We have, therefore, to consider next what is the relation of these peculiar gifts of the Spirit to that process of salvation in which Christ restores the wholeness of our nature, the process into which we enter through the baptismal rites of the Church.

IV

'SPEAKING WITH TONGUES' AS A GIFT OF THE SPIRIT. ITS ECSTATIC CHARACTER HIGHLY PRIZED IN THE FIRST PHASE OF THE SPIRIT-BEARING BODY, ALTHOUGH DANGERS OF MISUSE BECAME EVIDENT LATER. IN THIS FIRST PHASE REASONED CONVICTION AND HIGHLY EMOTIONAL TENSION GO TOGETHER. THROUGH THE LAYING ON OF HANDS THE NEWLY-BAPTIZED SHARED THE SENSIBLE EFFECTS OF THE SPIRIT'S FIRST IMPACT UPON OUR FALLEN HUMANITY. THE GIFTS RECEIVED CORRESPONDED TO A LAW OF GRADUAL ENLIGHTENMENT WHICH CHARACTERIZES THE LIFE OF THE CHURCH AS A WHOLE.

What happened on the Day of Pentecost? Anyone who has read recent critical discussions of this subject will know how obscure some at least of the facts can appear to be. In *The Beginnings of Christianity, I*, Vol. V, the authors have included a Note (pp. 111 ff.), covering ten pages, which discusses the difficulties fully from a modern point of view. For our present purpose the only matter which directly concerns us is the question as to what was the nature of the *glossolalia* or 'speaking with tongues' which in Acts 2 is described as a direct consequence of the Spirit's descent upon the apostolic company. It is natural to compare this phenomenon with that which St Paul describes very fully in 1 Corinthians 14. In both cases the speech is clearly 'ecstatic' in character. For at Corinth it was such as to give the impression of madness in the speakers, at least to a stranger entering the Christian assembly —'Will they not say that ye are mad?' (14^{23}). Similarly at Jerusalem, in the Pentecostal scene, some of those who formed the listening crowd thought that the apostolic speakers were drunk (Acts 2^{13}). Another point of similarity between the two descriptions is the fact that in both there are some hearers present who claim to be able to understand this form of speech.

On the other hand there is a difference. For St Paul sharply distinguishes *glossolalia* from prophecy, assuming that the latter is intelligible to all who hear without need of an interpreter, whereas St Peter in applying Joel's oracle seems to regard speaking with tongues as a form of prophecy. Prophecy, however, could take a variety of forms. When prophets first appear in the Old Testament they are perhaps not far from the level of the dervish (1 Samuel 10^{10-13}, 19^{20-24}). It is to be noticed also that in Acts 19^{6} *glossolalia* and prophecy are mentioned together as joint-effects of the laying on of hands. It is possible that we are confronted here with a genuine historical difference. It may be that 1 Corinthians represents a more developed stage of pneumatic *charismata* than that of the early tradition which St Luke is following in his descriptions. For our present purpose, however, what is important is the clear indication given by the narrator that the outward signs of the illapse of the Spirit upon the Day of Pentecost continue to be manifested and recognized as such during the ensuing development of church history covered by the Acts. This is clearly stated by St Peter himself in his account of Cornelius's entry into the Church: 'The Holy Spirit fell upon them *as also upon us in the beginning*' (11^{15}).

The main difference between 1 Corinthians and Acts in respect of *glossolalia* lies in the fact that in the epistle St Paul has clearly reached the conclusion that this particular gift had ceased to be edifying and was not to be encouraged, whereas Acts reflects a situation in which 'speaking with tongues' was highly prized by the church as a whole. What then are we to make of this marked divergence of opinion? We certainly ought not to conclude that one of the two opinions is more reliable than the other. That way would lead to hopeless scepticism like so many judgements of the 'either . . . or' type. It seems much more reasonable to conclude that here we are confronted with two quite different phases of early Christian experience. As regards actual facts the two accounts have been judged to be by no means mutually inconsistent.[1] Moreover St Paul freely acknowledges that *glossolalia* is a gift of the Spirit. He claimed to possess this gift himself and refused to forbid its exercise.[2] Experience and lapse of time, however, had shewn that it could be misused. St Luke, on the other hand, must not be assumed to be giving his personal opinions. As the late W. L. Knox has shewn, this author certainly sets himself to follow reliable traditions. He must have known something of St Paul's opinions on such a matter. But his business is that of a historian who seeks to present objectively the judgements and beliefs of those about whom he writes.

There are good grounds for believing that within whatever limitations he has served history well in this matter. It is easy to form *a priori* judgements about what we might think the earliest Christian experience of the Spirit should have been. To do so, however, would be an act of treachery towards the particular form in which the revelation took shape and towards the actual process through which the new life in Christ moved from stage to stage. The best commentary upon this subject with which I am acquainted is to be found in a few pages of a book written a generation ago. I refer to *The Ministry in the Church in Relation to Prophecy and Spiritual Gifts* by H. J. Wotherspoon, Lecture III, pp. 87–97. In St Luke's account of the pentecostal *glossalalia* the phenomenon had two contrasted effects. While some mocked, others among the 'devout' bystanders were deeply impressed. In whatever way it happened, they found themselves to be confronted with 'the wonderful works of God'. They were made to be conscious of a divine agency. A radically new force was present, creating a deep psychological disturbance. For it would seem that the deeper effects of the Spirit could not easily appear at once. He must needs work from the surface of human personality towards the centre.

Ecstatic gifts by their very nature belonged to an emotional level afterwards transcended when the Spirit took hold of will and

[1] *Beginnings I*, Vol. V, p. 118. [2] 1 Cor. $14^{18, 39}$.

character; but time would be needed for such a momentous change to take effect. One of the most significant features of St Paul's argument in 1 Corinthians 14 is the fact that he distinguishes 'spirit' and 'understanding' as though they were wholly different functions of human personality. Yet in both the biblical languages the words for 'spirit' are applied alike to the Spirit of God and to higher manifestations of the human spirit. In the apostle's argument it is assumed that one can offer prayer publicly with one's spirit and yet be wholly unintelligible to the ordinary listener. Yet earlier in this same epistle he had spoken of the 'spiritual' man as one who 'judges all things, but is himself judged by no one' because through the Holy Spirit he has access to the mind of God in Christ (chapter 2). The fact that the apostle could still regard *glossolalia* as a gift of the Spirit, notwithstanding the very different tone of such passages as the one to which I have just referred is an indication that the Holy Spirit can operate at very diverse levels in human nature. We seem, indeed, to be here in touch with a mystery of divine working which belongs to the very heart of revelation and of the ways in which our heavenly Father deals with his children.

I have written elsewhere at length concerning 'the form' of revelation and concerning its intimate connexion with the life of God's chosen people. 'Revelation is given, not only *to* those who make religious response, but also *in and through them*.'[1] This universal truth has its particular application and illustration in the facts which we are now considering. Revelation throughout its course was conditioned by the human nature in and through which it was given. This principle which is exhibited upon the largest scale in the Old Testament is not less truly operative in the history of the new Israel from its first beginnings. In the gospels we get glimpses of the slow mental processes into which the new revelation must enter, and by which its whole interpretation must be radically conditioned. But upon these processes there supervened the great illumination of Pentecost in a manner which transcends our powers of analysis. We can only observe its effects.

[1] *Revelation*, p. 22.

Now those effects as immediately manifested on the Day of Pentecost were twofold. Alongside the *glossolalia* we must set the speech of St Peter with its detailed exposition of the fulfilment of scripture in Jesus of Nazareth.

Both these effects suggest forcibly an enlightenment of the disciples by the Holy Spirit; and yet these two immediate results of the Spirit's outpouring are markedly different. Whereas the former illustrates the Pauline contrast between 'spirit' and 'understanding' referred to above, the latter, that is St Peter's argument, is a closely reasoned exposition of the manner in which the gospel events fulfil prophetic oracles. The speech gives evidence of earnest reflexion. It is the first classic proclamation of the Christian message, delivered with confident conviction. It is repeated with little variation in the later speeches of Acts. Yet an essential part of this reasoned address is the statement that Joel's prophecy is fulfilled in the ecstatic utterances which arrested the attention of the crowd. Thus it corresponds on the one hand to the fact that the risen Lord had 'opened their minds to understand the scriptures' (Luke 24^{45}), and on the other hand to the announcement made by him that 'ye shall be baptized with the Holy Ghost not many days hence'. The enlightenment of apostolic minds which began in the forty days after Easter did not come to fruition until the stupendous psychological event which generated the gift of tongues. The two effects, therefore, proceed from a single cause. They are two parts of one whole.

The next thing which is deserving of notice is that according to St Luke's reading of history both the two immediate effects of Pentecost set their stamp upon the life of the church as a whole. The speech attributed to St Paul in Acts 13 (verses 26–37) follows the Petrine model and reproduces the same argument concerning the fulfilment of Psalm 16. But also the *glossolalia* in which Peter found fulfilment of prophecy on the feast of Pentecost broke out afresh when Paul laid his hands on the Ephesian neophytes; moreover, in their case it was also combined with that gift of prophecy which Peter seems to have attributed to those who spoke with tongues. Thus the gifts of the Spirit bestowed through the imposition of the apostle's hands were precisely those gifts which were imparted to the new community by the ascended Christ when he gave to it its original endowment of the Spirit. These cross-connexions are all-important. The pentecostal gifts of the Spirit exhibit a high degree of emotional tension which corresponds to the confident proclamation of the apostolic *kerygma*, that condensed summary of the Good News concerning Jesus of which several examples are furnished in Acts. The reasoned argument in these statements produced conviction because it proceeded from a degree of Spirit-possession which went deeper than the level of conscious thought. For this very reason it could, at first, express itself, in part at least, only through ecstatic phenomena. Moreover, these effects of the great enlightenment are inevitably transmitted to those who at this stage are initiated into the Spirit-bearing community.

One of the most remarkable characteristics of St Luke's second volume is to be found in an apparent contrast. A main theme of the opening chapters is the topic of 'restoration to wholeness' which is symbolized by the healing of the cripple in chapter 3 in correspondence with the healing ministry of Jesus. Yet the inauguration of this salvation which leads to wholeness is accompanied by an outbreak of phenomena which might seem to indicate not wholeness but disintegration. Moreover, in those who are initiated into the new saving wholeness these tokens of disruption are repeated, and are clearly welcomed with satisfaction! It might almost seem as if the artificial surface-unity of our fallen nature had to be broken down by the first epoch-making entry of the Spirit, before the positive process of building up or 'edification' could proceed. It is this latter which becomes prominent in St Paul's epistles and which is so firmly stressed in 1 Corinthians 14. I cannot refrain from making a further suggestion about this whole subject which may or may not have been in St Luke's mind, but which certainly seems congenial to his technique. It concerns the symbolic connexion of the 'restoration' recorded in Mark 8^{22-26} with its sequel in the life of the church.

It will be remembered that one peculiar feature of the healing recorded in St Mark's story is its gradual character. In the gospels the laying on of hands is not often referred to in explicit terms; and there is no sort of parallel to its repetition in a single incident as we have it in this narrative of the blind man. The first imposition of hands gives him sight after a sort; but it leaves him in an abnormal state. In the Old Testament men are sometimes likened to trees; and there is an example in the first Gospel which might be considered relevant, inasmuch as it occurs in a comment of our Lord's where in a single breath he refers to the Pharisees as plants to be rooted up and also as blind men leading others astray (Matt. $15^{13, 14}$)! On the other hand St Mark's blind man sees men walking as trees before the second imposition of the Lord's hands enable him to see all things clearly. The bizarre picture of walking trees symbolizes the perplexity of the disciples before Christ was raised from the dead. But it may also serve to remind us that in her earthly pilgrimage the Church passes through stages of illumination. Moreover in each cycle of such a movement there may at first be deep perplexity and some disorder before the final clarification is attained. Thus the first phase of enlightenment both for churches and for individuals may be aptly symbolized by those first gifts of the Spirit which, through an *apostolic* imposition of hands, the newly-baptized were permitted to share with the rest of the Church.

Towards the end of § II in this chapter questions were asked concerning the significance of the apostolic imposition of hands in the Acts and concerning the corresponding gift or gifts of the Spirit. Actually the questions were posed in a wider form; and to this an adequate answer can be attempted only at the more theological level which we are now approaching. In the greater part of this chapter we have been occupied with the more pedestrian level of inquiry which seeks to form a just estimate concerning all the relevant facts of which the theologian must take account in reaching his ultimate judgements. At this point, then, it will be convenient to state a provisional conclusion. In our survey of the facts as set forth in scripture we have encountered no evidence which would justify an abandonment of the conclusion, traditional since Tertullian's day, that the laying on of hands recorded in Acts 8 and 19 is a form of the rite now known in Western Christendom under the name of Confirmation, the rite which is an integral part of our baptismal initiation as Christians. Recent suggestions to the contrary have not as yet taken serious account of the whole range of the facts which modern knowledge has made accessible.

Additional Note B. Two incidents in Acts

The stories in Acts 9 and 10 concerning St Paul and Cornelius contain features of special interest for our present inquiry. Both stories are concerned with Christian initiation under peculiar circumstances; and in both instances the baptism comes last in the order of events. In chapter 9 there is another detail to which attention must be drawn. In the ministry of Ananias to Saul of Tarsus after the latter's conversion physical healing is actually combined with Christian initiation. What was symbolized in Mark $8^{22\text{ ff.}}$ was effected in literal truth in this particular repetition of the Gospel. Ananias, divinely commissioned, laid his hands upon Saul, saying: 'The Lord hath sent me . . . that thou mightest receive thy sight and be filled with the Holy Ghost. And immediately there fell from his eyes, as it were, scales, and he recovered his sight; and he arose and was baptized' (vv. 17–19). The connexions here are all-important. Physical illumination and the influx of the Holy Spirit are closely united. They are the joint result of an imposition of hands by the Lord's *shaliach*. Baptism follows as a supplementary rite. Once more, as in John 9, we are confronted with what certainly looks like a primitive prebaptismal sealing. Saul is a Christian proselyte in whom the bodily and spiritual aspects of 'restoration' are identified in truly Hebrew fashion.

This incident forms with those in chapters $8^{14\text{ ff.}}$ and 10 a significant triad. In all three stories baptism is distinguished from the gift of the Spirit. In the first and second the gift is associated with the laying on of hands; in the second and third it precedes baptism like the proselyte's circumcision. Moreover the definite parallel between the two blind men healed by laying on of hands, in Mark 8 and Acts 9, has this further significance; it strengthens the case for a repetitive symbolism in Acts. For it provides a bridge between the healing in Mark 8 and the initiation in Acts 8 by combining the features of both stories in one! Also, by this combination there is further illustrated the theme of a total messianic 'restoration' unfolded in Acts 1–4, where a symbolic healing follows closely upon the Pentecostal outpouring. For, just as there Pentecost ushers in 'total restoration' in a healing (chapter 3), so here a restoration of the whole man which includes both parts of initiation ushers in (in chapter 10) 'a second Pentecost' (of the Gentiles) which is completed in the baptism of the converts. There is, perhaps, one further point to be noticed. The symbolic cross-connexions in this typically Lucan pattern of events are helped out by a strict economy of words. In the story of Saul's initiation there is a noticeable silence about external manifestations of the Spirit's presence. Attention is concentrated exclusively upon a symbolism of total restoration. By contrast, in the story of Cornelius the parallel between the two 'Pentecosts' is in this respect affirmed twice (10^{44-47}, 11^{15}).

BOOK II

THE THEOLOGY OF CHRISTIAN INITIATION

CHAPTER IV

THE ANALOGY BETWEEN CHRIST AND THE CHRISTIAN

I

OUR SURVEY HAS SHEWN A BAPTISMAL WHOLE IN TWO PARTS. OTHER EXAMPLES OF A 'UNITY WHICH INCLUDES DISTINCTIONS' TO BE FOUND ALIKE IN SCRIPTURE AND IN THE DEFINITIONS OF CHRISTIAN DOCTRINE. IN BOTH SPHERES REVELATION IS THE WHOLE TRANSCENDING KNOWLEDGE, YET ACCESSIBLE TO A SCRIPTURAL THEOLOGY. A SINGLE DIVINE PLAN FOR CHRIST AND HIS PEOPLE IS REPEATED FROM HIM TO US. SO THERE IS ANALOGY BETWEEN HIM AND US; AND THIS BEGINS, FOR EACH OF US, WITH THE RELATION OF OUR BAPTISM TO HIS INCARNATION.

The evidence of facts surveyed in the preceding chapters has shewn us Christian initiation as a single complex mystery, containing within itself a duality which may be regarded from various points of view. As a liturgical action it involves two stages of initiation. As a whole it has two parts, which, however, are not in compartments since they are mutually interpenetrating. The 'parts' are more like two foci of reference in one system, where each refers to the whole and represents the whole. The two are therefore mutually complementary. I am not forgetting that in practice the initiatory stages were sometimes held to be three or even four in number, as when the second stage was ritually divided into two parts, namely chrismation and imposition of hands, and again when first communion was regarded primarily, not as the first of a new series, but as the crowning point of the initiatory rites. Our present argument, however, is concerned, not with these details, but with the theological question concerning the status of confirmation and concerning its relation to baptism. That these two rites represent a duality within the one baptismal mystery will from this point onwards be taken for granted. What we have now to consider more fully is the problem as to how the two rites are to be distinguished with regard to the gifts of which they are respectively the channels or vehicles.

The reader may recall that in the course of the previous survey a comparison was made between the language of the fathers concerning the union of two natures in Christ and the language used by St Paul where it was believed that the apostle was indicating an analogous 'interchange of properties' between the two parts of Christian initiation.[1] The word 'analogous' is here introduced to provide a safeguard against misconceptions. For 'analogy' always implies difference as well as likeness in the comparison which is being made. Nevertheless, despite all differences between biblical idioms of thought and later doctrinal definitions the deepest mysteries in both of these spheres not infrequently take a form which might be described as 'unity in plurality' or a unity which includes distinctions within itself. Such a phrase clearly applies to the orthodox doctrines of the Trinity and the Incarnation; and it will be remembered that both doctrines were finally formulated only after prolonged conflict between opposing or contrasted tendencies. The difficulties were ultimately overcome, not simply by striking a balance between two complementary truths such as 'unity and distinction', but rather by shewing that, rightly understood, each truth implies as its counterpart the complementary truth. In fact each of the two contrasted truths could be correctly grasped only when it was seen to be definable in terms of the other truth which was its complement.

The successful formulation of those two primary doctrines was an outstanding example of faithfulness to revelation in more senses than one. For not only did the definitions drawn up by the Councils of the Church preserve the substance of revelation by safeguarding it from false or inadequate interpretations. It would also be true to say that the actual forms taken by the de-

[1] See above, ch. II, last two pars., and ch. III, § i, last two pars. with note.

finitions corresponded to the characteristic forms in which the revelation itself was given. This statement must now receive further elucidation. Dogmatic definitions, as such, have a logical and abstract character which differentiates them sharply from the concrete, pictorial imagery of scripture. Yet in the orthodox definitions the abstractions of logic are subordinated to the mysterious wholeness of revealed truth. The truth revealed is mysterious because its wholeness transcends the human intellect. In its unity this wholeness cannot be *com*prehended by the mind of man; it can only be *ap*prehended through the interrelation of the distinctions which lie within it. Similarly, the revelation contained in the bible has a unity which transcends all particular presentations of it in the parts of scripture. Logic can all too easily make it appear that any one part is incompatible with any other part; and the unity of the whole will then have been lost to sight. Orthodoxy, however, will in its apprehension of truth correspond to such an approach to scripture as may find the unity of revelation implicit in the correlation of its parts.

The truth about Christian initiation, as about other parts of the revelational whole embodied in Christian faith and practice, may be expected to manifest itself to us as we approach it with these considerations in mind. There is, however, a further aspect of 'unity in plurality', as that concept is here understood, in which not only a parallel but also a close inter-connexion may be observed to-day between problems arising in the sphere of biblical studies and those which belong more properly to systematic theology. Until quite recently in the modern era sacred study of all kinds was too exclusively analytical in its interests and in its techniques to pay adequate attention to the higher theological unities involved. Nevertheless, as we now learn to recognize the significance of such unities alike in scripture and in doctrine we may hope for a closer correlation of both in a scriptural theology which is not less thorough in regard to the minutiæ of scholarship because it also sees the parts related within a far-stretching whole. We have for some time been learning that particular doctrines cannot be adequately understood and appreciated as so many separate units.

For everything becomes more significantly intelligible just so far as we can discern its relation to the totality of revelation. That totality, however, belongs essentially to scripture; and it is only a scriptural theology which can be at home in it.

Accordingly it is in scripture that we must look for the substance of that unity which includes distinctions. In particular, it is in scripture that we see the Christological whole wherein Christ and the Church together form a single organism of new creation moulded through cosmic victory over evil. Within this new whole, as redeemed humanity is gathered in, there is taking place a fulfilment of the divine plan in its totality; and since the plan is one there is discernible a repetition of its outline from head to members. This is the ground upon which we may rightly expect to find some analogy between Christ and the Christian such as may throw light upon the order of Christian initiation. At one point in the gospel story suggestions of a parallel force themselves upon our attention. Jesus is baptized and receives a gift or endowment of the Holy Spirit. Here is surely a foreshadowing of the manner in which we became Christians. Such a parallel has perhaps always been present to the mind of the church; and lately some discussion of these two gospel incidents has entered prominently into contributions concerning problems of Christian initiation. It is, I believe, unfortunate that in what has been written recently upon this subject the biblical setting of the discussion has been unduly restricted.

The grounds of this criticism must now be explained more fully. In what has been written about our Lord's baptism in relation to ours the gospel event has very rightly been connected with all that followed from then onwards to the Day of Pentecost, particularly with the death and resurrection of the Saviour. I venture to think, however, that if attention had also been paid to all that preceded it in the gospels this enlarged background would have opened out new vistas of truth. It is all too commonly assumed that the mission of St John Baptist and the character of his baptismal ministry with their Jewish background, are the only matters which call for discussion in the preceding events or in the immediate context. This would be, in effect, to imply that St Mark's Gospel provides a sufficient evangelical context not only for judgements concerning our Lord's baptism and its sequel, but also for the relation of these events to corresponding events in the Christian life. It is sufficient, here, to point out that in the fourfold gospel the descent of the Spirit upon the newly baptized Saviour is not the only event of such a kind to be taken into account. For according to the first and the third evangelists Jesus was 'conceived by the Holy Ghost, born of the Virgin Mary'.

Jesus was baptized, and so were we. But analogy always involves difference as well as likeness, and so it is here. Our baptism marked the beginning in us of a newly-created humanity; but this was not so with our Lord. For the beginning of that new humanity which he brought to the world was effected by his Incarnation; and this in turn was brought about by the creative activity of the Holy Spirit. Thus it appears that whatever be the relationship between our initiation and the baptism of Jesus the analogy which we are now considering begins further back. It might provisionally be defined in some such words as these: At the Incarnation by a creative act of the Holy Spirit the Son of God entered into our humanity; and so too at our baptism by a creative act of the Holy Spirit we entered into our Lord's humanity. When the parallel is presented in this form it confronts us with a number of fresh problems which remain concealed as long as the analogy is confined to the two events of our Lord's baptism and his endowment with the Spirit. The first question is: What relation had the baptism of Jesus to that creative act of the Spirit by which the Son of God became incarnate? The second question then arises. It is this: what is the relation of the Spirit's descent after the baptism to the original act of the Spirit whereby the Incarnation was effected? Clearly these questions must be answered before we proceed further.

II

THE BAPTISM OF JESUS THE CLIMAX OF A STORY WHICH BEGAN WHEN HE WAS CONCEIVED BY THE HOLY SPIRIT. IN MATTHEW 1–3 THE PROMISED MESSIAH IS SHEWN TO BE THE SUFFERING SERVANT. THE VOICE FROM HEAVEN AFTER THE BAPTISM PROCLAIMS THE TWO TYPES AS ONE, BECAUSE IN HIS BAPTISM THE SON HAS ACCEPTED THE SERVANT'S VOCATION. THUS THE BAPTISM OF JESUS SYMBOLIZES THE SACRIFICIAL UNITY OF HIS LIFE-STORY. IN *OUR* BAPTISM, HOWEVER, WE ENTER THAT SACRIFICIAL MYSTERY BY AN ACT OF THE SPIRIT WHICH CORRESPONDS TO HIS VIRGINAL CONCEPTION

For the former of our two questions an answer is supplied mainly by the first and the third gospels. Briefly we may say that in different ways both evangelists make it clear that the baptism of Jesus is the climax of a first stage in the incarnate life. It is, therefore, to be regarded in the first instance as the last event in a series which began with the act of new creation when Jesus was conceived by the Holy Spirit. In St Matthew the series is primarily messianic, but in the new Christian sense. For Jewish expectation has here been transformed by the identification of the Messiah with the suffering Servant. This identification has coloured the whole content of chapters 1–3. The genealogy is, in its details, an ironic comment upon the 'scandal' of the Virgin-Birth. By entering the family of Joseph, David's descendant, the Son of God identified himself with the blemishes in that line of descent. Among the ancestresses of Joseph were at least two Gentiles and three women whose sexual associations had been shameful. In chapter 2 the messianic child is first glorified by the Magi and then hunted out of the holy land. Thus the pattern of the Servant prophecy already appears.[1] Humiliation is the key-note of this messianic story.

Accordingly, it is not surprising that in the third chapter of his gospel the evangelist should record an incident which carries forward the theme of messianic humiliation a stage further. In the little dialogue between Jesus and John which precedes the baptism

[1] For details see *The Dominion of Christ*, pp. 87–89.

of the former two things are made clear. First of all John regards Jesus as an unsuitable subject for a baptism of repentance. Their positions should be reversed. It is John who is the sinner; Jesus has no need of repentance. Secondly, Jesus does not repudiate the implications of John's remark. Yet 'so it is befitting for us to fulfil all righteousness' is his reply. The words must be interpreted in the light of the context. Jesus, who needs no baptism of repentance for himself, yet counts it fitting that he should associate himself with those who do. For he is the 'righteous servant' who is to be 'numbered with the transgressors' (Isaiah $53^{11, 12}$). If he begins now to identify himself with sinful Israel he will be fulfilling the rôle of the Servant in whom the prophet saw the Righteous One[1] who 'makes many righteous'. Matthew's preoccupation with prophecy is well known. Later on he quotes a 'Servant' prophecy fully in application to Jesus ($12^{18 \text{ ff.}}$). Here he fits the story of our Lord's baptism into the same frame, for which he prepared the way in chapter 2.

At this point it is worth noticing that in the opening statements about St John the Baptist in the four gospels St Mark alone quotes a group of prophetic oracles (perhaps already combined in a *testimonia* document). The other three evangelists all concentrate upon the 'Voice of one crying in the wilderness'. The part of the *testimonia* here omitted by Matthew and Luke will be utilized by them in a different context. The isolated quotation of the 'Voice' oracle, however, is perhaps due to something more than literary considerations. For this 'voice' sounds forth in Isaiah 40, and is thus quite closely connected with the Servant prophecies which follow. When, therefore, that particular prophecy is singled out for application to the Baptist, this feature of the description has the effect of intensifying the thesis, so congenial to St Matthew, that Jesus is the Servant. It is equally important, however, to notice how fundamental to this evangelist's thought is the unity of the book of

[1] This title for our Lord is employed in Acts three times: (1) by St Peter in a 'Servant' context (3^{14}); (2) by St Stephen with the same associations (7^{52}); (3) by St Paul, reporting the words of Ananias to himself before his baptism (22^{14}).

Isaiah with regard to prophecies bearing upon the person and mission of the Christ. In this respect, also, he is heavily influenced by the Septuagint.[1] This appears in two details. His quotation of the Emmanuel prophecy introduces the key-word 'virgin' from the Greek version, with which it is all but verbally identical.[2] Secondly, his repeated use of *paidion* for 'young child' in chapter 2 corresponds to the repeated use of this word by the Septuagint in Isaiah 7–11 and to its recurrence in Isaiah 53^2 in application to the Servant.[3]

This last feature has the effect, cardinal to the evangelist's implicit thesis, of uniting the messianic prophecies and the Servant prophecies so that they all refer to one person. Jesus, the Virgin-born Emmanuel, is also the Servant who suffers for our sins; and the two types, Davidic Messiah and Suffering Servant, are blended into one. The fulfilment of the two pictures in one person constitutes a divine revelation concerning the mystery of the Incarnation and its fundamental implications. At this point, however, we must notice that the particular fusion of types which we are now considering in its fulfilment is not peculiar to the first gospel. For it is implicit in the words of the heavenly voice addressed to our Lord when the Spirit descended upon him immediately after his baptism. In St Mark's version the sentence reads: 'Thou art my beloved son, in thee I am well pleased.' The title 'beloved son' recurs in the same gospel without further qualification in two contexts. The first occurrence is in the words of the heavenly voice at the transfiguration; the second instance is in the parable of the vineyard where the 'son' is contrasted with the prophetic 'servants' who preceded him (9^7, 12^6).[4]

Clearly the title is messianic.[5] But also it has the sacrificial

[1] Or by another Greek version in verbal agreement on these points. See further below.

[2] Matt. 1^{23}; Isa. 7^{14}.

[3] Cp. above, the first note to this section.

[4] The former is reproduced in Matt. 17^5; the latter in Luke 20^{13}.

[5] The LXX version of Psalm 45 (44) has a superscription which makes this Davidic rhapsody a 'song for the beloved one' (ἀγαπητοῦ). The alternative reading in Luke 3^{22} gives to the title the messianic associations of Ps. 2^7, for which see *The Common Life*, p. 272, note 1 and context.

associations of the ancient story concerning the sacrifice of Isaac (Genesis 22). This twofold significance of the title belongs also to the other part of the words uttered by the heavenly voice after our Lord's baptism. The phrase which we render: 'in thee (in whom) I am well pleased' corresponds verbally to words applied to David by himself in the Greek version of 2 Samuel 22^{20}.[1] On the other hand the same phraseology (with the same key-word) appears in St Matthew's quotation of Isaiah 42^{1}, the opening verse of the first 'Servant' song. Moreover the first evangelist was not alone in adopting that rendering in his quotation; he is supported by Theodotian in a Jewish Greek version of the following century.[2] The double nuance of the key-word in question (*eudokein*) could be further illustrated from a manifold use of the corresponding noun in the New Testament.[3] The fourth gospel also contains an illuminating comment in the words of Jesus: 'For this cause the Father loveth me, because I lay down my life' (John 10^{17}). The Son is the beloved one *precisely because* his filial obedience leads him to fulfil the mission of the Servant. Identification of content as between the two titles could scarcely go further!

We are now in a position to give a preliminary answer to the former of our two questions, as formulated at the conclusion of § I in this chapter. We have yet to examine St Luke's contribution. But already St Matthew's interpretation makes clear a point of fundamental importance. The baptism of our Lord was *not* primarily a new beginning (as ours is). It was rather the climax of a first stage in that voluntary self-humiliation which began at the moment when the Son of God became incarnate. By a creative act of the Holy Spirit the Son became the promised Saviour through a unique entry into our humanity. Here we can rightly connect the naming of 'Jesus' by the angel at the beginning of this first stage with the words of our Lord to John immediately

[1] In the extra psalm (151, LXX) the same language is applied to David by implication.

[2] For details see *The Cairo Geniza* by P. E. Kahle, pp. 166–169, especially the suggestion by Sir F. Kenyon (on p. 168) concerning a pre-Theodotian Greek version of OT, known to the Church.

[3] For which see *The Common Life*, p. 175, note 1.

before the baptism. If Jesus was to 'save his people from their sins' (1[21]) he must follow the path of humiliation and suffering which was involved in his self-identification with sinners. The baptism, therefore, was our Lord's public acceptance of the Servant's mission, to which, however, he had already been committed from the first by the creative act of the Spirit in his conception. It follows that the descent of the Spirit upon the newly-baptized Saviour signified the Father's recognition of His Son's perfect self-donation; and this recognition was rendered explicit in the words of the heavenly voice.

Our analysis of St Matthew's opening chapters has already led us further afield. For example, this evangelist's thesis may serve to clarify the implications of St Mark's brief prelude, limited as the latter was by his plan to recording the original proclamation of the apostolic eye-witnesses with regard to things seen and heard. The voice from heaven presupposes a great deal concerning the person and character of the Son who is declared to be 'beloved' and 'well-pleasing'. Moreover, the statement that Jesus was baptized by John follows paradoxically upon the preceding statement of the Baptist depreciating his own person and ministry by comparison with the coming one who 'will baptize you with the Holy Spirit'. The paradox is surely intended by the evangelist; and it implies the mystery of voluntary humiliation which becomes explicit in the fuller narrative of St Matthew. So also the words of the heavenly voice imply that the Son has already embraced the mission of the Servant. It is in consequence of this fact that the heavens are rent asunder. Nothing can come between the filial oblation of the Son and the love of the Father who receives that oblation. Furthermore, we can now see why the bestowal of the Spirit must *follow* the baptism. In his symbolic descent into the waters Jesus made himself to be the divinely-appointed victim; and for the mission thus accepted he needed to be equipped, in accordance with prophecy, with the anointing grace of the Spirit. Since the Son has now by his own act become the Servant, two lines of prophecy meet. The messianic endowment of Isaiah 11 and the Servant's anointing in Isaiah 61 become one in the fulfilment.

In the last paragraph we came within sight of an answer to our second question which formulated a query concerning the relation between two bestowals of the Spirit in the gospel story.[1] That question, however, could not profitably be considered until we had contemplated the spectacle of God-made-man embracing the Servant's vocation. The unity of theme which we have been tracing has its symbolic centre in the Lord's baptism. But, as we can now see, it has its full explication in the gospel story as a whole. In other words the symbolic event of the Lord's descent into Jordan points back to the creative event of the new beginning as surely as it points forward to the redemptive conclusion of the Servant's mission. The baptism has this inclusive character because in it the Son of God, as it were, passed sentence of death upon himself. In so doing he disclosed the essentially sacrificial character, both of the redemptive economy as a whole, and of that event in which the new creation had its beginning. The *kenosis* in which the Son of God 'poured himself out unto death' was inaugurated by the Creator-Spirit in the virginal conception; it was sealed formally by the Son's own act in the baptism; it was consummated in death and resurrection. Into this total mystery we were plunged at the moment of *our* baptism, and that too by a creative act of the Spirit corresponding to the original act with which the messianic life-story began.

III

RELATION OF CHRIST'S BAPTISM TO THE NEW BEGINNING IN HIM AND IN US. IN ST LUKE'S GOSPEL THE GENEALOGY SHOWS THE 'BELOVED SON' TO BE 'SON OF ADAM'. THE CONTEXT IS SACRIFICIAL, FUSING FOUR OT TYPES. 'THE SEED OF THE WOMAN' BRUISES THE SERPENT'S HEAD AND INAUGURATES THE SERVANT'S MISSION. THE VOICE FROM HEAVEN IN THE ALTERNATIVE VERSION QUOTES PSALM 2[7]. THE HISTORICAL BACKGROUND OF THIS AS INTERPRETED IN PSALM 89. THE DECLARATION OF SONSHIP A FATHERLY RESPONSE TO THE FILIAL CRY OF THE BAPTIZED SAVIOUR. THE FATHER'S 'FIRSTBORN' IDENTIFIED WITH SINFUL ISRAEL.

[1] See above, § 1, final par.

At the conclusion of the preceding section we arrived at a position which indicated a complex relation between three events, namely (1) the beginning of the new humanity in the Christ through his incarnation, (2) the baptism of the Christ in which that new beginning came to expression, and (3) the beginning of the new humanity in the Christian through the baptism which he in turn undergoes. The relation of the second event in this series to the first and the third might also be expressed by saying that the baptism of Jesus rendered explicit the sacrificial destiny involved in the Incarnation and therefore also in every Christian baptism. For through identification with the incarnate Saviour we are by our baptism committed to a sharing in that self-oblation to the Father which came to open expression in his baptism. Moreover, that self-oblation was in its essence a filial response to the Father's will, a response which was both acknowledged and interpreted in the words of the Voice from heaven. Into that filial response we enter through faith and baptism, as St Paul declares in Galatians $3^{26, 27}$: 'Ye are all sons of God through faith in Christ Jesus. For as many of you as were baptized into Christ did put on Christ.' The whole gospel story, however, is a record of filial response from the Son to the Father in terms of our humanity. What this implied, both for him and for us, must now be considered more fully in its several stages under the guidance of St Luke, whose Gospel sets the whole series of events in a new and yet wider context.

The opening chapters of the third gospel have two special features which stand out. The first of these is the very full treatment of the birth and childhood of Jesus himself and of his forerunner. The second special feature is the genealogy, and that too with regard both to its character and to its position. Both of these peculiarities have a bearing upon our present investigation. We may begin, therefore, by noticing their relation to the Marcan cycle. Whereas St Matthew succeeds in weaving together very closely his first three chapters in the manner already indicated, such a result would scarcely have been possible, at least to a like extent, under the Lucan plan. For, whatever be the precise literary history of St Luke's first two chapters, they certainly form an artistic whole in which all the sections after the preface are carefully arranged in symbolic correspondence.[1] Moreover, the distinction between our Lord's family history and his public ministry is further emphasized by the elaborate chronological note with which the latter is introduced at the beginning of chapter 3. Nevertheless, the carefully sustained parallel and contrast between the respective biographies of Jesus and John is continued into the Marcan sequence. Furthermore, in agreement with the first evangelist, as against St Mark, St Luke quotes in isolation the oracle of the voice in the wilderness from Isaiah 40.

As in the first gospel the last-mentioned feature prepares us for an interpretation of the baptism in terms of the Servant prophecy. This expectation is not disappointed if we follow the weight of manuscript evidence which repeats verbally the Marcan form of the words uttered by the heavenly Voice. There would then be an impressive unanimity in the collective synoptic witness at this point. As we shall see, St Luke continues to emphasize the Servant typology at the next stage of his narrative, and this fact may militate against the authenticity of the alternative version of the sentence uttered by the heavenly Voice.[2] Either version, however, bears witness to the messianic sonship of Jesus; and this fact has an important bearing upon our understanding of the genealogy which the evangelist inserts immediately afterwards. In this genealogy our Lord's legal descent is traced back to Adam; and doubtless that fact justifies a reference to the 'universalist' tendency of the Lucan gospel. Such a comment, however, will give no help in explaining why the genealogy with its peculiar ending should have been placed just where it is. The ending is peculiar because it affirms that Adam was 'the son of God'. But further, to this 'son of God' the legal descent of Jesus is traced immediately after he himself has been pronounced to be 'the beloved Son' of the Father.

[1] The details of this symmetry were impressively worked out by Eric Burrows in *The Gospel of the Infancy* (London, 1940).

[2] Quoted from Ps. 2^{7} which refers back to 2 Sam. 7^{14} and context. Its probable Christian fulfilment is shewn in Rom. 1^{4}: for which see above § ii, par. 5, conclusion of the first note.

The exact phrase in all three gospels is 'my son, the beloved one' and is verbally identical with the threefold repetition of this expression which occurs in the Septuagint version of the story concerning the sacrifice of Isaac (Genesis 22, verses 2, 12, 16). There first the divine voice and then an angel, addressing Abraham, refers to 'thy son, the beloved one'. The Hebrew text has each time 'thy son, thine only one'; and it is recognized that the Greek also will bear this meaning. By the time that the gospels were being written it is probable that the Christian meaning of this expression was moving into that deeper connotation which is clearly borne by 'only-begotten Son' in the fourth gospel. What then could be St Luke's purpose in connecting such a title of the Christ with the filial status of Adam in relation to his Creator? For a provisional answer I cannot do better than repeat what I have written elsewhere. The title 'Son of man' which Jesus applied to himself comes from the Greek version of the Old Testament, where it frequently occurs as a rendering of the Hebrew phrase: 'Son of Adam.'[1] This suggests a connexion between the ending of the Lucan genealogy and the Pauline doctrine of the Second Adam who reverses the tragedy of the Fall.

Does the evangelist intend to suggest that Jesus is the Seed promised to Eve, the son of Adam who was to bruise the serpent's head? If so the genealogy is in its right place. For it leads straight into the story of the temptation in which the serpent's head is very firmly bruised. If I have rightly interpreted the connexion with what follows, perhaps we may now make a corresponding connexion with what precedes. The beloved Son is 'the only Son'; yet he became 'son of Adam' in order that he might fulfil Adam's destiny as son of God by creation. If this is a correct reading of the evangelist's mind, then we cannot stop short at that point. For in both versions of Luke 3^{22} Jesus fulfils the Isaac type. He is the only son whom his father surrenders for sacrifice, and who, according to Jewish tradition, meekly accepted his sacrificial destiny. It follows that even if we accept the western reading in 3^{22} with its

[1] Cp. Ps. 8^4. In the Hebrew (8^5) the parallelism makes 'son of Adam' = 'man'. For what follows see *The Dominion of Christ*, pp. 54 (with note) and 94.

messianic quotation from Psalm 2[7] we still cannot exclude a reference to the Servant prophecy. For the Isaac type still remains in the text; and this means that the messianic reference must be interpreted sacrificially. In other words in this section of St Luke's gospel we have a deliberate fusion of four types, namely Isaac, the messianic Son, the suffering Servant and the son of Adam who fulfils the promise concerning the seed of the woman.

Something further must be said concerning the manner in which this blending of types is presented in the fulfilment. The temptation scenes in the Gospels inevitably recall the story of Adam's seduction and treachery. The more obvious contrasts are already present in St Mark's brief but terse statement. The Voice which called, 'Adam, where art thou?' now commends the faithfulness of a beloved Son. But unfallen Adam is immediately driven by the Spirit into a wilderness to which our fallen humanity properly belongs. There, however, he enjoys authority over the wild beasts and the friendly guardianship of angels, both of which were lost by his outlawed predecessor. When we turn to the two longer accounts we note that both start with an emphasis upon the title to sonship just previously announced; but there is a characteristic difference of development. In St Matthew's version the climax is represented as a rejection of the worldly kingdom, a victory of the true Messiah. St Luke is, perhaps, nearer to the original Marcan description. He shows the second Adam accepting wilderness hunger, content with the kingdom of unfallen man, and refusing to claim angelic protection for a presumptuous theophany. But further, for a temple theophany of the Son (as proposed by the tempter) he substitutes in the next scene a synagogue mission of the Servant who was anointed for service to all mankind. The familiar pattern of prophecy is fulfilled when the Servant is first 'glorified' and then rejected (4[14–29]). So the Son of Adam is also the Servant. Only so can he fulfil his destiny as son of God by creation, a destiny which became his when he was conceived by the Holy Spirit. Concerning St Luke's interpretation of that earliest phase in the incarnate life there is much to be said.

But first we must return to the declaration of sonship by the heavenly voice. The Marcan form of the saying has already been considered. If this was what St Luke wrote his interpretation of the whole series of incidents cannot be appreciably different from that which we have deduced from the first gospel. The western reading, however, cannot be simply ignored. It is twice quoted by Justin as the authentic saying of the Voice (*Dialogue*, chapters 88, 103). It is accepted by several other fathers from the second century onwards.[1] Its association with our Lord's baptism must be very early, despite the alternative association of Psalm 2^{7} with the resurrection of Jesus reported by St Luke himself in his summary of St Paul's synagogue address in Acts 13^{33}. This parallel connexion of a messianic oracle both with the beginning and with the end of our Lord's public ministry is in itself significant, since Jesus himself referred to his approaching passion in baptismal language (Mark $10^{38\text{ f.}}$, Luke 12^{50}).

The explanation of these phenomena must be sought in the Old Testament; and, in particular, attention must be given to the historical background of Psalm 2 which is to be found in the incidents of 2 Samuel 5–7. David conquers Zion and makes it a holy city; he then receives a promise of perpetual sovereignty for his dynasty. Moreover the son of David who succeeds to the throne is to be treated as God's own son. So the Epistle to the Hebrews (1^{5}) quotes Psalm 2^{7}: 'Thou art my son, to-day I have begotten thee', and immediately connects it with 2 Samuel 7^{14}: 'I will be to him a father, and he shall be to me a son.' These words referred directly to Solomon, himself a type of messianic sovereignty and wisdom; but the context here and in 1 Chronicles 17 suggests that the promise as a whole refers to the Davidic house in perpetuity. We must not, however, fail to notice the language of Psalm 89, a messianic hymn which is peculiarly relevant at this point. From verse 19 onwards the Davidic promise is renewed; and the announcement of a father-son relation between the deity and David's heir takes a form which almost amounts to a dialogue:

[1] See Otto's notes to Justin, *ad loc.*, and Lukyn Williams, *op. cit.*, p. 190.

He shall call me, 'Thou art my father, my God and the rock of my salvation';
I also will make him my firstborn, high above the kings of the earth.[1]

For the title: 'firstborn' we may quote the following: 'Israel is the firstborn of Yahweh among the nations (Exodus 4^{22}), and the seed of David among dynasties.'[2] In the psalm, however, the accord of this title to a 'son of David' is presented as though it were a response to a filial cry or prayer. Now in St Luke's gospel it is stated that immediately after the baptism Jesus was praying; and to this prayer of David's son all that follows comes as a divine response, namely the opened heavens, the descent of the Spirit in bodily form as a dove and finally the Voice from heaven. If the words of the Voice were believed to be a repetition of Psalm 2^{7}, this would seem to be an exact fulfilment of the sequence quoted above from Psalm 89. In this way we can see that the alternative version of Luke 3^{22} is something more than a messianic text applied to Jesus at a critical point in his earthly life. It becomes an assurance of fatherhood to one whose baptismal oblation finds expression in a supreme filial appeal. The difference between the two versions of what was happening dwindles to vanishing point. Nevertheless, whichever version we follow the characteristic Lucan reference to the praying Christ suggests a parallel with Gethsemane, where the filial cry, 'Abba, Father', renews what must already have been in our Lord's mind as in his baptism he identified himself with sinful Israel. Here the two traditional meanings of 'firstborn' come together. The Son of David now becomes 'firstborn' as well as 'beloved Son' in a wholly new sense because he has identified himself with unworthy Israel, the original firstborn, in a solemn repudiation of Israel's sinful past.

IV

SUMMARY OF ST LUKE'S INTERPRETATION, WITH ITS COMBINATION OF OT THEMES. THIS SUGGESTS AN EXTENSION OF OUR ANALOGY BACK TO THE

[1] vv. 26, 27 (EVV), 27, 28 (H. and G).

[2] A comment of the Hebrew Lexicon (BDB) upon the Hebrew word employed in our quotation.

CREATION, WHICH IN TURN WILL INVOLVE CLOSE ATTENTION TO BIBLICAL CATEGORIES AND MODES OF THOUGHT. THIS COMPLEX ANALOGY WILL COVER ALL REVELATION AND EXHIBIT ITS UNITY. ITS APPLICATION TO ST LUKE'S OPENING CHAPTERS. A JEWISH-CHRISTIAN UNDERSTANDING OF GENESIS 2[6, 7] OUTLINED.

This analysis of the gospel story in its synoptic form has now reached a point where we can begin to see clearly what answer should be given to the second of two questions posed earlier in this chapter.[1] That question involves a reference backward which may be taken in two stages. Our interpretation of the events by the river Jordan has brought to light the fact that the descent of the Spirit upon Jesus immediately after his baptism was complementary to the latter event in the sense that it was the Father's response to the Son's act of self-oblation. Having freely accepted the Servant's vocation in his baptism Jesus was immediately anointed with the Spirit in order that he might be equipped to fulfil his appointed mission. This conclusion agrees with both the relevant prophecies, namely Isaiah 11 and Isaiah 61. In the former the 'son of David' who is the predestined Messiah is endowed with gifts of the Spirit suitable to his kingly office. In the latter the Servant of the Lord is anointed for his mission. Here we may note that in St Luke's arrangement of order a synagogue sermon upon the second prophecy is the first recorded incident of our Lord's ministry. Moreover, the version of this prophecy thus presented by the evangelist as our Lord's text corresponds very closely to the actual details of that ministry which follow. It would then seem to be clear that we are intended by the author to connect the fulfilment of the prophetic oracle in Isaiah 61 with the preceding event of the Spirit's descent upon the Christ.

Between these two events, however, namely the anointing of the Servant and the beginning of his mission, there is interposed the Son of Adam motif in the genealogy and its sequel, the temptation. This alternation of themes secures the proportions of revelation. For, as we have seen, in St Luke's plan all the greater types come together. Thus the only Son is the Servant because,

[1] § 1. last par.

like Isaac, he is destined for sacrifice; and again this sacrificial interpretation of sonship belongs to the original plan of creation. For the sonship of Adam by creation was mediatorial, and its priestly service was renewed when the conflict with the serpent was resumed in the wilderness. This combination of themes is in the great tradition of scripture. It is one of the characteristic marks of unity in the biblical revelation. Everywhere, and in both Testaments, the two concepts of creation and redemption are intertwined, because all redemption is both a renewal of divine creativity and a restoration of creation's true order.[1] It is in accord with St Luke's literary genius that by careful arrangement of his material he can suggest such an inclusive combination of themes so as to exhibit the wholeness of revelation in Christ through the very diversity of its Old Testament background. Of this literary technique, however, there are consequences to which we must now give our attention.

If the human descent of Jesus is traced back to Adam, who was son of God by creation, then we are clearly being invited to see an analogy between the beginning of our Lord's earthly life and that first beginning of our race which was effected in the creation of Adam. Further, when the evangelist prefixes to the Adam genealogy a curious reference to 'Jesus himself beginning', it may even be that he was influenced, consciously or unconsciously, by the biblical associations of such phraseology. We remember that in his great Christological statement in Colossians St Paul plays upon the double theme of Christ as 'Beginning' of both creations. But, however that may be, it is in any case most probable that the evangelist finds a new beginning in the messianic life-story at the point where the Spirit descended to equip the beloved Son in fulfilment of prophecy. Thus we are faced once more with the fact of two beginnings in that life-story, each of which was inaugurated by the Holy Spirit. To the former, the virginal conception, the story of our Lord's childhood is traced in 'the gospel of the infancy', whereas the latter event, on Jordan's

[1] For details I must refer once more to what I have written in *The Dominion of Christ*.

banks, is the starting-point of the public ministry. The elaboration of typology in this gospel, however, suggests that our analogy between Christ and the Christian cannot be adequately stated without attending to a corresponding analogy between the Christ and the old order which preceded him.

In tracing out this analogy between the old and the new, however, we must bear in mind what was said above concerning the two themes of creation and redemption which are constantly interwoven in the Old Testament as well as in the New. The very notion of a second Adam, as developed by St Paul, implies, on the one hand a parallel between the two orders of creation and their respective heads, and on the other hand a contrast which requires to be developed further through the symbolic figures of Israel's redemptive history. Moreover, it has to be remembered that in this sphere of type and fulfilment there is no mechanical exactitude. A picture from the Old Testament carries a suggestion which may have more than one application in the fulfilment; and in the realm of suggestion there is never more than partial correspondence. On the other hand in the case of two major types, Adam and Israel, there is this great advantage that each is a figure which can be understood in both an individual and a corporate sense. In this way each of these types provides a background for the concept of the *totus Christus* which has been gradually coming back into its own during the past half century. I refer, of course, to the concept of the Christ as the entire organism of redemption, Jesus and his church regarded as a single redemptive mystery to which all Christians belong in such a sense that the law of the whole is reproduced in each one of its parts.

What we are now studying, then, is in reality a single complex analogy which covers the whole field of revelation, and which carries the inspired images of scripture over in detail from the old to the new. The analogy, in fact, does something which is at the same time both simpler and more profound than what has just been suggested. In its scriptural form it would be truer to say that it makes a simple identification between the messianic history in the new covenant and the various images of the Old Testament which show a significant similarity in respect of this or that detail. By this stress upon simple identification a single Old Testament image may apply equally to Christ and to the Christian, or it may significantly suggest the relation in which all Christians stand to the Christ. An outstanding example of this scriptural method is to be found in the Pauline use of the Adam image in application first to our Lord as an individual person and secondly to the church as the body of that same new Adam, whose members we are. In the present work we have already noticed two applications of the story in Genesis 2 concerning Adam's creation. The first of these was St Paul's statement concerning baptism in 1 Corinthians 12^{13}.[1] The second was Justin's application of the creation story to the details of Christian initiation. In the latter instance creation and redemption were interwoven by the combination of Adam's creation with the symbolism of the Exodus.[2]

There is no point at which primitive Christian thought in the first two centuries shows a more striking continuity than in this analogy between the two creations with some form of the new Adam motif as a recurring factor. In its application to the first two chapters of St Luke's Gospel, however, we must be careful not to overstate the argument. It is a characteristic of scripture that its implications do not lie on the surface, and that an implicit reference to an image from the Old Testament may sometimes be present in some New Testament passage without the author being necessarily conscious of the fact. The most that one can say in the instance we are considering is something like this: if we read Luke 1–4 in the light of the creation stories in Genesis the idea of an analogy between the two can be seen to be appropriate, But if we proceed on this cautious basis we must also allow full force to any supporting parallel in Israel's history. The interweaving of creation and redemption becomes relevant again here because such parallels

[1] Cp. ch. I, § iii. For fuller developments of the Pauline theme see *Revelation*, especially chs. V and VI.

[2] Cp. ch. II, § iv, pars. 7, 8. The gap between these two instances is partly filled by St Luke and the Ep. to Hebrews, for which see *The Dominion of Christ*, pp. 52–55 and pp. 71–83. After Justin comes Irenaeus whose contribution is outlined in the refs. given under note 1 above.

had significance for the biblical writers themselves, and may have influenced their way of telling their story, whether they knew it or not.

With these considerations in mind we turn to the narrative of Adam's creation in Genesis 2. In verses 6 and 7 we have a statement which shows at least two, if not three stages. It says:

There went up a mist from the earth, and watered the whole face of the ground.
And the Lord God formed man of the dust of the ground,
and breathed into his nostrils the breath of life; and man became a living soul.

How would this statement be understood by the earliest Christian community? Part of the answer to that question has been already outlined in chapter I, § III of the present work, when we were considering its bearing upon a passage in St Paul (1 Corinthians 12[13]). The 'mist' becomes a 'fountain' in the Greek version; and this might suggest the familiar biblical way of speaking as though the Holy Spirit were a celestial fluid.[1] Moreover the Greek word for 'formed' in the next line (from which comes our word: 'plastic') would suggest a process of moulding the wet earth into a human form by the Creator-artist. Thus we have here two creation-images, representing two quite different stages in the formation of the first man.

The second stage occurs only after the first stage has been completed, and is quite distinct. The medium is now, not watered soil, but divine breath. Moreover, whereas the first stage represents a prolonged process, the second stage is described in a way which suggests a single act accomplished in a moment of time. The symbolism of the story can also be estimated from another point of view. What is the purpose which the Creator is conceived to have in view in each of the two stages? Here we must bear in mind that the first Christians would understand the two stories of Adam's creation as referring to the same event, and would interpret each

[1] Cp. Isa. 32[15], Joel 2[28] (3[1]). In Isa. 30[28] the 'breath' of God is an 'overflowing stream'; and this might indicate that the two images of 'water' and 'breath' in Gen. 2[6, 7] both refer to the Holy Spirit, since 'breath' and 'spirit' are the same word in the bible languages.

version by the other. Also, we have to take account of yet another factor. *We* interpret the language of Genesis $1^{26, 27}$ concerning 'the image of God' in man spiritually. But it seems certain that the Hebrews understood it much more literally. In the vision of the prophet Ezekiel the deity is represented as appearing in 'the likeness of the appearance of Adam'. A literary connexion with Genesis 1 is rendered probable, not only by the reference to Adam in the Hebrew text of Ezekiel 1 but also by the occurrence of the same word for 'likeness' in both passages.[1] It would seem to follow that in a Jewish-Christian community the process described in the first half of Genesis 2^{7} would be understood to mean that the creator was shaping the figure into the likeness of his own image.

But further, there was also a specific purpose in the second stage of Adam's creation. Before the divine breath was breathed into the face, the clay figure was conformed indeed to that image which Ezekiel saw; yet the created likeness of deity was not yet endowed with life. Then the divine breath was infused, and the clay image became a living personality, not only 'like' his Creator but also capable of fulfilling certain functions for which he had been destined all along. What then were these functions? The living Adam was to be a viceroy of deity, a mediator between God and the rest of creation, a priest-king and servant of his maker, to whom he offered the worship which is proper from creature to Creator. It was not enough that he should be made 'in the image'. After that process was completed, he must be rendered capable of fulfilling his mediatorial functions in the world as the Servant of deity. In this analysis of Genesis $2^{6, 7}$ there is implied a clear distinction between two different functions of God's Spirit. In the former picture water makes possible the moulding of dust-particles into a clay figure, whereas in the latter picture this figure becomes endowed with a capacity to fulfil an appointed task. The application of this distinction to St Luke's version of the gospel story must be reserved to another section of this chapter.

[1] This is true of both biblical languages. For further details see *The Dominion of Christ*, pp. 92–94 (and notes), where the connexion with St Luke and St Paul is indicated.

V

THROUGH PARALLELS IN ISRAEL'S HISTORY ST LUKE SHOWS THE MOULDING OF THE HOLY CHILD TO THE 'NEW CREATION' FORM. TO TWO STAGES OF THE CREATION STORY CORRESPOND TWO FUNCTIONS OF THE SPIRIT IN RELATION TO THE TOTAL CHRIST-MYSTERY. DESPITE THE CONTRAST WITH THE FIRST ADAM JESUS WAS FIRST MOULDED TO THE SERVANT'S VOCATION, AND THEN ENDOWED FOR ITS FULFILMENT. SO THE HOLY CHILDHOOD FORESHADOWED A SACRIFICIAL DESTINY; AND IN HIS BAPTISM THE LAMB STRUCK A BLOW AT THE DRAGON.

In seeking for an analogy between Genesis and St Luke's Gospel we shall follow the principles of application already laid down. Later on we shall also have to reconsider the extension of the analogy to ourselves, already partially traced in our previous handling of 1 Corinthians 12^{13}. When we read St Luke's first two chapters we do not find any explicit reference to the idea which comes to the surface at the end of the genealogy. There is a wealth of Old Testament background; but it belongs wholly to the types and images furnished by Israel's history. Nevertheless the actual material used in this way may carry suggestions which are relevant to the first part of the creation story, that is the conception of a human figure moulded to a specific form. It is relevant to point out that St Luke alone, among the four evangelists refers to our Lord's human development from childhood onwards, and illustrates the character of that development in the final anecdote of chapter 2. Moreover, most prominent amongst the items from the Old Testament utilized by the evangelist is undoubtedly the story of another birth and childhood, namely that of the prophet Samuel.[1] The many points of literary connexion which have been noticed in this particular parallel come to a climax in the close correspondence between the incident of our Lord's boyhood (2^{41-51}) and the story of Samuel's call to be a prophet (1 Samuel 3). In both there is a conflict between divine and human authority. In both the child is being shaped for destiny by divine hands.

[1] For details see the volume by Burrows already cited.

It is at this point that we may, perhaps, see how readily the plasmic imagery of the creation narrative adapts itself to that more spiritual moulding of individuality of which the parallel last mentioned provides a good illustration. After Samuel came David, the shepherd-boy who was shaped for kingship by years of difficult testing. So in the gospel narrative the angelic annunciation identifies the child who is to be born with that messianic child of David's line who is proclaimed beforehand by prophecy (Isaiah $9^{6, 7}$).[1] Moreover David's original heir, King Solomon, confessed himself 'a little child' and asked for a 'listening heart'. In reply God bestowed on him a gift of wisdom (I Kings 3^{4-12}); and the whole incident provides a likely background for that suggestion of dialogue at which we have already glanced in Psalm 89.[2] When we thus connect the psalmist's interpretation of the original messianic promise to David with the actual dialogue between the deity and David's son we have yet another appropriate background for the concluding section of St Luke's story concerning the holy child. As Jesus 'advanced in stature' he was 'being filled' with that messianic wisdom which was originally bestowed upon David's son. Moreover it was a wisdom appropriate to sonship in one who was already calling upon the Father whose concerns were pre-eminently his own.

Having thus indicated clearly the process by which sonship was moulded in a new Son of Adam to the fulfilment of the old covenant in the new, the evangelist passes on at once to the situation in which sonship, thus tested and shaped, is endowed with the Spirit for the fulfilment of the specific functions proper to the Adam of the new creation. Here we may see how the two stages of the creation story serve to clarify further the distinction between two donations of the Holy Spirit, the former of which inaugurates a creative process, whereas the latter bestows the endowment appropriate to that which has thus been brought into existence. Before we explore further the details of this analogy, however, it will be well to reflect upon its wider bearings and their

[1] Luke $1^{32, 33}$. The Davidic descent of Joseph is also stressed twice (1^{27}, 2^{4}).
[2] Above, § iii, last two pars.

theological significance in the totality of revelation. For this purpose attention may first be drawn to a single striking difference between the two versions of man's creation as told respectively in Genesis 1 and 2. The former version simply says that 'God created man in his own image'. This might suggest a divine *fiat* which took place once for all in a moment of time, whereas the other version, which we have been considering, might indicate that the work of the divine artist covered a prolonged process. This contrast may throw light upon two corresponding aspects of the new creation.

The Son of God became incarnate at the moment of the virginal conception; and this is attributed by the angel of the annunciation to the agency of the Holy Spirit (Luke 1³⁵). So also each person who is made a Christian is incorporated into the virgin-born Redeemer at the moment of baptism; and this effect is attributed by St Paul to the agency of the Holy Spirit, as we found recorded in the first part of 1 Corinthians 12¹³.[1] On the other hand each of these two creative events is brought to fruition in an extended development. We are at present considering this development in the pattern of the incarnate life. The perfection of our Lord's sinless humanity did not exempt him from such a work of moulding and shaping as is represented in the story of the first Adam's creation. There is, however, a difference which corresponds to St Paul's saying: 'The first man is of the earth earthy. The second man is from heaven' (1 Corinthians 15⁴⁷). The earthy form of Adam was moulded to the heavenly image, whereas the eternal Son of God *is* that heavenly image in his divine person. In him, therefore, the uncreated image entered the Adamic form that he might mould that form to his own creative purpose. By entering it he re-created it, and also involved himself in all the conditions of our earthly development, sin excepted.

In him the image and likeness were always flawless, and therefore perfection belonged to every stage of the developing process. The perfection, however, was manifested in this humanly developing form as the remedy for our fallen state. Having assumed

[1] Ch. I, § iii, pars. 4 and 5.

the form of the Servant which is proper to the sons of Adam he was himself moulded in it to its predestined end. For this reason it was as the sacrificial victim that he approached the baptism of repentance appointed for his people. By that act of self-humiliation he entered upon the messianic vocation of the beloved Son; and for this he received immediately the appropriate endowment of the Spirit. Thus the distinction between two stages in the scriptural account of creation was reproduced in the order of redemption. St Luke's interpretation of the two stages in their incarnational form might be summed up in some such words as these: humanity re-created in the person of our Saviour was first moulded to the Servant's destiny and then anointed for that destiny. It is from this point of view that we may discern in the story of the holy childhood premonitory signs of that act of self-oblation which St Luke, like the other evangelists, found in the baptism to which Jesus submitted himself.

The foreshadowing signs of coming sacrifice are indicated chiefly in imagery drawn from the traditional cultus. In 1^{35} the blessed Virgin is told that she will be overshadowed like the tabernacle by a Shekinah cloud of the divine presence; and in the next sentence the child to be born is referred to in language which recalls the 'sanctification' of all firstborn males to the Lord (Exodus $13^{12, 13}$). The tabernacle was the place of sacrifice; and if Mary was the sanctuary her promised Son was already announced as the victim. All the firstborn sons of Israel were redeemed by sacrifice. Jesus, however, was to be the true sacrifice by which alone all are to be redeemed. It is also to be noticed that in these chapters the promised Messiah is surrounded by a significant blending of priesthood and prophecy. This is evident, first in Zacharias and his son, and then in the temple scene where old Simeon prophesies over the newly dedicated child. The central scene of all shows a king born in poverty; and Simeon's prediction of judgement, scandal and grief completes the stern premonition of all that is to come. Before the veil of silence falls the Son has spoken of his Father in the temple and then retired into lowly obscurity and submissive obedience. In ironic contrast the silence of years is broken with a list of earthly potentates followed by the solitary voice which heralds the approaching Servant of the Lord.

When we turn to the fourth gospel we find indications which tend to confirm the point of view already deduced from the other evangelists. In his own characteristic way St John connects the rebirth of Christian believers primarily with the virgin-birth of the Word incarnate (1^{12-14}). The witness of the Baptist is more fully stated, but follows the lines previously traced. John identifies himself with the Voice in the wilderness; and, in a scene later than the baptism of Jesus, identifies him with 'the lamb' of the Servant prophecy. The total impression of the Baptist's witness does not differ in principle from what is implied in St Matthew's record of the little dialogue before the baptism (Matthew 3^{14}).[1] There is, however, one point at which all four evangelists are in explicit agreement concerning John's testimony. It is this: the Baptist affirms emphatically that he himself baptizes only with water in contrast to 'the coming one' who will baptize 'with the Holy Spirit'. The whole meaning of John's baptism lay not in a sacramental endowment, but in an act of repentance. Jesus, therefore, did not come to Jordan to receive the Spirit but to identify himself with penitent Israel. In so acting, however, he entered of his own volition into the Servant's vocation for which his incarnation had predestined him and for which the Father's hands had shaped him during the intervening years.

At this point it will be fitting to introduce from primitive sources outside the canonical scriptures one further suggestion concerning our Lord's baptism which provides an interesting pointer to biblical interpretation in the patristic period. One of these sources is a group of early Christian hymns known as *The Odes of Solomon*, but very probably used in connexion with the initiatory rites of the Church. Elsewhere, and possibly here, there occurs the striking notion that when Jesus stepped down into

[1] The variant reading in John 1^{34} does not affect our argument. Whether under LXX influence (for Isa. 53) or through Aramaic background the messianic Son and the elect Servant have become one in Johannine thought. Moreover this fusion corresponds to our main conclusions concerning the Voice from heaven in the synoptic record.

Jordan's waters he trod upon the head of the ancient dragon and shattered it;[1] thereby he cleansed the waters of this world that they might become for us the laver of divine forgiveness.[2] Along the line of interpretation which we have followed in this chapter such a conception of new creation victory *before* the descent of the Dove occasions no difficulty. By his self-oblation at that moment the Lamb of God entered the arena of conflict and struck a deadly blow at the ancient enemy. For him, as for us, baptism was an act of renunciation, faith and self-giving. In him it was an act of filial response proper to the image restored to our humanity in his own person, and therefore already engraced by the Spirit. In us it is an event made possible by the Saviour's great work of restoration. What else this analogy implies for us must be considered more fully in the chapter which follows.

[1] Cp. the quotation from Moses Bar Kepha cited by Rendel Harris on p. 121 of his book referred to in the next note.

[2] A similar implication may possibly be found in the 22nd and 24th of the *Odes of Solomon*, taken together. For this see the volume entitled *The Odes and Psalms of Solomon* by J. Rendel Harris (2nd ed. Cambridge, 1911), pp. 120–123 and pp. xxv ff., xxxiii ff. The notion is assimilated to ancient dragon myths, but is also based upon passages of scripture, e.g. in Job and the Psalms, as we may see from its treatment by St Cyril of Jerusalem (*Catechesis* III, cap. xi).

CHAPTER V

THE ANALOGY COMPLETED

I

CORRESPONDENCE BETWEEN DIFFERENT FORMS OF 'UNITY IN PLURALITY'. THE GOSPEL HISTORY, LIKE THE BAPTISMAL MYSTERY, PRESENTS (*a*) A WHOLE IN TWO PARTS, AND (*b*) UNITY EMBRACING A SERIES OF EVENTS. A SYMBOLIC PARALLEL BETWEEN TWO SEQUENCES OF EVENTS AT THE BEGINNING AND END OF THE MARCAN GOSPEL IS SUPPORTED BY OTHER NT EVIDENCE. IN SUCH A PARALLEL EACH SEQUENCE WOULD ILLUMINATE THE OTHER. THE UNITY OF ALL REDEMPTIVE EVENTS IN ONE MYSTERY, SYMBOLIZED IN THE TRANSFIGURATION, EXEMPLIFIED IN PAULINE THEOLOGY, AND REALIZED IN PRIMITIVE LITURGICAL PRACTICE.

In Book I of this volume the facts surveyed suggested the conception of a single baptismal mystery which is actually realized in two parts. In chapter IV this concept of a whole actualized in two stages was referred back to the gospel records; and there we found a corresponding mystery in the life-story of our Lord himself. For in the analysis undertaken in that chapter the baptism of Jesus was seen to be the crowning event of that first period belonging to the incarnate life in which our Saviour was undergoing preparation for his public ministry. Similarly the descent of the Spirit which followed immediately afterwards was recognized to be the starting point of that ministry which had its culmination in death and resurrection. The conclusion drawn from this analysis makes the distinction thus emphasized between two parts of the incarnate life correspond to the idea of a single whole enacted in two stages, an idea which we had previously found to be required by the scriptural and primitive Christian evidence concerning our baptismal initiation into Christ. Thus the idea of 'unity in plurality' which is dominant alike in Scripture and in Christian doctrine[1] is seen to provide a major clue

[1] Ch. IV, § i.

to the mystery of the *totus Christus* both in the head and in the members.

In that conception, however, the all-inclusive unity is as vitally important as the distinctions which it includes. It will be recalled that when this concept of 'unity in plurality' was introduced at the beginning of chapter IV its relevance both to biblical idioms and to doctrinal definitions was emphasized. This fact, again, was held to justify a somewhat bold transference of a technical phrase from the sphere of dogmatic definition to provide an explanation of a certain phenomenon in St Paul's teaching concerning Christian initiation. So we found an 'interchange of properties' within the baptismal mystery as expounded by the apostle in his Epistle to the Colossians.[1] We shall find as we proceed that this inclusion of the manifold within the unity of a whole takes a variety of forms in the Christian revelation; and if no single instance proves to be irrelevant to our investigation, that will be so because we are confronted here with something characterizing the order of creation as such, and therefore likely to be exemplified in the whole range of God's dealings with us his creatures. We will proceed now to details which illustrate this conception and which bear directly upon our investigation.

In the preceding chapter it was suggested that the baptism of our Lord symbolized the sacrificial unity of his whole life-story here on earth as set forth in the gospels. Again it was indicated that the inner meaning of that event, as an act of voluntary self-oblation, connected it alike with both the beginning and the end of the gospel story. Moreover it was hinted that in this respect the Saviour's baptism foreshadowed ours, inasmuch as through baptism into the Christ we enter into that total mystery of redemptive history which Jesus both enacted and summed up in his own person.[2] In him it was a characteristic act of filial response proper to the image of the Father, restored to our humanity in the beloved Son and engraced by the Holy Spirit. In us it is an event made possible by the Saviour's great work of restoration whereby

[1] Ch. IV, § i, par. 2 with note.

[2] Chap. IV, last par. of § ii and first par. of § iii.

we are identified with him in that filial response with all its consequences. Among those consequences was that whole sequence of redemptive events which began in the story of Holy Week and reached its climax when the ascended Christ poured down the promised Spirit upon his disciples on the Day of Pentecost. As the Lord approached those events he referred to their imminence in terms of a 'baptism' with which he was to be baptized;[1] and it is possible that this thought may have left its mark on the gospel narratives of his baptism in the river Jordan.

We know that for St Paul Christian baptism meant an identification with Jesus in his death, burial and resurrection. It is possible that this way of regarding the sacrament should be traced back to the above-mentioned baptismal sayings of the Christ. For those sayings suggest that from the first our Lord associated the event of his baptism with the necessity of a sacrificial death in fulfilment of the Servant's destiny. Such considerations raise the issue as to whether in his account of the baptism St Mark's narrative was moulded, consciously or unconsciously, by similar associations. The evidence for such a possibility, in any case, would be all but confined to a single word.[2] If, for the evangelist, the 'descent' of Jesus into Jordan symbolized his future death and burial, then the word employed for his 'ascending' out of the water would carry the sequence on to the 'ascension'. The vision of 'the heavens opening' follows appropriately; and 'the Spirit descending upon him' carries through the analogy (if such it is) to the Spirit descending from him to us at Pentecost. Such a symbolical implication of 'ascent' and 'descent' would correspond to the manner in which the phraseology of Psalm 68 ('he ascended up on high' . . .) is interpreted in its Christian fulfilment by the Epistle to the Ephesians, where the 'ascent' of the Christ is coupled with his 'descent' into hell (4^{8-10}).

In St Luke's two volumes there is no parallel to this symbolic language, although in Acts $2^{34\text{ f.}}$ he uses St Mark's word in a comment on Psalm 110: 'David did not *ascend* into the heavens.' In his full treatment of our Lord's ascension the third evangelist

[1] Cp. above, ch. IV, § iii, last par. but two.

[2] Repeated in Matt. 3^{16}

draws upon Old Testament backgrounds which require a different terminology, whereas the comment in Acts 2^{34} occurs in a speech by St Peter which he may have drawn from a traditional source. As regards the feasibility of recognizing such verbal symbolism in the New Testament we have the much more manifest literary habits of the fourth evangelist whose symbolic play upon words is not open to doubt; and there is good ground for thinking that he plays upon this same Marcan word which we are considering. The word occurs twice in the record of our Lord's appearance to St Mary Magdalene on Easter Day, where Jesus says: 'I have not yet *ascended* to the Father . . . I *ascend* to my Father' . . . (20^{17}). There it has its normal meaning; but in John 7^{8-10} there is every appearance of symbolic by-play in what may well be the best authenticated text: 'Go ye up unto the feast; I go not up unto *this* feast.'[1] Jesus was on his way up to the eternal feast in heaven, of which the Jewish feasts were only types. So after a literal statement about the brethren's movements we are told that 'he went up, but as it were in secret', with which we may compare the parallel saying in 12^{37}.[2]

The symbolic character of the evangelists' literary style is slowly penetrating the modern consciousness of biblical students. We have travelled a long way from Dr Bernard on St John to Dr Farrer on St Mark. The latter is not every man's meat; but at least the author has shown that the raising of Jairus' daughter is told in a manner which points forward to our Lord's resurrection. The account of an exorcism immediately after the transfiguration is, perhaps, even more unmistakeable in its symbolic use of words for 'dying' and 'rising' (two expressions for each of these notions in two verses, $9^{26, 27}$). These instances are not unlike what is being suggested concerning St Mark's way of wording his story of

[1] I follow the more difficult reading. The symbolism was too much for the transcribers who reduced the saying to a dull commonplace of literalism.

[2] In St John there may be a further elaboration, built upon the Hebrew idiom of a sacrifice 'going up' to heaven; e.g. in 1 Kings $18^{29, 36}$, where LXX renders this expression with the Greek word used by St Mark and the other NT writers in the passages cited. The sacrifice of Christ 'goes up' to the Father with a sweet savour (cp. Eph. 5^{2}).

Christ's baptism and its sequel. They at least show that such suggestions of literary symbolism cannot lightly be dismissed. But what precisely would such symbolism signify? This much, at least: that the evangelist saw a significant parallel between two chains of events, namely (1) the descent of Jesus into the water, his ascent from the water, the opened heavens and the descent of the Spirit; (2) the descent of our Saviour into the waters of the abyss in death, burial and journey to Hades, his return from that abyss, and ascension into heaven to send down the Spirit upon his disciples. Possibly we might venture to add to each list one further item; the words of the Voice from heaven proclaiming our Lord's titles would then be paralleled by the voice of the Church proclaiming the *kerygma*, that kernel of truths about Jesus of which specimens occur in the Pauline Epistles and the Acts.[1]

The parallel shows two sequences of events; and if such a parallel was actually implied by the evangelist, it will have been made for reasons which deserve investigation. It may be presumed that in some way the two sequences are supposed to throw light upon one another. If the earlier sequence foreshadows the later, that will imply a unity of design in the gospel story taken as a whole. Such an implication was suggested earlier with regard to the baptism of Jesus. Indeed it is now widely recognized that the baptism as well as the last supper points forward to Calvary. Here, however, we are envisaging a parallel, not between single events, but between chains of events. Moreover, there is reason for thinking that the illumination given in the parallel flows in both directions, that is, backwards as well as forwards. Elsewhere I have suggested that this two-way illumination operates, as between the transfiguration on the one hand and the events of Holy Week and Easter on the other; and it is significant that the symbolic handling of the exorcism in Mark $9^{26,\ 27}$ contributes greatly to that particular form of two-way enlightenment.[2] The

[1] Such a parallel between deity and the church goes no further than the parallel between Christ and his disciples which is drawn out so admirably by Dr H. Riesenfeld in his contribution to *The Root of the Vine*, a volume of Swedish essays in biblical theology (Dacre Press, 1953).

[2] *The Dominion of Christ*, ch. VI (and cp. above, last par.).

transfiguration, like the baptism symbolizes a far-reaching unity of revelation. But further it suggests that humiliation and glory, death and resurrection cannot, in the gospel revelation, be understood apart from one another. This truth may be extended to the whole of the second sequence in the parallel set forth above in the preceding paragraph. In the story of Christ's sacrifice and its glorious sequel there is a mysterious unity embracing the whole series of events which it includes. Is the same thing true, then, of the other sequence?

The analogy implies that it is. But further, at this point we must recall the fact that our parallel between two stages of redemptive history is to be embraced within a yet wider analogy which includes the initiation of Christians into the Church. With that mystery of initiation the second sequence in the above parallel is firmly united and interwoven by St Paul's teaching about baptism in Romans 6. This does not explicitly correspond to the whole of the second gospel sequence. But it suffices for our present argument. In Christian baptism we are united with Christ in his death, burial and resurrection. The single event of baptism with water in the Name identifies us with that single mystery which, nevertheless, is a manifold in three stages. Here we may take note of two other facts which are highly relevant. The first is this; throughout the Pauline Epistles wherever the death of Christ is mentioned, his resurrection is either mentioned or implied in the context. There is, perhaps, only one clear exception to this, namely the saying in 1 Corinthians 11[26]: 'Ye do show forth the Lord's death till he come.' But even there the saying concludes with a reference to the living Christ. To this phenomenon of inspired writing there correspond certain liturgical facts of primitive Christianity. In early days the initiation of new Christians took place at the paschal season; and in the Christian commemoration of our redemption at that season there was not at first a spacing out into the days of a 'holy week', but a single commemoration of all the saving events in the solemn paschal vigil culminating in the eucharist of Easter-Day.

II

INCLUSIVE UNITY IN THE GOSPEL STORY. THE SEVENFOLD GIFT OF THE SPIRIT MANIFESTED IN JESUS BEFORE HIS BAPTISM (LUKE $2^{40, 52}$), BUT BESTOWED AFRESH AFTERWARDS FOR MESSIANIC VOCATION. THE HOLY SPIRIT AND CREATION. GRACE AS THE COMPLEMENT OF THE DIVINE IMAGE IN MAN. THE CREATION STORY, REPEATED PARTIALLY IN ISRAEL, IS FULFILLED IN CHRIST. THE INCLUSIVE UNITY OF THE CHRIST-MYSTERY IS PRESENT IN BOTH PARTS OF THE BAPTISMAL MYSTERY.

The 'major clue to the mystery of the whole Christ', referred to at the beginning of the present chapter, has now been illustrated by means of what appears to be a scriptural concept, that is to say, the concept of a single mystery embracing a series of events in history in such a fashion that no one of such events can be rightly understood except in relation to the whole series. We recall here an earlier observation that what has just been referred to as true of events in redemptive history has also been found in experience to be true of the relation between particular doctrines.[1] It is one thing, however, to recognize such general principles; it is a more difficult matter to see precisely how they are to receive a correct application. We must, therefore, proceed with caution if the analogy between Christ and the Christian is to be brought to a sound conclusion. Our next task will be to examine more closely the nature of that inclusive unity which embraces the earlier and later parts of the gospel whole at the point where they seem to meet, on the banks of the river Jordan. For this purpose we can get no further by dwelling upon the symbolic centrality of our Lord's baptism. For, notwithstanding that centrality, the baptism was seen to be the climax of a first stage in the divine-human life, whereas we are now seeking to know how that first stage is interwoven with the second or later stage in one all-embracing unity.

For this purpose we shall do well to concentrate our attention upon the event which followed upon our Lord's baptism, namely the descent of the Holy Spirit; this we understood to be the ful-

[1] Ch. IV, § i, par. 4.

filment of two prophecies which are to be found respectively in Isaiah 11 and 61. The former prophecy is the more detailed, containing as it does a list of spiritual gifts which were to be bestowed upon the messianic king when the Spirit rested upon him. The list reached a traditional form in the Septuagint version where the gift is sevenfold; and traces of all the gifts are to be found in the apostolic writings, especially perhaps in Ephesians. The Greek version of the list passed into the Latin prayer recited by the bishop over candidates for confirmation in the western liturgical tradition of Christendom. These facts provide an important historical link in the application of our analogy to the second stage of the baptismal mystery. At present, however, we are concerned with its application to our Lord himself in the gospel history. It is here that St Luke's picture of our Lord's boyhood is of peculiar importance in determining more exactly the relation of the second donation of the Spirit to that earlier endowment which graced the incarnate Saviour from the beginning of his earthly existence.

The sevenfold gift of the Spirit has two main aspects, illumination of the mind and strengthening of the will; and these graces were manifestly present in our Lord before he came to Jordan to be baptized. St Luke makes this perfectly clear in two statements concerning the development of the Holy Child:

> The child was growing and being strengthened, being filled with wisdom; and the grace of God was upon him (2^{40}).

> Jesus was advancing in wisdom and in stature, and in favour with God and men (2^{52}).

These sentences give a general picture of flawless and harmonious development such as would correspond to perfect and sinless humanity. There are, however, several matters of detail which must claim our attention. In the first place the opening clause of the first quotation repeats verbally the corresponding statement concerning our Lord's kinsman, John, the child who became his forerunner. This belongs to the parallel which is carefully drawn by the evangelist between the two childhood stories along with some pregnant contrasts. All the more significant is a verbal difference here. The clause concerning John says that 'he was being strengthened in spirit', whereas 'in spirit' is omitted in the above quotation concerning Jesus.

We cannot suppose that the spiritual strengthening supplied to John was not granted to Jesus. It may be that the evangelist felt it unnecessary to repeat the whole phrase the second time; or it may be that what was a vital necessity for one of Adam's fallen race, to repair the ravages of sin, would have such a different significance in the sinless humanity of Jesus that it might even prove misleading to repeat it in the same phrase. Whatever be the reason for the omission, however, it may be thought to strengthen the impression of harmonious development in a fashion wholly consistent with the Hebrew background which is so pronounced in these two chapters. For the natural Hebrew presupposition of such a statement would refer it to the entire personality of the Holy Child, unless there were explicit statement to the contrary. A similar detail occurs in the second quotation. The word rendered 'stature' can refer both to physical size and lapse of time like our word 'span'. It could, therefore, be rendered 'maturity' as in other instances.[1] Such a rendering would fit well with the emphasis upon 'wisdom' and 'favour' divine and human. Moreover the word which must mean 'favour' in the quotation from 2^{52} is practically identical with 'grace' in its original Hebrew meaning. For God bestows 'grace' upon one who is 'well-pleasing' to him. So the Spirit descended, after the baptism, upon One in whom the Father was well-pleased. It remains to point out that the illumination and strength received led the Holy Child into the docile 'subjection' of the years at Nazareth (2^{51}).

As the Holy Child increased in wisdom and in spiritual power so he learnt obedience, until the day when his total self-identification with a sinful people as the sin-bearing Lamb brought his filial response to the point which caused the heavens to open. Then in reply came the descending Dove bringing gifts of illumination and strength which corresponded to the accepted

[1] E.g. Eph. 4^{13}, and possibly Matt. 6^{27}.

vocation. What then was the differentiating factor in this second donation of the Spirit? Upon our answer to this question must depend the whole upshot of the analogy between him and us. It is clear that the gifts bestowed after the baptism were not in themselves different from those already received. But here is the vital point: *the same gifts may be given for different purposes.* The full significance of this fact must be unfolded by stages; and the proper starting-point for us is the doctrine concerning man which is implicit in the creation narratives, although it can be further elucidated from the scriptures as a whole. One of the most fundamental truths of scripture is that one which could be defined by saying that man is incomplete without God. This truth is implicit in the symbolism of the creation narratives taken together. But for our present purpose we may fix our attention upon one of its several aspects.

Man is incomplete without the Holy Spirit. This aspect of the biblical doctrine concerning man is adumbrated in Genesis 1 and 2, at first indirectly and obscurely, but eventually in an unmistakeable manner. In the former chapter the Spirit broods over chaos to bring order into it; and in scripture as a whole this picture finds its authentication in the inner life of man as well as in his material environment. Secondly, the symbolism of water, introduced at the beginning of the second narrative, provides a starting point for that imagery which depicts the activity of the Spirit in terms of the various uses to which water can be put. It is only by virtue of this far-reaching fact that the symbolic application comes into recognition as a possible interpretation of the creation-story itself. At the third stage, however, the symbolism is decisive in its own right. 'Breath' is 'spirit' in bible language; and if there were no other biblical examples of its application to the Spirit of God the picture of divine inbreathing in Genesis 2[7] would still mean that man's life is not his own but a gift of God, and that too such a gift that in it the deity imparts something of himself to this most privileged of his creatures. In Hebrew idiom, moreover, man is 'flesh' and God is 'Spirit'. So, as the revelation unfolds it comes to mean that man's true being and destiny is nonexistent apart from the Holy Spirit. If, however, this is true at all it must be a dominant truth which has decisive effects upon our interpretation of revelation throughout its whole course.

We conclude, then, that the grace or gracious activity of the Holy Spirit is the proper complement of the divine image in man, a truth upon which St Athanasius insisted in that great phrase which may be rendered 'the grace accorded to him who is made in the image'.[1] If then in mortal man as such the divine image implies the graces of the Spirit, how much more must this truth hold good of him who is the uncreated image? At this point, however, we must observe that the activities of the Holy Spirit are as wide in scope as the universe; yet in scripture we see them operating at different levels and for diverse ends. 'The Spirit of the Lord hath filled the world', so that the psalmist could cry: 'Whither shall I go from thy Spirit?'[2] Of all living creatures it could be said: 'Thou sendest forth thy Spirit, they are created'; and individual man could say: 'The Spirit of God hath made me, and the breath of the Almighty giveth me life.'[3] But alongside such statements, universal and individual, we find clear indications of a more specialized sphere of the Spirit's presence. The following passage is distinctly reminiscent of Genesis $2^{6,\,7}$; yet it refers to God's creative grace at work upon 'Israel whom I have chosen':

> Thus saith the Lord that made thee, and *formed* thee from the womb . . .
> I will pour water upon the thirsty land[4] and streams upon the dry ground:
> I will pour my Spirit upon thy seed. . . .
>
> (Isaiah 44^{1-3})

Here we have the plasmic moulding of a people in language suitable to the birth of their ancestor; for they were in Jacob, as we were all in Adam. Then the imagery of the creation story is completed with the double reference to watered land and the Spirit. There is this difference, however; Israel shaped by the Creator's

[1] τὴν τοῦ κατ' εἰκόνα χάριν (*Orat. de incarnatione verbi*, 7—PG. XXV).
[2] Wisd. 1^7; Ps. 139^7.
[3] Ps. 104^{30}; Job 33^4.
[4] So RV margin; and see BDB, p. 854, Col. 2. The italicized word in the first line is the same as in Gen. 2^7 in both Hebrew and Greek.

hand still awaits completion through the promised outpouring. Meanwhile, Israel during the long moulding process was undoubtedly the sphere of the Spirit's special activities, witness the phenomena of prophecy and the anointing of individuals, who thereupon received the Spirit for particular functions in the theocracy. It is the last-mentioned item which has special relevance to our present argument. The prayer of Moses: 'Would God that all the Lord's people were prophets, that the Lord would put his Spirit upon them',[1] continued to recur in effect as the objective for which the prophets hoped. Yet along another line they concentrated upon the promise of an ideal king or at least an individualized figure anointed with the Spirit, and so equipped with spiritual gifts to bring Israel's vocation to fulfilment. Israel was already the matrix of the new creation and the home of the Spirit's gifts. Moreover a partial manifestation of those gifts gave hope of a more complete manifestation either in individual or in universal form. In the fulfilment the sphere of creative grace was first narrowed to the person of our Saviour and then universalized in his Church.

We have now reached a point at which the last stage in the analogy may be considered in detail. Jesus is Israel in his own person and in the Church, his body. By virtue of his incarnation he is the new creation, the sphere of the Spirit's new creative activity. The graces which he exhibited in his earthly life are now accessible to every initiated Christian by virtue of membership in his body. Baptism admits us into the sinless humanity of the new Adam. As the graces proper to the image of God were manifested in his developing humanity from the first, so also the powers of the Spirit begin to work upon every baptized infant for illumination of the mind and strengthening of the will. But further, as the humanity into which we were grafted by baptism was once for all 'conceived by the Holy Ghost and born of the Virgin Mary', so also it was afterwards anointed with the Spirit. In baptism, therefore, we entered a domain which had already been first re-created by the Spirit and afterwards endowed for the messianic

[1] Num. 11^{29}.

vocation. Moreover, we also entered by baptism into our Lord's fulfilment of that vocation through out identification with him in his death, burial and resurrection. These facts about our union with Christ suggest that if we rightly distinguish between the two parts of our initiation, we must also recognise the complementary truth that there is a sense in which the whole mystery of the Christ is present in each of those two parts.

III

THE ANALOGY COMPLETED IN THE BODY OF CHRIST. THE CHRISTIAN LIFE THE SAME FOR ALL; YET IN IT WE ARE SHAPED TO THE UNITY OF AN ORGANIC WHOLE INVOLVING FUNCTIONAL DIFFERENCES. TO THIS PLURALITY IN UNITY CORRESPONDS A MANIFOLD ENDOWMENT OF THE SPIRIT'S GIFTS PROCEEDING FROM THE TRIUNE LIFE OF GOD. THE OT BACKGROUND SHOWS IMPARTIAL DISTRIBUTION TO ALL WITH LEVITICAL DEDICATION OF SOME IN A WORSHIPPING COMMUNITY, THUS FORESHADOWING TOTAL DEDICATION OF HEAD AND MEMBERS WITH SPIRITUAL ENDOWMENT FOR ALL. A SKETCH OF THE COMPLETED ANALOGY.

The new Israel is Jesus *and* his church; and this must be understood to mean also Jesus *in* his church. For the completion of the analogy, therefore, we must transfer our attention to the Body of Christ. Here as elsewhere, analogy implies both likeness and contrast. In the order of St Paul's thought Jesus is first envisaged as the Whole to which we belong (1 Corinthians 12), and then as the Head upon which we depend (Colossians). In Ephesians the latter image is shown to imply that the church, as body and bride, is the complement of the Head. In either of these two forms the image is seen to involve a contrast between the One and the many and an utter dependence of the many upon the One. What once happened to him also happens to us in him. For our being derives from him, and our life in him corresponds to what he now is. In the words of another apostolic writer: 'As he is, so also are we in this world' (1 John 4^{17}). Along with these implications of the revelation concerning 'the whole Christ' there is one other consideration which must be taken into account as we proceed.

The analogy was drawn, in the title of chapter IV, as 'between Christ and the Christian'. This emphasis upon the individual was deliberate. Now, however, we have to see how what happens to the individual initiate is related to his membership with others in that Body which is also a new family and community.

In the apostolic epistles generally, and perhaps most clearly in passages descriptive of the Church as Christ's Body, we may distinguish two different ways of speaking about the Christian life. The first way of speaking refers to those fundamental aspects of the new life in which it is the same for all of us. All baptized persons are members of the one Body, and as such all have the same status. All alike have been translated out of the realm of darkness into the kingdom of light. All have died to the old sinful life and have been re-created in Christ; all have been made sharers in his atoning sacrifice and admitted to the privileges of the redeemed community, such as forgiveness, reconciliation with God and free access to the throne of grace. These are so many aspects of the status or condition shared by all. But further, the new status is a new life which involves a life-long process of development. Here we are once more at the point sketched out by St Paul in 1 Corinthians 12[13]. It will be remembered that he there first stated the fact of our common admission to membership in Christ, a fact which reduces to insignificance all natural differences of race or social status. In the second part of the statement, however, we gave reasons for thinking that the apostle may have had in mind the creation-picture of a process by which a human figure was being moulded into shape.[1]

The fulfilment of this creation-image has also confronted us in another form, namely in connexion with St Luke's picture of the process by which the Holy Child was shaped for destiny in his early years. There are, in fact, no less than three aspects of this biblical image corresponding to three distinct forms in which it may be conceived to find fulfilment in the new creation. The moulding of the Christ to the form of the Servant has its individual counterpart in the Christian life. The third aspect of this process

[1] Ch. I, § iii.

was touched upon in our comment upon a prophetic oracle concerning the shaping of old Israel.[1] Significantly that passage referred to the moulding of a people in terms of the gestation of their ancestor. So also, here; as Israel was in Jacob, so the new Israel is in Christ. As he was shaped by his Father's hand for the fulfilment of his vocation, so also in his body the church (a new chosen people) is being shaped to fulfil the bridal destiny of being his perfected complement or counterpart. The moulding of the individual Christian life is from one point of view the same for all of us. For all are being restored to that image of God's Son in which we were originally created.[2] On the other hand the Church is not a mere collectivity, that is a collection of individuals like a heap of pebbles. We are organically united in one Body. All are being shaped to the larger Whole; and in this process individual differences are vitally important.

In a living organism there is both sameness and difference. All the parts are formed ultimately from the same material substance; and although this takes widely different forms, yet all share in one organic life. There is an identity of substructure, and also a similarity of process by which relative permanence is maintained. There is, however, a great diversity of functions, and there are also individual characteristics or circumstances attaching to each. These differences are indispensable to organic unity. For, on the basis of a structure which is broadly identical in character, the differences are mutually complementary within the whole. In such an organism, therefore, no unit can find its completion in isolated development. For the perfection of each unit consists in its flawless fulfilment of the special function assigned to it in the whole. So also the perfection of the whole body depends upon the harmonious co-operation of all its functional units. This is the picture which St Paul applies to the Church, although it must be remembered that in its first and most detailed formulation Christ himself *is* the Body, and the Church has no existence apart from him. From this point of view, clearly asserted in 1 Corinthians 12[12], the creation-image in the following verse would imply a

[1] Above, in this chapter, § ii, last par. but two, etc. [2] Rom. 8[29].

moulding of Christ, the second Adam, which is also a shaping of his Church. To this corresponds the teaching of Ephesians notwithstanding the new emphasis upon Christ as Head.[1]

This image of the human organism, vitally important as it is, is subject to the limitations which characterize all such picture-thinking. It cannot contain the whole truth concerning the Christian community and its relation, on the one hand to Christ, and on the other hand to its individual members. The personal factor is wanting. Later this was supplied, for the relation to Christ, in the nuptial imagery of Ephesians. In I Corinthians, however, the body-parable is only one section of the treatise on the Church (chapters 12–14), and its limitations are helped out by several other pictorial associations. For example, in the section preceding the body-parable (12^{4-11}) there is furnished a list of diverse gifts of the Spirit bestowed upon the Church. This list illustrates what has been said above concerning differences of function in the Body of Christ. Moreover to the details concerning these gifts there is prefixed a supremely important 'trinitarian preface' (verses 4–7). The preface is important for two reasons: first because it suggests an analogy between the functional character of the Church and the triune life of God himself; and secondly this preliminary statement contains a key-word which is repeated in each of the three trinitarian clauses. The word in question owes its importance, in part at least, to certain Old Testament associations which it possesses through the usage of the Septuagint.[2]

The meaning of the key-word can be fixed with reasonable certainty from St Paul's use of the corresponding verb at the conclusion of this section, where we read (verse 11): 'all these [gifts] worketh the one and the same Spirit *distributing* to each one severally as he wills.' The correspondence is unambiguous. The emphasis in the 'trinitarian preface' is not upon the variety of the gifts, etc., but upon their distribution or apportionment from a

[1] In Eph. 1^{23} the Head attains fulfilment in his complement, the body.

[2] For what follows I am greatly indebted to the I C Comm. by Robertson and Plummer.

divine source. The gifts are certainly various; and that corresponds to the diversities of human nature, and ultimately of the Creator's plan. This is implied throughout, and perhaps especially in the third trinitarian clause: 'there are distributions of workings, but the same God, who worketh all in all' (verse 6). The clause last cited carries the triune analogy to its ultimate ground in the fatherhood of God, the order of the divine Persons being reversed in order to begin with the gifts of the Spirit which are the main topic (verse 1), and which lie nearest to the interior life of the Church. The theme of variety, however, is subordinate; the major emphasis lies along two lines of thought. On the one hand the equipment of the Church proceeds from a divine source; and on the other hand there is a contrast between the manifold character of what is bestowed and the single source of the bestowal.

The many gifts are distributed by the same Spirit, and the many forms of ministry have their source in the same Lord. There is here a subtle correspondence between the many and the One. The Holy Spirit is himself referred to frequently as God's gift, and the Lord Jesus spoke of himself as 'he who ministers' (Luke 22^{27}; cp. Mark 10^{45}), The context of these latter sayings shows that the emphasis lies upon 'service' rather than upon an official order of ministers. So too, here, in the epistle the commentators rightly point out that the gifts and ministerings referred to in St Paul's list are not confined to the ordained ministry. Their scope is as wide as the Church, and they transcend wholly the distinction between clergy and laity. The entire section, like the parallels elsewhere,[1] refers to the unity of the Church in terms of the endowment bestowed upon all its members. The manifold gifts express and foster a fundamental unity which proceeds from a divine source; and this plurality in unity corresponds to the very being of God in whom unity is triune. The fact that in such lists official forms of ministry are mentioned is not, however, without significance. For this fact suggests an important parallel between

[1] E.g. Rom. 12^{6} ff. Eph. 4^{7} ff. The more official list in the latter passage (v.11) is intended to illustrate the wider principle laid down in v.7.

the more specialized character of the Apostolic Ministry and the functional structure of the Church as a whole. This parallel has its counterpart in the Old Testament background to which we now turn.

The thrice-repeated key-word[1] of verses 4–6 and the corresponding verb rendered 'distributing' in verse 11 occur in the Septuagint where they have two principal applications connected respectively with the names of Joshua and David. (1) Joshua 'divided' the holy land by lot into portions which he 'distributed' to the twelve tribes. Here the noun employed by St Paul (as also its Hebrew originals) has an objective sense. Each 'apportioning' is a portion of land. Moreover it was apportioned by lot, a procedure which, as we see in the choice of St Matthias (Acts 1^{26}), was believed to indicate the divine will. Thus each tribe received a divinely apportioned gift of land to be subdivided among the heads of families. How sacred such an apportionment was conceived to be appears in the story of Naboth's vineyard. (2) In 1 Chronicles David is represented as 'dividing' the priests and levites into 'courses' which carried out by rota the various fixed duties of the temple worship. There is also a significant connexion between the two principal meanings described above. The tribe of Levi received no portion of land; for 'the Lord was their portion'. Moreover the levites had been offered to God by the other tribes to represent them vicariously; and in the ritual description of this event the people laid their hands upon the levites *as upon victims selected for sacrifice.*[2] If the Lord was their portion, they also were his. Thus we have two complementary apportionings. God distributes portions to all his people according to their need; and they in turn offer to him a representative portion of their whole number for his service.[3]

The correspondences between the old and the new Israel are never exact; yet they can never be safely ignored. In the present

[1] Rendered: 'diversities' in RV and 'varieties' in M.

[2] Num. 8^{10}. Cp. above, ch. III, § iii, note to par. 1.

[3] For detailed references corresponding to this paragraph see the LXX Concordance (Hatch and Redpath), Vol. I, pp. 302, 303.

instance we can see certain guiding lines which lead directly into the new covenant. Each of the twelve tribes, and by consequence every family, received a portion of land as its inheritance. So also in the apostolic statements concerning gifts of the Spirit there is a sustained emphasis upon the principle that every Christian is endowed with such gifts.[1] Yet the levitical exception pointed forward to something higher. Whereas other tribes tithed the produce of their portion, the total levitical dedication foreshadowed the total self-donation of the new Israel in head and members. There is a verbal indication of this which is, perhaps, not wholly fortuitous. A description of the Christian life in Colossians 1 contains one clause (verse 12) which may be rendered thus: 'Giving thanks unto the Father who made us meet for our *share* in the *inheritance* of the saints in light.' The italicized words belong to the regular terminology of the 'apportionment' theme where it occurs in the Greek version of the Old Testament. Moreover, the two words occur together more than once in statements which withhold from the levitical tribe share or inheritance in the land.[2] The apostolic utterance, however, is positive. The new Israel, wholly levitical in its dedication, is also wholly spiritual in respect of the rich inheritance of charismatic gifts in which all its members share.

We are now in a position to sketch briefly the substance of the analogy which is brought to fulfilment in the Church. In baptism we were identified with that sacrificial dedication which extends over the incarnate life of Jesus from his conception to his ascension, a dedication which he embraced in his baptism and fulfilled in his life, death and resurrection. In response to his baptismal surrender accomplished in the power of the Spirit, he was equipped with the gifts of the Spirit for the fulfilment of his messianic vocation as the Lord's Servant. So also we, who by baptismal grace are sharers in his total dedication, are equipped in confirmation with those same gifts of the Spirit which the incar-

[1] 1 Cor. $12^{7, 11}$, Eph. 4^{7}, 1 Peter 4^{10}; and, by implication, in Rom. $12^{6 \text{ ff.}}$ from 'everyone' in verse 3.

[2] Deut. 18^{1}, Josh. $14^{3,4}$.

nate Lord received, and with which the ascended Lord dowered his Church. As he was anointed after baptism, so are we. But there is this difference. His anointing enabled him to fulfil the whole mystery of redemptive sacrifice whereby the Spirit's gifts became available for us. Our anointing by him through his apostolic ministry qualifies us to fulfil our individual share in that mission of the divine bridegroom wherein his bride the Church is for ever united with him. We are so qualified by receiving our 'portion' of the charismatic gifts in order that we may severally contribute to the fulness of the Christ that individual oblation which corresponds to our personal vocation. The offering thus made by each one is indispensable to the perfected worship of the new temple which is Christ's Body.

IV

IN NT THE OFFICIAL MINISTRY IS INSEPARABLE FROM A 'NEW CREATION' STRUCTURE IN WHICH EVERY CHRISTIAN REPRESENTS CHRIST; AND THAT NOTWITHSTANDING A CONTRAST BETWEEN THE NEW ADAM AND THOSE WHO ARE BEING CONFORMED TO HIS IMAGE. HE IS THE WHOLE MAN WHO INCLUDES WITHIN HIMSELF THE HARMONIES OF CREATION RESTORED IN A WORSHIPPING COMMUNITY. THIS SCRIPTURAL REVELATION CONCERNING 'THE WHOLE CHRIST' EXCLUDES AN INDIVIDUALISTIC DOCTRINE OF PERFECTION, BUT AGREES WELL WITH A GATHERING OF MANY INTO THE ONE IN THE TWO STAGES OF THE BAPTISMAL MYSTERY.

For the completion of the analogy it will be necessary to amplify in certain respects the sketch with which the last section was concluded. For this purpose we must recur to two images drawn from the Old Testament, namely, first the creation-story and secondly its symbolic counterpart in Israel. There are only two passages in the New Testament which could be said to reproduce *verbally* the symbolism of Genesis 2^{7}.[1] Of these 1 Corinthians 12^{13} has already been examined, and we shall return to it again presently. In John 20^{22} we read that the risen Lord breathed upon his disciples and said: 'Receive ye the Holy Spirit'; and the words which follow have the character of a

[1] John $9^{6\ ff.}$ does not come into this category.

ministerial commission. The mediatorial and priestly function of Adam, restored in Jesus, is now extended into the Church.[1] There is, however, another facet of this symbolic event which must be kept in mind. In Ezekiel 37⁹ the prophet, under divine direction, invokes the Spirit to come and breathe upon the dry bones of Israel's dead; and a general resurrection follows. It would seem, then, that in the Johannine scene the ministerial commission is, as it were, enfolded within a 'new creation' act which extends the risen life of Jesus to his people. This makes the ministerial function of the apostolate to be inseparable from the 'new creation' life of Israel as a whole. That function is at once distinctive and representative in the new creation, just as in St Paul's teaching we found it corresponding to the functional structure of the entire organism.[2]

It will be noticed that the Johannine use of Genesis 2⁷ is directed towards the apostolic ministry, whereas the Pauline text is applicable rather to the Body of Christ as a whole. Moreover the symbolism of the creation picture with its two phases is divided between the two apostolic writers so that each has a different phase of that miniature story in mind. If we applied Pauline language to the Johannine picture we might say that the Head breathed into certain organs of the body, thereby making them to be channels of a power which was proper to the Head. In that respect St John's Easter story presents a final section of the momentous chapter of redemptive history which began, for this evangelist as for the other three, with the descent of the Spirit upon Jesus at Jordan. From this point of view the anointing of Jesus with the Spirit was a commissioning for his ministerial function as the high priest of restored creation. Yet once again that high function includes within its scope all members of the redeemed community. Thus the specialized ministerial organs are integral to a body in which all members are functional on behalf of the priestly life of the body as a whole. It is in accord with these facts that elsewhere in the New Testament the sacerdotal character

[1] For fuller treatment of this incident I must refer to what I wrote in *The Apostolic Ministry*, pp. 99–104.

[2] See above, § iii, last par. but three, and note.

of the whole Church is expressly affirmed in language drawn from the story of Israel's initiation into the old covenant.[1]

Yet, notwithstanding the declaration under both covenants to which we have just referred, the Israel of God, old and new, has always had its specific organs of ministry, those of the former covenant foreshadowing the messianic headship of the Christ and those of the latter flowing from it and representing it. The difference here is radical, however, and is seen most clearly in the picture of Christ's Body with its interior unity of life and its consequent identification of every member with the Head in whom all ministerial functions are summed up. It was suggested above that this difference could be expressed by saying that, whereas in old Israel a levitical tribe represented vicariously the dedication of God's people, in new Israel the entire people of God are one with their high priest in a total dedication which transcends all external differences and all differentiations of status. It is this which makes it reasonable to find a parallel between the anointing of the Christ after his baptism and the anointing of the Christian at the second stage of his baptismal initiation. Although certain functions are reserved to the official ministry, every Christian represents the Christ in some particular function which corresponds to his or her particular vocation.

As the argument of this chapter has developed, it has proceeded along a line which has brought to light with equal clarity two characteristic traits of the new Israel. These are, first a clear distinction between official and unofficial ministries, and secondly an equally clear affirmation of their togetherness in the functional structure of a single organism, This analogy within analogy throws light upon a recent tendency to think of confirmation as a kind of 'lay' ordination. Such a use of the term 'ordination' may easily lead to false conclusions. Moreover we have found reason for thinking that St Luke discriminates very carefully between ordination and that laying on of hands which bestowed gifts of the Spirit upon newly-baptized Christians.[2] Nevertheless, the

[1] I Pet. $2^{5, 9}$; Rev. 1^{6}, 5^{10}; following Exod. 19^{6}.
[2] Ch. III, § iii, pars. 1 and 2.

above-mentioned tendency is not without some justification; and it must now be our concern to define more precisely what this really implies. As before, we must take account of three biblical images, presented respectively in the first part of the creation text, in the 'Davidic' ordering of Israel as a worshipping community, and in the organism of Christ's body. As we have already seen, there is good ground for thinking that the two former pictures are presupposed in St Paul's earliest statement concerning the third.

Unlike John 20^{22}, 1 Corinthians 12^{13} is not concerned with a ministerial commission. The context is baptism in its relation to Christ's body; and the background of the final clause is the first half only of Genesis 2^{7}. In our earlier exposition of this Pauline text it was suggested that the two parts of the statement indicate two quite distinct functions of the Holy Spirit. First he is the agent of our incorporation into Christ, and then he is the binding force whereby individual units are moulded together into a single shape. The figure thus formed is the body of the second Adam. Accordingly there are at least two important aspects of this Pauline creationist imagery, only one of which was seriously examined in our original analysis. For we there concentrated almost entirely upon the two different representations of the Spirit's being, namely, first as the divine agent to whose action baptismal water is instrumental, and then as himself a celestial fluid entering into the earthy units of humanity. Nevertheless a second aspect of the imagery was there envisaged as part of the picture. An illustration was introduced which referred to the process whereby new members are 'assimilated' to the ways of a voluntary human society. As individuals we are incorporated into Christ; as *members* we undergo conformation to a larger Whole. This sociological aspect of the new life must be more fully explored.

From one point of view the Body-of-Christ doctrine has affinity with that whole line of thought, ancient and modern, which draws a parallel between human society on the one hand and the individual human organism on the other. Thus in the providence of God this illuminating illustration entered into the stream of biblical revelation. It entered, however, as one element amongst others. It happened to be congenial to that Hebrew way of thinking in which a people is sometimes personified and sometimes identified with an individual figure. Yet other aspects of revealed truth were dominant, notably the biblical conceptions of creation and man. In the result St Paul was constrained to combine in one picture a new creation and a new Israel, identifying both with the body of a new Adam. Implicit in this complex picture was a conception of the divine image in man which, as the Church received it, had three aspects: (1) Christ is that image in a sinless individual development; (2) in the Church that image is extended from the Christ into a society of redeemed sinners; (3) in the Christian that image is being restored through re-integration into a perfected Whole which is Christ in the Church.[1]

Between the Christ and his Church there is contrast as well as identification. In his life-story we see at every stage a perfect conformation of sinless humanity to the uncreated image of the Father in the person of his Son. In the society of redeemed sinners, on the other hand, we see something aptly signified by a mass of lowly earth-particles which are being welded together by the perennial fountain of the Spirit's graces. In themselves they are a mere collection of individual entities in which the divine image cannot be manifested. Yet the moulding process implies that they are being shaped into an organism in which one day the image will be fully revealed. There is here a double theme with a common background of Hebrew presuppositions. The creation-story implies that the image is to be manifested in the Adam figure *as a whole* when the moulding is completed. This conception is clearly present in St Paul's mind in his epistles, since (as I have written elsewhere) he 'finds the *perfect* manifestation of the divine image only in Christ and its *complete* manifestation only in the general resurrection of the just'.[2] This, however, indicates an ultimate restoration of the image in each redeemed person; and this result

[1] For what follows the reader is referred also to *Revelation*, ch. VI, especially §§ iii and v.

[2] *Op. cit.*, p. 171.

would be one aspect of that salvation which, for each one, is to consist in being made whole.

The complex picture which we are examining was said to have three aspects. It is not only the body of the new Adam, but also a new creation and a new Israel. The individuals who enter the Church are all alike in their helplessness and in their earth-bound character as fallen sinners. Yet they are God's creatures, and as such have in them all the possibilities of a restored creation, that is, of a manifold order which includes harmoniously within itself every sort of diversity. Such a manifold is exemplified in the illustration from the human body. But that illustration occupies one short section only of the apostle's argument. As we have seen, it is preceded by a statement about gifts of the Spirit which has for its background another sort of manifold, namely the theocracy of old Israel, that is a divinely ordered kingdom. It is also succeeded a little later (in chapter 14) by a diagnosis of disorderly worship at Corinth; here St Paul seems to have in mind a musical concept of order as manifest in orchestral harmony. In these two pictures we have glimpses of a new Israel and a new creation, in both of which the harmony of many in one is that of a worshipping community. Moreover in the second picture the apostle may well have in mind, by way of contrast, the wordless and soundless harmonies of creation's worship in the orchestra of nature (Psalm 19).

There is a harmony in creation designed by the Creator; but only at the human level does it become vocal and rational. As Adam named the animal species in his kingdom, so Adam's children lead the praises of the created universe.[1] So too human skill can evoke intelligible sounds from lifeless objects;[2] and human co-operation can produce musical harmonies, orchestral or choral. In the worshipping community such ordered beauty is dedicated to the Creator's service in grateful response to revelations of his love. Such was the ideal expressed in Israel's temple-worship as reflected in the books of Chronicles. But in the new Israel the temple is the Body of Christ and the entire life of his members is worshipful in its essence. Engraced by the Spirit each is empowered

[1] Ps. 8^3 (LXX).	[2] 1 Cor. $14^{7\ ff.}$

to make his contribution to the corporate oblation of the whole Church. Moreover it is only through such co-operation that the individual can fulfil his destiny in the new creation. The parallel with the original order of creation persists, a fact of which we are constantly reminded at every stage in the biblical writings: 'The stars shined in their watches and were glad: when he called, they said, Here we be; they shined with gladness unto him that made them.'[1] Israel's ideal of a worshipping community is here reflected back into all orders of created being.

The worshipping community is a family in which all members share one life, the life of the new Adam in whom there is constituted a new creation. This again implies an ordered kingdom in which Christ is king, and a single organism of which he is head. All these aspects of the *totus Christus* are set forth in St Paul's First Epistle to the Corinthians,[2] and all are equally necessary to the proportions of truth in scripture as a whole. Together these various images combine to exclude the notion of a mere collectivity, that is a collection of individuals who move along parallel lines of isolation, like monads, to an individual state of perfection. In so far as the Church has been thought of along predominantly individualistic lines such one-sidedness has in practice been mitigated by mutual charity. It is significant, however, that in the above-mentioned epistle the hymn to charity is set at the centre of that cluster of images in which the new creation exhibits social order and functional unity as well as identity of life. This manifold revelation, to which no single image can do justice, is a unity in plurality of which the baptismal mystery is the appropriate counterpart.

In that mystery there are two aspects of initiation corresponding respectively to baptism and confirmation. In the former of these aspects we see an individual belonging to a fallen and sinful race incorporated into the new humanity of the Christ by a creative act of the Holy Spirit. He is now no longer a mere fallen indi-

[1] Baruch 3^{34}; cp. Judith 9^{6}; both statements are apparently based upon Isa. 48^{13}.

[2] See especially chs. 10–15.

vidual. For although the evil legacy of the fall has not thus far been wholly eradicated in him, yet he has been re-created as a member of Christ, and that too in a manifold sense which corresponds in its rich significance to the entire complex of relevant biblical images. He lives in the new world of the Spirit's gracious creativity. But further the divine humanity into which he has been grafted was anointed for service with the seven-fold endowment of the Spirit. In his baptism, therefore, he was plunged into the heart of the messianic mission, as surely as, at the Lord's bidding in John 9, the man born blind dipped himself into the pool called 'Sent'. At this point we turn to the second aspect of the mystery. It is precisely because we are, through baptism, members of the anointed Messiah that we need to be equipped, as he was, by an individual anointing with the Spirit for the fulfilment of our vocation as organs of his Body.

We are to become whole through our unification with the messianic Whole of the new creation's order. Thus the completion of our baptism is fittingly effected through the intervention of the bishop whose apostolic authority is the indispensable link between the individual parts and the Body as a whole. We can, therefore, heartily agree with the authors of *The Beginnings of Christianity* I, (vol. iv) that, as once at Ephesus, so now in every episcopal act of confirmation 'the laying on of hands is regarded as the climax of baptism'.[1] In such an act the Apostolic Ministry equips the member of Christ for a ministerial function as vital in its own order as that of the official ministry itself. For wholeness of salvation and wholeness of organic functioning in the Body of Christ are inseparable. The entire baptismal mystery is eschatological in its reference; and so in its 'completion' the neophyte is 'sealed' by the Holy Spirit of God 'unto the day of redemption'.[2]

[1] Above, ch. III, § ii, par. 1 f.

[2] Eph. 4^{30}.

CHAPTER VI

THE MEANING OF CONFIRMATION

I

THE THREEFOLD PARALLEL OF BIBLE, CHURCH AND INITIATION IN RESPECT OF 'UNITY IN PLURALITY'. DIVERSITIES IN THE MANIFOLD TEND TO DIVERGENCE IN A DIVIDED CHRISTENDOM. NT ALREADY SHOWS THE POSSIBILITY OF DIVERGENCE, E.G. WITH REGARD TO INFANT BAPTISM. CHILDLIKE DEPENDENCE FUNDAMENTAL TO THE PLAN OF CREATION. 'BELIEVERS' BAPTISM' IGNORES DOMINICAL TEACHING AND THE ORGANISM OF CHRIST'S BODY. THE UNITY OF THE BAPTISMAL MYSTERY SUBJECTED TO FAR-REACHING EROSION IN HISTORY.

In the present volume we have been almost wholly occupied with the teaching of scripture in its bearing upon Christian initiation. The church, however, is 'a witness and a keeper of holy writ'; at this point, therefore, in our inquiry it will be convenient to return once more to a connexion between the bible and the church to which attention has already been drawn. In the opening paragraphs of our first chapter something was said about a parallel between these two fundamental sources of authority. In that context we were considering the unity of scripture as conveying a single revelation, a revelation which could be apprehended as a whole, albeit through many diverse parts belonging to different stages of development. A difficult problem confronted us here concerning the relation existing between that 'whole' of revelation and its parts; and it was in reference to this problem that attention was drawn to 'the exposition of a parallel theme in scripture itself'. The theme in question was that which St Paul unfolded concerning 'the principles operating in the Body of Christ'. The analogy between the bible and the church thus introduced was at the same time connected with 'the mystery of Christian initiation' in which we have also found a 'complex whole embracing a plurality of parts'.

In reference to this threefold parallel it was remarked that we might 'find occasion to develop more fully the analogy between scripture and the Body of Christ'; and we have now reached a point in our argument where this line of thought can profitably be pursued. The analogy, however, may be considered from two points of view, the one negative and the other positive; and this use of terms must now receive a fuller explanation. We will begin with the negative aspect. If there is a correspondence in unity or wholeness between the written Word and the People of God to whom that Word has been committed, then we might expect that breaches in the unity of Christendom would render more difficult a right apprehension concerning the wholeness of revelation once for all enshrined in the sacred writings. Elsewhere[1] I have discussed the general truth of the particular proposition implied in the preceding sentence; and our immediate task will be to consider its application to the baptismal mystery. That, however, will be no more than a necessary preliminary. It is a good thing to be humbled by facing up to the grim realities of a divided Christendom. Such a discipline of faith might effect in us a more chastened and reverent regard for those ultimate mysteries of revelation which confront us here as certainly as in every other part of Christian faith and practice.

The divisions of Christendom are manifested most obviously in diversities of practice; and such diversity is perhaps reflected nowhere more characteristically than in the divergences which have arisen with regard to the rites of initiation and the conditions under which they are administered. It may be that only one of these divergences can be traced with some degree of probability to the first Christian century, namely the choice between two alternative methods of administering confirmation, that is to say, by chrism or by laying on of hands. But even this alternative rests heavily upon the argument from silence, whereas in the healing ministries of Jesus and his disciples both these outward means were employed (Mark $6^{5, 13}$). Moreover, in this connexion we shall do well to bear in mind a shrewd observation by the

[1] *Revelation*, ch. III.

authors of *The Beginnings of Christianity*, I (vol. v, p. 134) concerning 'associated ideas, any one of which might in any single narrative be either omitted or emphasized'.[1] This utterance may possibly throw light upon the fact that, whereas in 2 Corinthians 1^{22} St Paul connects the gift of the Spirit with 'anointing' and 'sealing', in Acts 19^{6} he is represented as conveying that gift through the laying on of hands.

Nevertheless the situation disclosed in the New Testament already shows a possibility of problems arising to which gravely different answers might be given in the ever-changing circumstances of history. Of these problems the most momentous are probably those which have sprung from the practice of infant-baptism, precisely because the apostolic writings, in their explicit statements, envisage only adult neophytes with a corresponding emphasis upon individual faith and repentance as necessary presuppositions. That teaching corresponds to the situation which obtains at all times in a purely missionary church. Such teaching in fact, like the transient character of the more ecstatic gifts of the Spirit, compels us to remember that the New Testament embodies, not only the final revelation, but also the first epoch only of Church history. For our Lord, in blessing little children, had already foreshadowed the limits of such a situation. The dominical saying: 'Suffer little children to come unto me and forbid them not' is a foundation text which may well be thought decisive. The children whom our Lord blessed with the laying on of hands were young enough to be taken into his arms. They were certainly not old enough to understand what was happening. Moreover our Saviour's action was accompanied by the saying: 'Whosoever does not receive the kingdom of God as a little child shall not enter therein.'[2]

It would seem that the little child has qualities of special affinity with the kingdom which adults must desire to possess, and without which they will be disqualified. Adults, therefore, are at a

[1] The passage was quoted in full above in ch. III, § ii, par. 4.

[2] For the connexion of Mark 10^{13-16} with Acts 8 and 19 see above, ch. III, § iii, pars. 3, 4.

disadvantage; and in order to overcome this disadvantage they need the discipline of the catechumenate and the cultivation of those graces of repentance and faith which will restore to them the childlike character. For original sin has undermined in them the attitude of childlike dependence upon God which belongs to the original plan of creation. We recall here the fact that in scripture the order of creation constantly provides the background for a true perspective concerning the order of redemption. The fathers sometimes taught that Adam and Eve possessed a childlike innocence which was lost in the fall;[1] and in the psalm of creation a high significance is attached to the incipient speech of babes and sucklings (Psalm $8^{3(2)}$). So it was fitting that the Son of God should inaugurate the new creation by becoming a helpless infant, and that later on he should see something symbolic and prophetic in the praises of children in the temple courts (Matthew $21^{15, 16}$). In the order of creation we are not primarily adults or children but helpless creatures; and our utter dependence upon 'the grace which corresponds to the image'[2] is reflected in that same order of creation by our mutual dependence upon one another in family and society.

By contrast with these scriptural themes the 'believers' baptism', for which the Baptist community stands presupposes a conception of the church characteristic of the reforming movement in the sixteenth century. This conception does not proceed from the biblical associations of creation and new creation, but from a much later emphasis upon individual experience. The church is now thought of as the sum total of converted sinners, brought to faith in Christ through God's electing and predestinating grace. This was in fact to substitute a collectivity of individual units for the scriptural conception of an organism. Moreover quite naturally it carried with it a rejection of confirmation which derives so much of its significance from the associations of wholeness and unity in the one Body, wherein the individual is to find fulfilment of

[1] Details are given by N. P. Williams in *The Ideas of the Fall and Original Sin*, Lecture IV.

[2] Cf. above, ch. V, § ii, last par. but two with first note.

vocational endowment. Behind the individualism of the Reformation, however, lay the various changes of emphasis which Christendom underwent from the time of its first emergence in the so-called 'peace of the church' during the fourth century. It is upon this background that we must consider the divergences of custom which now obtain with regard to the initiation of neophytes into the church.

The first new development which is relevant to our subject was the emergence of the parish priest to whom was now delegated much of the sacramental ministries formerly administered by the bishop himself. In various degrees the bishop became a more remote personage, although certain functions were believed to be inalienably his; and amongst these was the consecration of the chrism for the sealing of the newly baptized. By the method of delegation the unity of baptism and confirmation could thus be preserved as a single mystery, visibly one in its significance, although the vital function of the bishop as the centre of unity in his flock was no longer manifested in a personal contact with the newly-made Christians. Moreover, the laying on of hands, whereby Jesus blessed little children and the apostles bestowed the gifts of the Spirit, was no longer a normal method of confirmation until it was revived in the early middle ages for western Christendom only. For purely practical reasons that revival of a scriptural form carried with it, as it seems inevitably, a non-scriptural separation in time between the two parts of what had thus far been manifestly the single mystery of Christian initiation.

At this point we seem to have reached a definite parting of the ways. The Orthodox Churches of the east had at least preserved the outward symbolism of 'unity in plurality' by their method of initiating Christians, whatever we may think of the practice by which consecration of the chrism has been reserved to the patriarch. In the west, however, the separation in time between baptism and confirmation was accompanied by other changes which, taken together, have a decidedly ominous character. The total effect of such changes, in so far as they bear upon the baptismal mystery, tended to obscure the theological significance of confirmation.

But, in the opinion of the present writer, that particular obscuration formed one factor only in *a process of erosion* which was destined to affect adversely the whole notion of 'unity in plurality' and that on the widest scale. It is certainly this aspect of Christian initiation which has so largely fallen into the background in western Christendom. It is important to observe, however, that what I have called a 'process of erosion' has, in the course of centuries, gathered volume in its progress like a moving snowball. It has left its mark, not only upon liturgical practice, but also upon our methods of handling scripture and apprehending doctrine. Fortunately there are not wanting signs that the tendencies which have characterized this process are being reversed. From such a reversal we may hope for beneficial results alike in the sphere of sacramental theology and of its liturgical expression.

II

PRIMITIVE TEACHING CONCERNING CONFIRMATION OBSCURED IN THE WESTERN MIDDLE AGES WITH DISASTROUS RESULTS IN A DIVIDED CHRISTENDOM. BY CONTRAST SOME CONCLUSIONS OF THE PRESENT TREATISE RECALLED CONCERNING CHRISTIAN WITNESS IN THE FIRST TWO CENTURIES. A FOURFOLD FORM OF 'UNITY IN PLURALITY' APPEARS IN SCRIPTURE, THE GOSPEL SEQUENCE OF EVENTS, THE BODY OF CHRIST AND THE BAPTISMAL MYSTERY. THE WEAKENED THEORY OF CONFIRMATION FURTHER AGGRAVATED BY A GROWTH OF 'PAPAL PRESBYTERIANISM'. THE SYMBOLIC SIGNIFICANCE OF THE EPISCOPATE TRAGICALLY OBSCURED THROUGHOUT CHRISTENDOM. THE TWOFOLD DISTORTION IN THE WEST TENDED TO GENERATE AN UNSCRIPTURAL CONCEPTION OF THE CHURCH

One of the problems which has eluded any adequate solution in recent Anglican discussions has been the question as to what is the distinctive gift of the Holy Spirit in confirmation; and closely bound up with this is the further question concerning the relation between that gift and the benefits bestowed in baptism. Presently we shall attempt to define our answer to these questions more exactly in the light of the evidence already collected in this volume. First, however, we must complete what I have called the negative part of our argument. The 'process of erosion' in western Christendom, in so far as it affected the theology of Christian initiation, was surveyed in masterly fashion by the late Dom Gregory Dix in a lecture published under the title: *The Theology of Confirmation in relation to Baptism*.[1] He found the first beginnings of the process in the 'presbyterian' leanings of St Jerome, and traced it, through a fifth-century Whitsun sermon which was later incorporated into the forged decretals, down to the authoritative utterances of Peter Lombard and his scholastic successors. The essence of the change effected in this movement was an almost total evacuation of the theological significance assigned, in the teaching of the primitive church, to what we now call 'confirmation'.

Whereas, for example, Tertullian following St Luke had affirmed that the Holy Spirit is not given in the water of baptism, but in the subsequent laying on of the bishop's hands, the new mediaeval doctrine affirmed that confirmation was merely the 'increase' and 'strengthening' of gifts already received in baptism. The development of this teaching coincided with a separation in time between infant baptism and the episcopal laying on of hands restored to the west in the Carolingian period. When once the process of separation had got under way in the administering of the two sacraments, it was doubtless inevitable that baptism with water should tend to be regarded as complete in itself. It would then seem to follow that there was nothing new to be added; and the more ancient conception of confirmation as the 'completion' of baptism would become less intelligible. It would even come to be supposed that such a notion of 'completion' actually cast a slur upon Holy Baptism. Certainly modern attempts to revive the more ancient doctrine have been regarded as paradoxical, or even as slightly shocking.[2]

The mediaeval change of doctrinal emphasis with regard to

[1] Dacre Press, 1946 (now published by A. & C. Black).

[2] The drawbacks attending separation of the two rites are not a sufficient reason for a drastic change in Anglican practice. On this point I am in general agreement with the concluding pages of Dix's lecture (*op. cit.*, pp. 31 ff.).

confirmation was a momentous step away from the wholesome diversities of the New Testament. It was also a tragic step forward into the unwholesome diversities of modern Christendom. For in our present situation the diversities of a divided Christendom have the appearance of rival theses, each of which claims to be true to the exclusion of the other. Either baptism is exalted or confirmation; either the infant or the adult is put forward as the suitable neophyte. This is a conflict of unwholesome diversity from which we shall do well to seek deliverance in the Word of God and in the apostolic tradition of the church. We need to retrace our steps out of a net of baffling contradictions into the mysterious harmonies which are implicit in the original revelation. The mediaeval notion that confirmation conveyed only an increase or strengthening of what had already been bestowed in baptism implied that in Christian initiation there is only one donation of the Spirit and that this is conveyed through the waters of baptism. In our previous survey of the biblical evidence we have found ample grounds for rejecting such a theory.

Let us recall some of the principal conclusions reached in the preceding chapters, conclusions which point in a direction quite contrary to that of the mediaeval simplification. First then we found in St Paul's epistles clear indications that there are two stages in Christian initiation. Secondly, this impression was strengthened by reference to the Johannine writings. In particular we found in the Apocalypse an emphatic concentration upon the practice of 'sealing' the forehead and in the Epistle a corresponding emphasis upon the 'anointing'. These two expressions also occur together in a Pauline reference to Christian initiation (2 Corinthians 1^{22}). Moreover a connecting link between that utterance of St Paul and the Johannine passages is to be found in the two references to the 'seal of the Spirit' in Ephesians (1^{13}, 4^{30}). The connexion lies in the strongly eschatological tone of all the passages cited. For just as Revelation $7^{1\text{ ff.}}$ has its background in the sealed remnant of Ezekiel 9 and in the Exodus story, while the anointing in 1 John 2 is a safeguard against the coming of antichrist, so also in Ephesians the sealing is 'unto the day of redemption'.

Thirdly, we found in Justin's *Dialogue* an elaboration of the biblical imagery employed by St Paul in his Epistle to the Colossians with the twofold background of Joshua and Ezekiel. The argument of our second chapter thus served to strengthen still further the impression of two stages in the Pauline conception of the baptismal mystery. At the same time it also underlined a probable continuity of image-thinking, connecting the New Testament with patristic modes of thought concerning Christian initiation in the third century. Fourthly, the analogy between Christ and his people was seen to point to a twofold donation of the Spirit with a distinction between 'being' and 'mission' alike in him and in us. What we are by grace corresponds to what he became by divine condescension; and this correspondence, in turn, opened the way to a further engracing of the many for sharing in the vocation of the One. There is one factor in this analogy which will require further consideration. It was touched upon in the final section of chapter V in the remark that 'between the Christ and his church there is contrast as well as identification'.[1] To that we shall return presently.

Finally, as the argument developed there recurred repeatedly a dominant clue in the concept of 'unity in plurality'. This concept with its manifold applications was found to be a connecting link between scripture, the Body of Christ and the baptismal mystery. This threefold parallel, adumbrated in the opening pages of this book and resumed at the beginning of the present chapter, can now be further elaborated into a fourfold form. For in the original Pauline formulation Christ *is* the Body of which we are members. The mystery of the Body, therefore, is the mystery of the whole Christ; and our completion of the analogy between him and us was introduced by a summary statement to the effect that 'the gospel history, like the baptismal mystery, presents', not only 'a whole in two parts', but also 'unity embracing a series of events'.[2] We remember that according to St Paul the waters of baptism effect our mystical identification in a moment of time with a whole series of redemptive events, namely death, burial and

[1] Ch. V, § iv, par. 7.

[2] Ch. V, summary at head of § i.

resurrection; and this simultaneous conjunction of the individual neophyte with a temporal sequence in redemptive history stands over against the simultaneous unification of all Christ's members with the One Head of the Body.

Here we are already passing over to the positive aspect of the parallel between scripture and the Body of Christ which we set out to consider in the present chapter. Before proceeding further with that task, however, we must take note of some other factors which were present in the process of erosion as it developed in the course of the middle ages. We have noticed that a temporal separation between the two parts of the baptismal mystery may have assisted the process by which confirmation was evacuated of its true meaning. That unity in plurality which belongs alike to revelation and to its ecclesiastical vehicle was in other respects becoming obscured. Its preservation in the common life of the church depended upon a balance of forces exceedingly difficult to maintain in our present fallen state. The development of rivalry between the great sees of Christendom was an ominous sign of things to come; and after the great schism the steady increase in the papal claims tended to obscure the apostolic character of the episcopal office. The whole history of mediaeval thought in the west on the subject of the ministry shows a tendency towards a papal version of 'presbyterianism' in which the claims of the papacy on the one hand and the *sacerdotium* of the presbyterate on the other reduce the office of bishop to one of convenience rather than of principle.[1]

With this further distortion of primitive ecclesiology the ministry of the church tended to become a graded sequence of earthly rank and preeminence in society rather than an organic structure in Christ's Body fulfilling a series of functionally differentiated services appropriate to the welfare of the organism as a whole. In fact it became 'authoritarian' in the sense against which our Lord uttered a solemn warning.[2] The primitive bishop

[1] The facts are set forth in an essay by Dr Jalland in *The Apostolic Ministry* (Hodder and Stoughton, 2nd ed. 1947). See especially pp. 340 ff.

[2] Cp. *The Dominion of Christ*, p. 77 with note 1.

represented his local flock to the church universal, as he also represented the church universal in and to his own flock. For that very reason he was the fitting person to admit a new member of the flock to full communion with the church universal by confirmation, thus completing the neophyte's initiation. The manner in which this beautiful symbolism was obscured throughout Christendom belongs to the most distressingly tragic ironies of history. In the East the diocesan bishop was eventually eliminated from his proper symbolic function by a combination in which the patriarch blessed the chrism and the parish priest administered the chrismation; and *yet* the essential meaning of the rite as a 'completion' or 'perfecting' was retained. In the West, on the other hand, from approximately the period when the personal intervention of the bishop was being restored in the revived practice of laying on of hands, this outward symbolism was being largely nullified in two respects. For first the original meaning of the rite was already forgotten, and secondly the essential significance of the bishop who administered it in person was slowly but surely fading into oblivion.

As we contemplate this tragedy in its western form, we can see that it has the character of a vicious circle. The distortion has two sides, each of which tends to obscure one part of the truth. Yet the two negations—the one concerning the candidate for confirmation, and the other concerning the bishop's function in confirming—are complementary to one another and support one another. For example, if the candidate is simply being 'strengthened' for the battle of life he can receive such strengthening as effectively in Holy Communion administered by a priest. A distinctive function of the episcopate at this point is therefore otiose. Together the two new factors in the mediaeval set up were, therefore, combining to foster an unscriptural conception of the church. For now individualistic piety and authoritarian government were together displacing the Pauline conception of an organism in which individual vocation is fulfilled through functional service in accordance with gifts received. Under the weakened conception of confirmation the vocation of the individual initiate need not have a necessarily sociological significance. Moreover, just so far as the bishop ceases to be regarded as the centre of unity through whom such a vocation is mediated, individual Christians cease to that extent to be organic to the Whole. Their piety is individualized except so far as it finds security in unquestioning obedience to papal authority.

III

ANALOGY SUGGESTS THAT IN CONFIRMATION THERE IS A CONTINUITY WHICH IS MORE THAN 'STRENGTHENING'. FOR AFTER BAPTISM JESUS RECEIVED THE 'COMPLETION' PROPER TO HUMANITY. THE PERFECTION OF DEITY EXISTS IN PERSONAL RELATIONS; AND A FILIAL RELATION OF MAN TO GOD IN DEPENDENCE UPON THE HOLY SPIRIT IS THAT 'PERFECTION' OF HUMANITY WHICH JESUS EXHIBITED. SO IN CONFIRMATION THE HOLY SPIRIT IS GIVEN FOR 'PERFECTING'. IN THE BIBLICAL WORLD RELIGIOUS INITIATION WAS EXPRESSED IN TERMS OF 'PERFECTING'; AND IN THE EPISTLE TO THE HEBREWS JESUS THROUGH DEATH INAUGURATES THE TRUE SACRIFICIAL INITIATION INTO THE FINAL PERFECTION.

The mediaeval doctrine concerning confirmation is believed to have received its shape largely from a sermon in which it was said that in that rite the Holy Ghost 'provides an increase of grace' whereby we are 'strengthened for combat'. Those who adopted this teaching might with justice have pointed to some statements of St Luke concerning our Lord himself. For, as we saw previously, our Lord was being 'strengthened' in his childhood by the grace of God; moreover, further strengthening by the Spirit after his baptism armed him, as son of Adam, for combat with the serpent. In our previous analysis of this material the earlier 'strengthening' was referred back to an activity of the Holy Spirit which had its inception at the moment when the Incarnation took place. The analogy between Christ and his members, therefore, would, on the evidence of the third evangelist, strongly support a view which stressed to the fullest degree continuity as between the graces and gifts respectively of baptism and of confirmation. It is also true, however, that if 'confirmation' is taken to mean no more than 'strengthening' the Lucan form of the analogy would evacuate the rite which bears that title of any *specific* significance. For the evangelist affirms a 'strengthening' of the Holy Child *before* he received the second donation of the Spirit.

These considerations suggest that on the one hand confirmation may rightly be said to strengthen the regenerate life in all its aspects, but that on the other hand it would be fatal to limit its significance to such strengthening. This brings us to the point where another aspect of the analogy presents itself for consideration. The descent of the Spirit upon Jesus after his baptism was understood to be an endowment for the fulfilment of his messianic mission in accordance with prophecy. The first donation (at conception) disposed the developing humanity of the incarnate Lord to the acceptance of the Servant's vocation. The second donation could be bestowed only when that vocation had been deliberately accepted. Thus the two bestowals of the Spirit were for two quite distinct purposes. Yet that very distinction which we have just drawn inevitably implied continuity. Our Lord's self-oblation to be the Servant was 'completed' by the Father's acceptance of that oblation and by the endowment of the Spirit in which that acceptance was expressed and implemented. The oblation was 'strengthened' in purpose by its acceptance and endowment. But even more important is the truth that it was actually brought to fulfilment by the response from heaven. The perfect humanity of the Second Adam was 'completed' by the inbreathing of the Spirit.

In the concluding sentence of the preceding paragraph we returned to the analogy between the two creations which we found to be inextricably bound up with the analogy between Christ and his people. We have next to consider further what precisely is implied in the language in which this analogy has been expressed. A preliminary sketch was outlined in chapter V (§ II); but we must now go into the matter more fully. First of all, then, a question may be asked as to the sense in which it is legitimate to suggest that the incarnate Lord stood in need of completion. In what sense could perfect humanity be said to be at any time 'incomplete'? The answer to this question will depend upon a discrimination between various possible meanings of 'incompleteness'. Obviously what is 'perfect' cannot be incomplete in respect of anything proper to *this* perfection. But further, when that notion has been ruled out there still remain two possible meanings of the word which correspond to the biblical doctrine of creation. In the first place there is the basic biblical conception that man is incomplete apart from God; in the divine plan man was not intended to be complete in himself, but rather to find his completion in God. Secondly this creaturely dependence upon God is bound up with a creaturely development of humanity from first beginnings to a final goal. The original creative 'call' implies a vocation fulfilled by a perfected response to the call.

In the statements just made there is a correlation between 'perfection' and 'completion' which needs to be more fully expanded in view of the fact that both terms will be found to play an important part in the doctrine of Christian initiation. In the being of God 'perfection' consists in the mutual relations internal to the life of the Blessed Trinity. Such mutual relationship is complementary in the sense that each Person is the complement of the other two. In short the *completeness* of perfection consists in a reciprocity between the Persons. The doctrine of the Holy Trinity is thus the complete negation of that self-sufficiency which is idolized by fallen humanity.[1] By contrast the reciprocity of personal relations in the Godhead is the ground of creation in its nexus with the Creator. The mutual love of Father and Son is thus the basis of the heavenly Father's relations with his human family. The image of the eternal Son is reflected, however faintly, in man's dependence upon God. A total dependence of our humanity upon its Creator belongs to that very perfection in which and for which it was brought into existence. It is in fact a *perfection of dependence*.

Thus by another route we have returned to that great phrase of St Athanasius. A perfect manifestation of the divine image in man would appear in an unswerving dependence upon 'the grace

[1] Whereas the divine attribute of *aseity* has reference to the external relations of deity with creation. The all-sufficiency of the Godhead is an aspect of the triune life.

which corresponds to the image'. That is precisely what the Gospels show us in their portrait of Jesus. Of his childhood St Luke says quite simply: 'The grace of God was upon him' (2^{40}). Of his interior adult life St John reveals glimpses in sayings which recur in the great discourses such as the following:

The Son can do nothing of himself, except what he seeth the Father doing;
Whatsoever *he* doeth, these things the Son also likewise doeth (5^{19}).
The things which I heard from him, these I also speak in the world (8^{26}).
All things which I heard from my Father I made known unto you (15^{15}).

The Athanasian phrase referred to above is one way of expressing the truth that man's filial relation to God involves a dependence upon the Holy Spirit. For the created image corresponds to its archetype. The Holy Spirit proceeds eternally from the Father to the Son; and that eternal procession took historical form when the Son was 'conceived by the Holy Ghost'. So too the perfect humanity developing perfectly was in due course anointed with the Spirit to fulfil that perfect response to which the Son had been called.

At this point we may take note of the patristic doctrine that confirmation or chrismation of baptized persons is given for their 'perfecting'. This became a characteristic teaching of eastern fathers at least from the fourth century onwards. But it is also found in the West as early as the third century. In North Africa according to the Cyprianic tradition the newly-baptized were brought to the bishops 'to receive the Holy Spirit by the invocation and by the imposition of the hands and to be perfected by the seal of the Lord'.[1] The connexion of the 'perfecting' with the gift of the Holy Spirit is once more affirmed in Western teaching by St Ambrose who refers it explicitly to the seven-fold gift conferred through the sealing.[2] It seems clear that in the fourth

[1] Quoted by J. Daniélou on p. 163 of *Bible et Liturgie* (Paris, 1951) from Cyprian, Ep. LXXIII, 9. Cp. Mason, *op. cit.*, p. 71.

[2] *De Sacramentis*, III.8. For the patristic teaching on this part of my subject I am greatly indebted to the above-mentioned work by Professor Daniélou.

century this type of teaching could include the notions of 'increase of grace' and 'strengthening for combat' as the greater includes the lesser. The baptismal graces are quickened, the spiritual senses are awakened and the Christian, like his Saviour, is armed to resist the hostile power.[1] On the other hand later eastern teaching interprets 'the perfecting' of the fully initiated in terms of mystical contemplation.

A tradition of this sort could obviously take a variety of forms. For our present purpose, however, it will be more pertinent to return to the analogy in its scriptural form; and this will be found in the Epistle to the Hebrews. Running through the argument of that book there is a double doctrine of perfection which might well prove to be a starting-point of the whole patristic tradition. It will be well to remember, however, that through the Septuagint the relevant Greek terms could have a meaning corresponding to that of religious initiation into a mystery cult; and this aspect of 'perfection' is already apparent in St Paul's epistles.[2] It has been well said that St Paul applies such language to the Christian dispensation, 'that he may thus more effectively contrast the thing signified'.[3] In ancient religion the language of initiation signified admission to the knowledge of a hidden 'mystery'; and in the language common to the New Testament and to the 'mystery' cults the 'perfect' man was one who had attained a desired goal or 'end' by initiation into such a mystery. St Paul taught that Christ is the supreme 'mystery', the all-satisfying 'end' in which human life is fulfilled.[4] The distinctive theme in the Epistle to the Hebrews takes us a step further. Christ is our goal of perfection, because he himself was 'made perfect through suffering'. He is himself the perfect initiate.

In the light of explanations given in the last paragraph we are now in a position to examine what I have called the 'double

[1] Daniélou, *op. cit.*, p. 165.

[2] E.g. 1 Cor. 2^{6}, Col. 1^{25-29}. In LXX a striking example occurs in Num. $25^{3, 5}$ to which Ps. 105 $(106)^{28}$ refers; Hos. 4^{14} shows how sinister 'initiation' could be in OT religion.

[3] J. B. Lightfoot in his commentary on Colossians, p. 237.

[4] Col. $1^{26 \text{ ff.}}$, Rom. 10^{4}.

doctrine of perfection' set forth by this apostolic writer. In his use of words Christ is our 'pioneer-leader'. Like Joshua (4^8) he is leading us to our rest in the promised land. For this task he is qualified by having himself passed through the ordeal to which he now summons us. The parallel between him and us is noticeably stressed in those very passages in which the technical language of 'perfection' is most prominent, namely 2^{5-18} and 5^5–6^6. Moreover the second of these passages includes the classic statement of this epistle concerning Christian initiation.[1] There are, however, two other possible nuances in the writer's employment of this language. (1) Of the word rendered 'make perfect' in Hebrews 2^{10} Dr Moffatt wrote: 'The verb had already acquired a tragic significance in connexion with martyrdom', quoting in illustration from the account of Eleazar's heroic end the words of 4 Maccabees 7^{15}, 'perfected by the faithful seal of death.'[2] This association of ideas may possibly throw light upon a dominical saying in Luke 13^{32}, where our Lord says: 'I accomplish healings to-day and to-morrow, and on the third day I am perfected.' For the literary connexion between Luke-Acts, Hebrews and the Maccabean writings is now recognized.[3]

(2) Our Saviour was 'perfected' through death, but not simply as a martyr. In 7^3 the author informs us that Melchizedek was 'made like unto the Son of God'; the type was conformed to the eternal antitype. Priesthood in its essence is the prerogative of the Son of God. Yet he 'glorified not himself to become high-priest' because sonship means filial obedience. So the incarnate Son entered the lowly school of suffering, and having been 'perfected' in death he became the 'author of eternal salvation'. For the true priesthood of which Melchizedek is the type is that of a 'Son, perfected for evermore' (5^{5-10}, 7^{28}). Small wonder that the early church repeated the language of 4 Maccabees about the deaths of her martyrs, or that martyrs for Christ not yet christened were

[1] For completeness we may also mention 7^{28}. B. F. Westcott's Commentary has a valuable pair of additional notes on this terminology (pp. 63–67).

[2] IC Comm. *ad loc.*, p. 32.

[3] For which see the treatment by W. K. L. Clarke in *The Beginnings of Christianity* I, vol. ii, pp. 73–76.

held to have been baptized in their own blood! Nevertheless the Saviour's title to be accounted King of Martyrs was a consequence of his fulfilling the rôle of Adam's son who bruised the serpent's head, and thereby restored the universal priesthood over creation which was man's true destiny. This is the main theme of 2^{5-18} in which the note of 'perfecting' is first struck.[1] In the biblical background there may perhaps be one further detail. The great phrase in 7^{28} concerning 'a Son, perfected for evermore' makes a contrast with the evanescent character of the levitical priesthood. There might be here an ironic play upon the Greek version of Leviticus 21^{10} where the Hebrew idiom of consecration to the priesthood is expressed in precisely the same form of the 'perfecting' verb as the author of the epistle applies to the Christ.

IV

THE PERFECTING OF THE CHRIST BOTH FOR AND IN HIS MEMBERS. THIS BRINGS THEM TO THEIR TRUE END IN HIM FROM WHOM THEY ALSO RECEIVED THEIR NEW BEGINNING. THE SIX FUNDAMENTALS IN HEBREWS $6^{1\text{ ff.}}$ SET THE BAPTISMAL MYSTERY LIKE A BRIDGE BETWEEN THE FIRST AND THE LAST THINGS. THE BIBLICAL BACKGROUND OF BAPTISMAL 'ENLIGHTENMENT', AND THE AGREEMENT OF HEBREWS WITH ACTS CONCERNING ITS 'COMPLETION'. CHRISTIAN INITIATION IN ITS WHOLENESS ANTICIPATES THE FINAL GOAL.

In the preceding section mention was made of a 'double doctrine' concerning perfection in the Epistle to the Hebrews. This expression was intended to signify the fact that Jesus was himself 'perfected' in order that he might be thereby enabled to perfect us. There is, moreover, a sense in which the author evidently conceives these two aspects of perfection to be interwoven. For example in 10^{14} he says that our Lord 'hath by one offering perfected for evermore those who are being sanctified'. This corresponds to St Paul's teaching. All has already been accomplished in Christ's sacrifice. In him we are already perfected. Yet the process of sanctification is still going on. Moreover our

[1] For details see *The Dominion of Christ*, pp. 77–83.

author would doubtless have agreed with another aspect of Pauline teaching. When 'One died for all, then all died' (2 Corinthians 5^{14}). Yet also we died and rose with him in baptism. So the 'perfecting' accomplished once for all 'by one offering' is also effected in us at our initiation which inaugurates the process of 'being sanctified'. We have now, therefore, to give our attention to the description of that initiation which is set forth in 6^{1-6}. Before doing so, however, we must take note of another sense in which the teaching concerning perfection has a 'double' character.

In the Greek language the words which are used to express the ideas of perfecting and perfection have also a nuance of finality. For the basic word in this group of expressions is *telos* which means 'end'. Perfection, therefore, consists in reaching the desired end or goal.[1] The Christian religion is 'final' in the sense that Christ is the 'end' in which the old covenant finds its fulfilment (Romans 10^{4}). Moreover, because Jesus is the perfect man he is also the end or goal in which alone we can find our fulfilment. Nevertheless his perfect humanity was manifested in being made perfect, that process of finding 'completion in God' which we described as a 'perfection of dependence'. We, then, are to find our true 'end' in our identification with him in this perfection of dependence. For the full understanding of the teaching in Hebrews 6, however, we must take note of one more point. A familiar text in 12^{2} tells us that Jesus is the 'author and finisher' of our faith. Here are two of the author's key-words. Our Lord is both 'inaugurator and perfecter' of our salvation. This, once more, corresponds to the Pauline thesis in Colossians (1^{15-20}), where Christ is shewn to be 'the Beginning' of both creations, but also the End; for 'all things were created through him and unto him'. In Ephesians 1^{10} this version of the Alpha and Omega doctrine[2] is explained to mean that all things are to be 'summed up' in Christ.

The doctrine that Christ is 'the beginning and the end' seems to

[1] And in this sense the redeemed in heavenly bliss are said to have been perfected (Heb. 12^{23}).

[2] Rev. 22^{13}; cp. $1^{8, 17}$.

have influenced the form of words in which the author of Hebrews 6[1 ff.] opens his exhortation. He is about to warn his readers concerning their danger of falling away from Christ in open apostasy. He thinks that they have remained stationary or perhaps relapsed to a rudimentary level. Surely they do not need to be taught again the elementary truths learnt in their preparation for baptism! So he says: 'Let us leave behind the discourse concerning the beginning of the Christ and let us press on to the perfection which is our goal.' 'The beginning of the Christ' seems to mean the ABC of the Christian religion. But this strange expression might also serve to remind his flock of the time when they received a new beginning from him who is 'the Beginning'. In him they began to be what God always wanted them to be; and if they will press on they will be brought eventually to their true end in him. There is then set forth a list of six points which exemplify the ABC or elementary features of Christian belief and practice, things that had already been learnt at the beginning of the Christian life. Repentance and faith are the fundamental dispositions which are presupposed. Without them an adult candidate could not go forward to baptism. Similarly, the Christian life will attain its goal when in our resurrection bodies we stand before the judgement seat of Christ.

It is possible that the expression 'eternal judgement' points forward to the warning about to be given concerning the danger of apostasy. Otherwise the statement might have anticipated the final clauses of the later creed concerning resurrection and 'eternal life'. In any case the writer is clearly matching the two dispositions which belong to 'the beginning' with two statements concerning 'the end' toward which we are to 'press on'. This excellent rendering of the main verb in verse 1, vivid as it is, does not convey the possible echo of the same word in its earlier occurrence. The short prologue to the epistle speaks of the incarnate Lord as 'bearing all things along by the word of his power' (1[3]). But we are among the 'all things' so mentioned. 'Let us, therefore', says the author, 'be likewise borne along to the perfection which is our goal' (6[1]). If there is such a verbal connexion as I have here indicated,[1] then the thought is that 'the presence of the eternal Son' is the power which can and will bear us along from the beginning of the Christian life to its end, from the catechumenate to final judgement. His presence throughout that earthly course is, however, effectually indicated by the two terms which occupy the middle of the six-fold statement concerning the rudiments of Christianity.[2]

So we come to 'baptisms[3] and the laying on of hands'. The author is clearly referring to something familiar and customary in the church which he is addressing. The laying on of hands, like Christian baptism, belongs to the rudimentary elements of Christian practice for him, as for his readers. In short, this statement strengthens immensely the conclusions reached in chapter III concerning the laying on of hands in Acts 8 and 19. For the two authors concerned the reference is to the 'completion' of Christian initiation in the form in which it was familiar to them. As we shall see presently, there is also agreement between them in respect of the nature of the gift conveyed in that 'completion'. But first of all we must finish our survey of the six-point statement concerning elementals. It was hinted at the conclusion of the last paragraph that the two middle terms of that statement had a Christological significance. The language about 'beginning and end' with which this exhortation opens in 6[1] (it has been pointed out) introduces a statement covering the whole of the Christian life. In that statement the two middle terms, baptism and the laying on of hands, might be said to bridge the gulf between the dispositions of the catechumen and 'the last things', the two topics which are here set on either side of Christian initiation.

At this point we must take note of the fact that the two middle terms are bound together by the word 'teaching'. The emphasis lies not so much upon what is done, but rather upon what is signified by the facts of Christian initiation. Moreover, as we

[1] Suggested by Nairne in *The Epistle of Priesthood*, p. 334.

[2] I agree with Moffatt (ICC. *ad loc.*, p. 75) in thinking that, whichever reading we adopt in 6[2], 'it makes no difference to the sense'.

[3] The plural is adequately explained by Moffatt, *ad loc.*

consider what that teaching must have been we can confidently assume that it looks both backwards and forwards. There is a sense in which baptism looks back, not only to the beginning of the new creation in the Incarnation, but even further still to that creative act of God in which the deity bestowed something of himself upon his human family when he stamped his own image upon our human nature. That was the original 'enlightenment' of mankind when the uncreated Light of the world shone forth and bathed the created image in bright beams of gracious influences. Small wonder then that those in whom the Creator's handiwork was restored by baptism into the Christ were already coming to be known as 'the enlightened ones'; moreover, they are actually so designated in the ensuing description of the initiated which begins at verse 4. By the path of repentance and faith they returned to the Beginning in which they were created, that is to God's only Son. In him also they tasted 'the heavenly gift' which might be regarded as the rare and precious fruit of paradise regained.

We have now begun to interpret the 'teaching' concerning baptisms and laying on of hands by means of the explicit statement which follows in verses 4 and 5; and we have reached the point where baptismal 'enlightenment' is also interpreted in terms of 'refreshment'. This was a familiar biblical idiom of speech as we may see by turning to the Old Testament. In 1 Samuel 14^{29} Jonathan says to the people of Saul's victorious army, who were faint from lack of food: 'See how mine eyes have been enlightened, because I tasted a little of this honey.' The idiom is repeated in Psalm 34^{8} with the invitation: 'O taste and see that the Lord is good'; and this phrase is applied directly to baptismal initiation in 1 Peter 2^{3} where Christian neophytes are addressed as 'new-born babes' who are assumed to have 'tasted that the Lord is gracious'.[1] In the light of these facts we can say with a high degree of certainty that enlightenment and tasting of 'the

[1] The connexion of enlightenment with *honey* in Jonathan's words may well have a bearing upon the early Christian practice of feeding 'milk and honey' to the neophytes at first communion, the *milk* appearing appropriately in the exhortation of 1 Peter 2^{2}.

heavenly gift' together form a single statement in verse 4. Secondly, we may also conclude that this double description refers to the Christian version of 'baptisms' which preceded 'the laying on of hands'. Similarly it will be natural to see a reference to the second part of the baptismal mystery in the following phrase which runs thus: 'having become partakers of the Holy Spirit.' Since Acts and Hebrews appear to agree about the outward form in which the baptismal mystery is completed, it is reasonable to suppose that they also have the same teaching concerning the gift conveyed.

If the above analysis is approximately correct, it will mean that the authors of Acts and Hebrews have the same pattern of initiation, not only with regard to outward form, but also in their conception of the theological sequence involved. In both the gift of the Spirit is *in some sense* reserved to the second stage. As we have found distinct traces of this conception elsewhere in the New Testament it becomes a matter of first importance to consider its theological rationale, and that too in relation to Christian doctrine as a whole. To that task the final sections of this chapter will be devoted. Meanwhile there remains one further clause to be considered in our analysis of Hebrews 6^{1-5}. It is this: 'And have tasted God's good word and powers of the age to come.' At first sight the opening words look like a repetition of the previous expression concerning 'tasting'. In the clause as a whole, however, something new is added. 'Powers of the age to come' looks forward to the future, whereas 'have tasted the heavenly gift' suggests a present experience. But, more exactly, the original 'tasting' is here associated with baptism whereas the final utterance refers to an experience which followed the laying on of hands and which may therefore be most probably connected with the first communion.

There are, however, two distinct considerations to be weighed at this point before we pass on. In the first place, it is already clear that, if baptism refers back to 'the beginning' in more senses than one, the latter part of this description in verses 4 and 5 looks forward rather than backward. Jesus received the Spirit's endowment for fulfilment of vocation, and so do we. But further, 'the age to come' here, as elsewhere in the New Testament, is both present and future. We stand within its forecourts and have already begun to taste its fruits, yet only as an earnest of greater things yet to be. Its 'powers' are already at work in us with a view to our 'perfecting'. The laying on of hands equips us to go forward into that fulness which is still future, a fulness of which, nevertheless, every eucharist provides a foretaste. The second consideration refers to the repetition of the language about 'tasting'. It is possible that this peculiarity provides another example of that mutual penetration or reciprocity between the parts of the baptismal whole concerning which a good deal has been said in earlier chapters. To this we shall have to return. For the present it is sufficient to point out that 'enlightenment' is not a mere phase which passes. Clearly all that baptism conveys is carried on to higher stages in confirmation and in the communicant life.

V

A RESUMÉ OF EVIDENCE. WHY IS THE BESTOWAL OF THE HOLY SPIRIT RESERVED TO THE SECOND STAGE OF INITIATION? THE ANALOGY INCLUDES CONTRAST BETWEEN THE CREATOR-REDEEMER AND CREATURES REDEEMED FROM SIN. IN BAPTISM—UNLIKE THE SAVIOUR—WE WERE PREPARED FOR THE SPIRIT'S INDWELLING BY A RADICAL REVERSAL OF OUR CONDITION. IN HIS BAPTISMAL FUNCTION THE PARACLETE GLORIFIES THE CHRIST. BAPTISM, LIKE THE GOSPEL HISTORY, IS CHRISTOLOGICAL; AND REGENERATION CORRESPONDS TO THE NEW BIRTH OF THE ENTIRE MESSIANIC ORGANISM ON EASTER-DAY.

The meaning of confirmation has, in this inquiry, gradually emerged through attention to a whole series of biblical images, some of which have more than one possible application.[1] In the present chapter special attention has been given to a conception of confirmation as the 'completion' of baptism, the patristic statement of this notion in terms of 'perfecting' being traced back to biblical roots, especially in the Epistle to the Hebrews. In the

[1] This is notably true of Gen. $2^{6, 7}$, in connection with I Cor. 12^{13}; e.g. above ch. V, § iii, par. 3.

result the 'perfecting' of Christians is seen to extend backwards into the entire Christ-mystery; and yet is also seen to have its sacramental completion in that bestowal of the Spirit which in Acts is explicitly connected with the laying on of hands. We have found that explicit connexion to be indirectly supported by other evidence in the New Testament. Most notable in this respect are two factors which stand out. First of all there is the emphasis sometimes laid upon 'sealing' or 'anointing', neither of which is ever identified with the laver of baptism, whereas 'sealing' sometimes suggests a *concluding* ceremony,[1] and anointing is connected implicitly with a gift of the Spirit. The last point links up with a second factor in the evidence, to which we have now to give our attention, namely the recurrence of the conception that the specific endowment of the neophyte with the gift of the Holy Spirit belongs to a second stage in initiation.

This tendency to connect the Holy Spirit with the second part of the baptismal whole is unmistakeably present in the writings of three New Testament authors, namely St Paul and the writers of Acts and Hebrews. If the two last mentioned belonged in certain respects to the same church circles, and also were probably acquainted with St Paul's thought, yet they also show a marked independence in other respects. Moreover, we have also found a noticeable difference between St Paul and the author of Acts in the respective estimates which they present with regard to the value attaching to ecstatic phenomena in the Christian life. The total silence of the Pauline epistles concerning the laying on of hands is another indication of mutual independence. These differences make unanimity on the question at issue all the more striking. Moreover, at this point the evidence of 1 John becomes corroborative when weighed in the light of the biblical background as a whole. If, however, this evidence is to prove acceptable and intelligible to the Christian consciousness, some attempt must be made to show its theological harmony both with scripture as a whole and with Christian doctrine. A prolonged epoch of histori-

[1] As in Rom. 4. The synopsis of Contents will indicate the passages briefly summarized in this paragraph and the next.

cal research and literary analysis has thus far failed to grapple with this task. Let us now try to face it.

The fundamental point at issue must first be defined more exactly. In our survey of the analogy between Christ and the Christian it was made clear that in either case there were two operations of the Spirit, the former referring to *being* and the latter to *mission*. This is not now in question. It is here assumed that the Holy Spirit is the creative agent of all that is effected in baptism. It is, moreover, assumed that by incorporation into Christ we enter an organism which has been anointed with the full messianic endowment of the Spirit's gifts. Granted that all this is true, how comes it that an 'indwelling' of the Spirit or an entry of the Spirit 'into the heart' appears to be reserved to a second stage of initiation? The answer to this question which is here to be undertaken will send us back once more to some aspects of the analogy between Christ and the Christian; and further, the solution offered will be found to depend upon considerations drawn from the Christian revelation as a whole. Our starting-point has already been indicated in a previous statement that 'between the Christ and his Church there is contrast as well as identification'.[1] The analogy is drawn between God incarnate and redeemed sinners, between him who is both Whole and Head and those who are his parts and members.

It will be remembered that we found reason for supposing that in his first picture of Christ's Body in 1 Corinthians 12 St Paul had in mind the parallel with Adam's creation. In that connexion it will be convenient to repeat the contrast between the two Adams as stated in an earlier chapter:[2] 'The earthy form of Adam was moulded to the heavenly image, whereas the eternal Son of God *is* that heavenly image in his divine person. In him, therefore, the uncreated image entered the Adamic form that he might mould that form to his own creative purpose. By entering it he re-created it. In him the image and likeness were always flawless,

[1] Ch. V, § iv, par. 7. Cp. also ch. IV, § v, pars. 4, 5, from which a quotation follows here in the next paragraph of the text.

[2] See last note.

and therefore perfection belonged to every stage of the developing process.' In the new creation, we may say, Adam and his Creator are one person! Whether St Luke had this thought in mind in his pictures of the holy childhood we cannot tell.[1] What is assuredly true is that the thought in question provides an adequate clue to the Lucan picture of perfect humanity developing perfectly. Moreover the dependence of that development throughout upon the grace of God corresponds to all that has been said in this chapter and previously concerning the true relation of our humanity to the Holy Spirit.[2]

It follows from such an estimate that in the incarnate life continuity was at a maximum as between the two donations of the Spirit. The descent of the Dove after the baptism was not so much a bestowal of new gifts as a re-endowment for a new purpose. By that very fact it manifested the truth that the Holy Spirit is bestowed by the Father for the fulfilment of a particular vocation, a truth which is exemplified in ordination as well as in confirmation. From another point of view, however, it is vitally necessary to recognize the contrast which obtains between the person of the Redeemer and the sinners whom he has redeemed, when we try to envisage their respective relations to the gracious activity of the Holy Spirit. We cannot too strongly stress the analogy between the incarnation of God the Son and the baptism of each Christian neophyte, provided that we also stress with equal emphasis the contrast between the entry of the sinless Redeemer into our flesh and the entry of fallen sinners into his spotless Body. In his entry there was inaugurated a new creation, whereas our admission to that new creation is primarily a radical reversal of our previous fallen condition. He was the Creator renewing his own plan of creation in a yet more intimate fashion, whereas in us the ruin of the original plan was now being reversed!

The contrast which has just been stated may also be regarded

[1] St John seems to be thinking along these lines in the 'Adam' parallels of his Easter story (John 20^{14-23}). See above, ch. V, § iv, par. 1 and note.

[2] The whole of ch. V, § ii is here relevant, and also, in the present chapter, § iii, pars. 2–5.

from yet another angle. In the incarnate life the original creative act of the Spirit set in motion a flawless development of sinless humanity which led inevitably to the baptism and the consequent descent of the Dove. The ordeal of suffering and death followed later. With us the situation is reversed. The moment of our entry into the new creation is also the moment of our identification with the death of Christ. For we must be prepared for the descent of the Dove by a radical reversal of our whole condition. So in baptism we died to the old life of fallen self-love and buried its corpse in the Easter tomb. This was the negative side of our incorporation. In the alternative Pauline image we were the wild branches grafted into the good olive-tree; so that there then began a process of transformation by which the old wild characteristics were removed or overcome by the rich quality of the new life. In all of this the Holy Spirit is the agent. Why then is the Spirit never mentioned in the argument of Romans between 5^5 and 8^2? The whole of that long statement is concerned with our relationship to the person of the Christ and to his redeeming acts. As late as 7^4 we are still preoccupied with a death to the law 'through the body of the Christ'.[1]

Perhaps this silence or reserve in Pauline statements concerning the relation of the Holy Spirit to baptism may be fruitfully compared with a corresponding statement concerning the Paraclete in the Johannine discourse of the upper room:

When he, the Spirit of the truth, is come, he will guide you into all the truth;
for he shall not speak from himself, but whatsoever he shall hear he shall speak,
and he will show you the things that are to come.
He shall glorify me; for he shall take of mine, and shall declare it to you.
All things that the Father hath are mine;
Therefore said I that he taketh of mine and shall declare it to you (John 16^{13-15}).

In 14^6 Jesus says: 'I am the way and the truth and the life'; and this

[1] Even the interlude of $7^{7\,ff.}$ continues this theme, as appears (*a*) from the echo of Gal. 2^{20} in the phrase: 'no longer I', and (*b*) in the thanksgiving 'through Jesus Christ our Lord' (7^{25}).

saying gives a Christological turn to the first line of our quotation; The Spirit of the Christ will show us the way into the Christ in his wholeness. Moreover that wholeness is also 'the way' and 'the life'. So when we enter the Christ and share his life the Spirit leads us in and reveals to us all the treasures of this new sphere of existence. The witness of the two apostolic writers agrees. The function of the Spirit is fundamentally Christological; and to this the theology of baptism corresponds.

Nevertheless our Johannine quotation does *not* say that the Spirit will be silent concerning himself. In Romans 8, for example, and in the Acts of the Apostles he speaks of himself very fully through his inspired agents. At this point we shall find valuable guidance in the technical language of the developed doctrine of the Trinity. There is a 'coinherence' of the divine Persons, so that all three co-operate in the divine activities towards the creaturely world. Yet there is also an 'appropriation' of particular activities to particular Persons. The four gospels record the 'appropriation' of redemption to the Person of the incarnate Son. 'The Spirit was not yet, for Jesus was not yet glorified' (John 7^{39}). Moreover the gospel history was, from one point of view, the first part of the initiation of the original disciples. They were not ready or able to receive the indwelling of the Spirit until they had been eye-witnesses of the saving events of death, burial and resurrection. Only the risen Christ could complete the moulding process of the new creation by breathing upon them the Breath of God (John 20^{22}). This Johannine incident suggests a close continuity between the Christ history and the Spirit history which are divided into two Lucan volumes. 'Appropriation' is consistent with 'Coinherence'.

In a previous reference to this Johannine feature of the Easter story I remarked that here 'the ministerial commission is enfolded within a new creation act which extends the risen life of Jesus to his people' (chapter V, § IV, first paragraph). Elsewhere I wrote: 'In the gospel story we see the messianic organism, together with its human organs, passing through stages of growth and of testing. Integration is attained only at the point where the organs are finally enabled to represent functionally the maturity of that sacred whole to which they belong. This maturity (of the parts, as of the whole) was attained only through death and resurrection.'[1] This repetition of the creation story (Genesis 2^{7}) foreshadowed in its new communal form by prophecy (Ezekiel $37^{9\text{ ff.}}$) represents a new birth of that organism which is both the Israel of God and a 'new creation' whole wherein the priestly function of Adam is restored. The patristic suggestion that this event was the baptism of the church was, therefore, pertinent. The church entered the risen life as Christ's Body with its organs fully equipped. Easter Day constituted a new birth of 'the whole Christ', head and members, in the organic unity and in the functional structure which are proper to the entire messianic *mysterion*. The completion of this picture of contrast within the analogy must be reserved to a new section.

VI

NT WRITERS SHOW THE PRESENCE OF THE HOLY SPIRIT ALIKE IN THOSE EVENTS WHICH COMPRISE THE ONE MYSTERY OF REDEMPTION AND IN THAT PROCESS OF INITIATION THROUGH WHICH BOTH THE CHURCH AND THE INDIVIDUAL HAVE PASSED. WE CAME THROUGH EASTER TO OUR PENTECOST; AND WE ARE IN THE SPIRIT THAT HE MAY BE IN US. ST LUKE SHOWS A SINGLE CHRIST-MYSTERY IN MOVEMENT TO ITS COMPLETION (FROM THE HEAD THROUGH THE BODY TO THE MEMBERS). AS THE SPIRIT IN THE CHURCH IS COMPLEMENTARY TO THE CHRIST, SO IS CONFIRMATION THE COMPLEMENT OF BAPTISM.

The Johannine account of the Lord's death and resurrection appears, by a typical play on words, to intimate a connexion of the Spirit with the death of the Redeemer (19^{30}) before proceeding to associate the Spirit also with the risen life in the manner indicated above. As I wrote elsewhere, when 'the head was bowed in death, the Head of the Church inclined towards the mother and the disciple standing beneath him. Thus with his last breath he breathed down upon them the Breath of God'.[2] The second

[1] *The Apostolic Ministry*, p. 100, note 1.

[2] For details see *The Apostolic Ministry*, pp. 98 ff.

clause of Genesis 2^7 is operative here as well as at 20^{22}. In this symbolic effect we are reminded that 'the gospel history, like the baptismal mystery, presents unity embracing a series of events'.[1] Indeed, in this part of the fourth gospel there seems to be a suggestion that death, burial, resurrection, ascension and the gift of the Spirit form a series so inseparable that they all belong together in a single mystery of redemption. This dominance of the 'unity in plurality' principle would also justify a method of employing the original creation story which no longer seeks to preserve the chronological sequence of its parts.[2] A symbolic simultaneity is made to represent the oneness and wholeness of that Christ-mystery which includes history within itself. This corresponds remarkably to the Pauline conception of the neophyte's identification with Christ's death, burial and resurrection in a single moment of time.

Thus once more we return to a parallel with which this chapter began, and which was later elaborated into fourfold form. It is as though scripture itself is so shaped as to warn us against a merely chronological conception of either the creed or the sacraments. We have just seen, moreover, in the Johannine symbolism, an emphatic affirmation of unity between the Holy Spirit and the Christ at each stage in the crucial events from Good-Friday to Easter. Similarly the Pauline teaching connects the Holy Spirit with the Christological sequence of those events which are mysteriously comprised within the baptismal mystery.[3] With this aptly agrees the Johannine teaching in the discourse with Nicodemus. For there 'water and Spirit' are conjoined as closely as language would permit (3^5); and the whole statement is set between 'the temple of the body' and the uplifted Son of man. Once more, if in Galatians 4^{4-6} the 'adoption of sons' precedes the entry of the Spirit into the heart, we also find in Romans 8^{23}

[1] Quoted from the summary at the head of ch. V, § i; and for what follows cp., in the present chapter, § ii, par. 6.

[2] The second clause of Gen. 2^7 is the climax of that story. But in John 19^{30} and 20^{22}, as interpreted above, the divine inbreathing is referred to two distinct events.

[3] By comparison of Gal. $3^{2\ ff.}$, 1 Cor. 12^{13}, Rom. 5^5 and 6.

another aspect of truth. For here those who have 'the firstfruits of the Spirit' are still waiting for their adopted sonship to be brought to fulfilment. If, then, the Spirit is present alike in the events of our redemption and in the whole process of Christian initiation we have still to consider the relation of this truth to the remaining part of the fourfold parallel. What further light may we gain, in particular, from considering the complex of Christian initiation in its relation to the Body of Christ?

In the preceding argument a parallel has been suggested between the initiation of the Church and the initiation of individual Christians. The parallel would imply that a first stage in the initiation of the disciples was concluded upon Easter Day, but further that the true 'completion' took place upon the first Whitsunday. On this view Christian baptism is for the neophyte his entry into the new birth of the world through death and resurrection, whereas confirmation constitutes his participation in the pentecostal gift of the Spirit. This conclusion completes a further strand in the complex pattern of connexions between the Gospel and the Church, as will perhaps become clearer if the reader at this point glances back to the sequence of thought in chapter V, § I. It is significant that in Luke-Acts the second volume opens with a discourse of the risen Lord, thus securing continuity between the treatise 'appropriated' to the Christ, and its sequel which is clearly 'appropriated' to the Holy Spirit. So also the treatment of confirmation in the present work depends not only upon the conception of the baptismal mystery as a single whole, but also and equally upon that other form of 'unity in plurality' which may be called the Christ-mystery or 'the whole Christ' wherein Jesus and his church form one organism sharing one life.

The question is sometimes asked, whether the Holy Spirit begins to dwell in a person at baptism, or whether this particular imagery should more properly be confined to confirmation.[1] A careful study of the apostolic writings should make for caution in deciding this particular issue. Here are some relevant facts:

[1] Cp. Darwell Stone, *Holy Baptism* (3rd ed. 1901), ch. V and notes, where it is shewn that the patristic statements on this point are very diverse.

Generally speaking St Paul seems to regard the church as the temple of the Holy Spirit, rather than the individual.[1] Even in 1 Corinthians $6^{19, 20}$, in addressing a congregation, the apostle refers to 'your body' in the singular in contrast to the individual body of the sinner in verse 18. Here, as in Romans 8^{23}, he seems to think of Christians as sharing one body in Christ. If, then, we take the view that the Spirit dwells in the temple of Christ's Body, that is in 'the whole Christ', it will seem to follow that through membership of the Body we enter at baptism into a Spirit-dwelt sphere. We are now, at least 'in the Spirit' (Ephesians $2^{21, 22}$). From the moment of baptism we are surrounded by the Spirit's influences and activities. Moreover, we are now actually members of that organism which was anointed with the Spirit on Jordan's bank. Our new life is drawn from the Spirit and moulded by the Spirit. Yet there is a further stage of yet greater intimacy.

As we have seen, in Galatians 4^{4-6} the apostle writes as though at a second stage in our initiation 'God sent forth the Spirit of his Son into our hearts, crying, Abba Father'. This phraseology is repeated in Romans 8^{15} in the course of a much fuller statement concerning the Holy Spirit in the church. Now the main argument of Romans 3–8 has every appearance of being an expansion of Galatians 3^{23}–4^{7}. If this is so, the echo of Galatians 4^{6} in Romans 8 could be taken to mean that here also the exposition has reached a point corresponding to the second stage of initiation. If this is allowed it will follow that the marked emphasis upon the indwelling of the Spirit in Romans 8^{9-11} refers to confirmed Christians. It may be pointed out that in verse 9 the expression 'if anyone hath not the Spirit of Christ' suggests that the writer is thinking of an individual indwelling which would correspond to 'sent forth into your hearts' in Galatians 4^{6}. It must, however, be remembered that the first Christians did not commonly make sharp distinctions between the parts of initiation as we western Christians of a later date inevitably tend to do. We cannot therefore dogmatize with precision about their nomenclature in such a matter.

[1] 1 Cor. $3^{16, 17}$, 2 Cor. 6^{16}.

One thing, at least, can surely be said about this Pauline teaching. The Epistle to the Romans is addressed to fully initiated Christians in whom the baptismal mystery had been completed. In his exposition of what that mystery meant the apostle's thought passes quite naturally from the doctrine of the new beginning inaugurated by a Second Adam reversing the fall, through the facts of death and resurrection and their consequences, to the new life in the Spirit. In following this sequence he is rehearsing the events of our redemption from the incarnation to the pentecostal gift, and identifying his readers explicitly with each stage of the redemptive history so rehearsed. With this we may profitably compare the plan of 'Luke-Acts'. In the transition from his first to his second volume this evangelist is as much concerned as St John to exhibit a mysterious unity in the sequence of redemptive events. This interlocking of mysteries is equally noticeable in Luke 24 and in Acts 1 and 2. Moreover in both parts of the story there is an extended initiation of the disciples by the risen Lord, the fruits of which are seen in St Peter's proclamation after the initiation has been completed at Pentecost. St Luke then, like his fellow-evangelist, exhibits the unity of the Christ-organism by identifying the initiation of the church with the actual mysteries of our redemption.

In the Acts of the Apostles, however, the evangelist carries through this identification to a further epochal point. He first completes the gospel story by showing that the final stage of the redemptive history is also the final stage of the church's initiation. Having thus traced out the manner in which the dispensation of the Spirit was inaugurated he proceeds to an account of that dispensation in which it is made clear that the completion of the church's initiation at Pentecost is repeated seriatim in the initiation of individual Christians. The manner in which this plan is carried out in Acts has been sufficiently indicated in chapter III, especially in § IV.[1] On the background of the New Testament as a whole this 'plan' contributes notably to the pattern which we are now building

[1] And also in Additional Note B. What follows may be further illustrated by reference to *The Common Life*, pp. 82–105.

up, and that in more ways than one. In the first place it is made clear that at Pentecost the body of disciples became effectually the complement of the Christ in the messianic organism as a whole. A company of persons previously weak and ineffective had now become the living counterpart of the ascended Lord, understanding his mission to the world and entering into it as his representatives and agents. This extension of the Mission, however, is not confined to the apostles. For there is a repetition of Pentecost in every completed initiation of converts. The movement of completion passes from the ascended Head through the body to the members.

In this form of words we are interpreting the main theme of the Acts by reference to the image-thinking which is characteristic of the Epistle to the Ephesians, and notably perhaps to the statement which occurs in chapter 4 (verses 7–16). At this point we may take note of the fact that, whereas in the last section we were mainly occupied with the contrast between Christ and his members, we have in the present section returned to the positive aspect of the analogy. There is a sense in which the theme of Ephesians brings these two aspects together by a paradoxical volte-face. For here God incarnate finds his 'complement' in a world of redeemed sinners. As he was humiliated for our salvation, so he was exalted for our 'perfecting'; and our perfecting is *his* perfecting.[1] For he and we are one organism. The contrast between him and us was bridged by death and resurrection. So our baptism was both our humiliation and our exaltation, the cancelling of what we were that we might be wholly his. For what he is in his ascended glory needs us for his completion! In the Gospel the Spirit 'was not yet' in order that by the outpouring of the Spirit the treasures of the ascended Lord might be ours in the church.

He became poor that we by his poverty might be made rich (2 Corinthians 8[9]). There is a sense in which we are *in baptism* identified with his poverty in order that *in confirmation* we may be dowered with his riches. Paradoxical language of this kind is

[1] This is actually expressed by two different words in Eph. 4[12, 13], where 'the perfecting of the saints' has for its goal the fulfilment of the whole Christ. Our 'perfecting' is indispensable to the fulness in which he is perfected.

evoked by the strange modern notion that a 'completion' of baptism in confirmation is derogatory to baptism. We might just as well say that the Spirit-history in the Acts is derogatory to the Christ-history in the Gospels! This is the unwholesome idea of completeness which we found to be flatly contradictory to the perfection of the triune life in God.[1] As the Persons of the Godhead are complementary to one another, so the dispensation of the Spirit is complementary to the work of the Redeemer. So also our identification with the Christ in his life-story through baptism is crowned by *his* bestowal of the Spirit in confirmation. The notion which isolates the laver of baptism in a self-completing circle of its own runs counter not only to the evidence for two stages of initiation, but also to every other aspect of 'unity in plurality' surveyed in the present work. The whole plan of St Luke's two volumes is a case in point. How often has it not been pointed out that 'the things which Jesus began to do and to teach' during his life on earth (Acts 1[1]) were continued through his church as recorded in the second volume!

VII

A CONTINUITY OF LANGUAGE IN SCRIPTURE SUGGESTS A DESCENT OF THE SPIRIT UPON THE HEAD; AND TO THIS CORRESPONDS THE RITE OF CONFIRMATION. SO TOO THE INTERIOR CONNEXION OF THE MESSIANIC ANOINTING WITH A SACRIFICIAL VOCATION EXTENDS THROUGH THE CHURCH TO EVERY INITIATE WITH SOCIOLOGICAL IMPLICATIONS WHICH ARE CHRISTO-CENTRIC. THESE ARE REALIZED *IN MYSTERIO* AT EVERY EUCHARIST. BAPTISM AND CONFIRMATION CORRESPOND RESPECTIVELY TO TWO ASPECTS OF CHRIST'S BODY, THE ONE LIFE AND THE MANY GIFTS. SCRIPTURAL INDICATIONS OF THE END TOWARDS WHICH THE SPIRIT-FILLED BODY IS BEING LED.

Let us now, in conclusion, seek to define more precisely what is signified by the bestowal of the Spirit in the completion of baptism. Confirmation corresponds to the pentecostal outpouring upon the church as that in turn corresponded to the anointing of the Christ. It is, moreover, worthy of notice that in the biblical

[1] See, in the present chapter, § iii, par. 4.

descriptions of this series there is observable a certain continuity of language. In the messianic prophecy of Isaiah 11 it is said that 'the Spirit of the Lord shall *rest upon him*'. So also in Luke 3^{22} we read that 'the Holy Spirit *descended upon him* in bodily form as a dove'. Again in Acts 2^{3} we have: 'there appeared unto them tongues as of fire, distributing themselves among them;[1] and *it sat upon each of them.*' The series continues in Acts 8^{16}, where in the prelude to the laying on of hands it is said that the Holy Spirit 'had not yet *fallen upon* any of them'. Finally in 19^{6} we find: 'When Paul laid his hands upon them the Holy Spirit *came upon them.*' In this sequence there is a continuity of imagery suggesting a descent of the Spirit on to the head. So also the sealing of the new Israel in Revelation 7 is effected upon the forehead. Moreover these indications correspond to the physical actions in the rite of confirmation under the various forms which that rite has assumed in history.

Such details suggest an actual continuity which goes beyond mere outward expression, a continuity which goes back to the fulfilment of messianic prophecy at our Lord's anointing. This anointing is explicitly referred to by St Peter in Acts 10^{38} as the starting-point of our Lord's ministry, as though it were an important feature of the apostolic proclamation. Its relevance to that proclamation would be greatly enhanced if the same anointing were extended to the church at Pentecost and renewed at every confirmation. This would mean that, as Jesus accepted the Servant's vocation in his baptism and was equipped for it by his anointing, so it was also with the church, identified with the crucified and risen Messiah,[2] and anointed with the gift of his Spirit at Pentecost with a view to a sharing in his vocation. Once more, it would mean that in every baptism the candidate is identified with the Lord's acceptance of a sacrificial destiny; for, as we have said, he is there identified with our Saviour's voluntary

[1] So RV margin, preserving a verbal connexion with the Greek text of Col. 1^{12} and Heb. 2^{4}, in accord with the thesis of 1 Cor. $12^{4\ ff.}$ concerning 'apportionings', for which see above, ch. V, § iii, pars. 5 ff., where the trinitarian background was in evidence.

[2] In the sense defined in the final quotation in § v above (from my essay in *The Apostolic Ministry*).

self-impoverishment. So finally, when he is enriched with that messianic treasure which we call 'the sevenfold gift of the Spirit' this seals him for sacrifice. Confirmation endows him with the fulness of that 'grace which corresponds to the image of God', now once more restored in accordance with the plan of creation. By this means he is enabled to fulfil his part in the high-priestly destiny of the new Adam.

The manner in which the individual vocation is thus fulfilled has already been indicated in the later sections of chapter V. In those sections there was implied a whole doctrine of Christian sociology which, if it were realized, would provide the necessary solution to the characteristic problems of our present civilization. There has, indeed, during the past century been a considerable return to the distinctively social aspects of sacramental theology which are implicit in the New Testament; and it may be regarded as one part of the purpose with which the present work has been written to indicate the important place which confirmation may come to occupy in such a return to biblical conceptions. From the first days of the church the climax of Christian initiation was the first communion of the newly confirmed. The deeper entry of the Spirit into the heart of the neophyte was the gateway into total identification with the ascended Christ in his eternal high-priestly oblation. This crucial event, however, had its setting in the worshipping community of the new Israel, and that too in the most characteristic action of its common life, that is to say, the identification of the community with that one perfect sacrifice of the divine Priest-Victim which fills heaven and earth with its sweet-smelling savour (Ephesians 5²).

In that action each congregation is a microcosm of Christendom as a whole; and in each act of communion the worshippers are united in personal self-committal to that 'perfecting' of vocation which receives its whole form from Christ's victorious sacrifice. For this transforming process their initiation prepared them in two ways. In baptism they entered the divine-human being of the incarnate Lord, whereas in confirmation they were anointed with the Spirit for their share in the fulfilment of his mission. This distinction between the two 'moments' of initiation presupposes a certain contrast between two aspects of Christ's Body which we examined in chapter V, § III. I refer to the contrast between what is common to all the members and what is different for each individual Christian. In baptism we were all alike assimilated to the Christ in the new creation. In each of us there was a renewal of that image in which we were created, that image which belongs to God's Son and which is therefore the same for all. 'God sent forth his Son that we might receive the adoption of sons.' By this act of reception we were made sharers in that one filial nature which is the same for all. Here, then, all our natural human differences are wholly indifferent. We are like so many earth-particles taken into the fabric of the new Adam.

Yet here a new facet of the biblical imagery confronts us. The regenerate life is one; yet its unity involves diversity. Functional differences are vital to organic unity, and this implies a manifold of contrasts. In the apostolic descriptions of Christ's Body the Holy Spirit is pictured as a celestial fluid supplying the one organic life to support the manifold organic functions. For this purpose 'God sent forth the Spirit of his Son into our hearts' at the second stage of our initiation. Here once more the gift is the same for all; yet its application is wholly individual in the true meaning of that word. Each one receives that sevenfold endowment which is characteristically messianic in order that his personality in all its uniqueness may make that particular response to the call of God which was assigned to him by his Creator. Yet the one gift which is the same for all, like the 'apportionings' of land to Israel and like the tongues of fire distributing themselves at Pentecost, is also infinitely varied in its individual application. So diverse indeed are the 'gifts' of the Spirit that his crowning gifts of wisdom and charity are the indispensable bonds by which alone the unity of the Body is preserved.

The goal towards which the Holy Spirit is leading the worshipping community is an ordered harmony which is variously depicted in scripture. Fundamentally it is the manifold unity of a restored creation. But from another point of view it is the 'full-grown' or 'perfect man' of the Ephesian epistle to which every Spirit-endowed Christian makes his indispensable contribution 'according to the measure of the gift of the Christ'. The movement towards this goal is truly corporate precisely because it includes within itself, in principle, a total dedication of each individual to 'perfection of dependence' upon the Spirit of God, a dedication which represents essentially the true life of man according to the plan of creation. In the new creation, however, such dedication takes the sacrificial form which characterizes the whole redemptive process. As the gift of the Spirit in confirmation leads the initiated Christian into the fulness of sacrificial worship, so the entire community of worshippers forms the chosen temple within which the flame of the descending Spirit ever abides upon the whole burnt-offering of the Lamb. Where the Spirit is there is the Christ; and the interchanges within the Spirit-filled Body correspond to that law of complementary relationships which we have traced back to the life of the Blessed Trinity.

APPENDIX

THE SEAL OF THE SPIRIT

The present volume represents, primarily, a particular application of those principles of biblical study with which I have been occupied in previously published works. Such studies, however, are necessarily concerned with a particular situation in current thought; and in the present instance this means a particular book. *The Seal of the Spirit* by G. W. H. Lampe (Longmans, 1951) was briefly reviewed by me in CR, the Quarterly Chronicle of the Community of the Resurrection, June, 1952. There I gave reasons for repudiating the author's method of handling Holy Scripture, and I also drew attention to his misunderstanding of my own position. In so far as the present work has a connexion with current controversy it may be taken to represent, in part at least, my considered reaction to Professor Lampe's book taken as a whole. The fact that my own book is almost wholly occupied with biblical interpretation will serve as an indication that in my opinion the manner in which the scriptural revelation has been treated by the writer in question is the Achilles' heel of his entire position.

When I was nearing the end of my task there reached me, by the kind courtesy of its author, a printed paper entitled *The Sealing at Confirmation* by Fr Joseph Crehan, S.J., of Heythrop College, Chipping Norton, Oxon. This is a reprint from *Theological Studies*, Vol. XIV, No. 2, June, 1953 (Printed in U.S.A.). Fr Crehan, from whose pen came *Early Christian Baptism and the Creed* (London 1950), has followed closely recent 'baptismal' debates amongst Anglicans; and in the paper here referred to he has contributed his own comments upon *The Seal of the Spirit*. These comments provide a welcome reinforcement of my own conclusions, as will be clear from the following summary:

(1) The argument which synchronizes the baptism of Jesus with

the descent of the Spirit in Mark 1^{10} (see above, ch. II, § II, par. 3, and note referring to ch. IV) depends precariously upon assigning a strictly temporal meaning to a favourite Marcan adverb which is often employed without that implication; and *even then* the argument fails to reach its desired con clusion!

(2) The argument from silence, as applied to the laying on of hands in Acts, 'if used in this sweeping fashion, would lead to the conclusion that no apostle did any preaching save Peter and Paul.'

(3) Fr Crehan dissents from the view that in *Adversus hæreses* a reference to the apostolic laying on of hands by St Irenaeus refers to 'exceptional cases', whilst 'the briefer references to baptism in the *Epideixis* are quite indecisive about the parts or moments into which that rite was thought by Irenaeus to be divided'. This is an important consideration to which I shall return.

(4) On the correct text of the initiation prayers in the *Traditio Apostolica* of Hippolytus this authority brings forward important considerations in support of Dix against Lampe. 'The agreement of the Arian fragments with the Ethiopic version of Hippolytus is too remarkable to have been the result of a later deliberate adaptation.' Moreover, the 'liturgical formulæ for the blessing of the chrism and the conferring of the seal in confirmation' preserved in this version correspond precisely to the theological conclusions drawn from scripture in the present volume.

Fr Crehan's observations concerning Irenaeus and Hippolytus help to fill the gap between Justin and Tertullian which occurs in my own argument (above, chapter II). Moreover, whatever form the rites of initiation took in the practice of St Irenaeus, he clearly found no difficulty in accepting St Luke's testimony to the effect that the Holy Spirit was given through the apostolic laying on of hands. Whether he thought of this as a mode of confirmation or not he was certainly not possessed by the notion that the Spirit is given for initiation solely through the waters of baptism. For his treatment of 1 Corinthians 3^2 implies that, although baptized, the Corinthians had not received the Spirit. There is one further point to be noticed in this passage (*Adv. hær.* iv.38, 2; Fr Crehan's references follow Harvey's edition). The Corinthians' non-reception of the Spirit is here compared to Adam's incapacity to receive 'perfection' at the time of his creation. The comparison implies that although newly created in baptism the Corinthians did not then receive a gift of the Spirit which corresponds to 'perfection'. The language of this passage is reminiscent of Hebrews as well as of Acts, (cp. Heb. 5^{11}–6^2), and provides a link between one particular strand of NT teaching and the patristic connexion of 'perfecting' with confirmation from St Cyprian onwards (for which see above, ch. VI, §§ III, IV).

In *The Theology of Confirmation in relation to Baptism* the late Dom Gregory Dix remarked: 'How difficult it is to avoid misreading ancient evidence with modern eyes' (p. 12); and again: 'We only misunderstand really ancient Christian evidence if we try to interpret it by our own post-mediaeval ideas' (p. 14). These two sentences might fairly be taken as symbolizing much modern discussion concerning baptism and confirmation. For we not only tend to think in terms of two separate rites. Sometimes our modernity goes further and seems to lift the whole baptismal mystery out of its original setting, and that in more ways than one. In his discussion of details in the Hippolytan rites of initiation Dix shows by a single concrete example how from such causes misunderstanding may arise. In *The Apostolic Tradition* after the baptism in water there follows an anointing of the neophyte's head by a presbyter with oil previously blessed by the bishop; and this precedes the actual 'sealing' by the bishop. Such a presbyteral form of chrismation, however, was in some later centuries the only 'confirmation' given in the West. But further, though it could be called 'confirmation', it was 'performed by pouring a little chrism upon the head—in other words it is something like a "Baptism by affusion" in chrism'. Finally this part of the initiation was accompanied with the words: I anoint thee with holy oil *in the Name of Jesus Christ*. Upon these facts the following comments are made (*op. cit.*, p. 13). Referring to the formula of invocation just cited, Fr Dix wrote:

> That, as we all know, is a phrase of great significance in connection with 'Baptism' (with matter unspecified) in the New Testament evidence. It also played an unexpectedly large part in the Rebaptism controversy of the third century . . . opponents of Cyprian all insisted that what gave such efficacy as it might have to heretical Baptism was the fact that the recipients had been baptised 'in the Name of Jesus Christ'. It has long puzzled us that these opponents of Cyprian should have attributed such special force to this invocation, when it was virtually certain that neither the African nor the Roman rites contained anything of the kind at Baptism *in water*. I begin to suspect that we may have misunderstood what they were referring to, and with that a number of other points in the controversy.

I venture to think that the paragraph from which that quotation is taken is one of the most important contributions to our subject that has been made throughout the whole course of the modern discussions. Moreover the context brings out clearly the essential point. Christian initiation is a single baptismal mystery; and 'baptismal' language belongs to the whole and not simply to one part of it. We have sufficiently indicated what this means in the text of the present work from the evidence of the New Testament itself. It is, in this connexion, decidedly interesting that in the Introduction to *The Seal of the Spirit* the author makes the following comment upon Wirgman's reply to Mason's book about confirmation: 'He succeeded in demonstrating . . . the important truth that the Fathers had no consistent doctrine on the matter' (p. ix). Elsewhere he not infrequently accuses some of them of 'inconsistency' or 'confusion' of thought, when what in fact they are giving is simply an extension of those ancient modes of thought which are so characteristic of scripture. The modern puzzle concerning baptism 'in the Name of Jesus Christ' referred to by Dix in the above quotation is solved at once as soon as we realize that 'baptism' here stands for a form of chrismation with blessed oil. On the other hand, if we insist upon attributing to the fathers our modern habits of thought, we are certain to misunderstand them.

Perhaps the most important investigation which could at this juncture be undertaken by patristic scholars would take the form of an inquiry concerning the relation between the thought-processes of the fathers and those ancient idioms of thought and speech which can be illustrated from the bible. Such an inquiry would of course be complicated by the uniquely transforming processes which the Gospel introduced. The complex development of the doctrine of the Holy Spirit through such phenomena as 'Spirit-Christology' to later orthodoxy would come in for scrutiny from a new point of view; and we should learn a great deal more about the ways in which divine revelation passes into the mind of the church. We should certainly be saved from that sort of rationalistic criticism which tends to underrate what it has not learnt to understand. In an earlier phase of the 'baptismal' discussion this peculiar psychological problem had not come into view. The fathers were made to speak with mutually contradictory voices according to the presuppositions with which they were approached. The anthropological group of sciences, however, has provided new clues which may help us out of this impasse if we take the trouble to use them.

Such an inquiry would perhaps enable us to see more clearly how Origin could speak of our being baptized in water *and* chrism, and how Tertullian could write enthusiastically about the scriptural connexions of the Holy Spirit with water whilst affirming with equal conviction the bestowal of the Spirit through 'a hand laid upon us'. Above all, if the picture-thinking which is characteristic of scripture persisted in the minds of early Christians, we might find an adequate solution of some puzzling phenomena in their talk about 'the seal'. Professor Lampe thinks that the Pauline language about 'sealing with the Spirit' refers to 'the inward experience of which Baptism is the effective symbol' (*op. cit.*, p. 5). He then gives a very full list of ancient practices and uses bearing upon the 'seal' terminology, a list which does not contain a single example of 'inward experience'. He shows convincingly that *the sealing of a person* would suggest an outward mark applied to the body; and this has an obvious connexion with two biblical practices, namely circumcision and a 'mark' upon the forehead such as we find in Ezekiel 9 and Revelation 7. A corresponding connexion with the water of baptism is by no means equally obvious.

Yet if the water of baptism is the *only* outward fact corresponding to the seal of the Spirit, one would expect some definite indication of this in scripture, whereas we have found the evidence to point elsewhere. How then does it come about that in the course of the following century 'seal' terminology came to be applied to baptism in general or even to the 'water' of baptism in particular? We have already noticed that the earliest examples of such a use occur in literature which is as full of 'Semitic' idioms as scripture itself (ch. III, § I); and this is significant. For it will be remembered that in our analysis of Pauline modes of expression it emerged that the faith of the neophytes could stand for the whole baptismal mystery (ch. I, § II), even though that faith could not be regarded as symbolizing the specifically baptismal act. The possibility, therefore, presents itself that the application of 'seal' imagery to the water of baptism belongs fundamentally to the same group of phenomena. It is noticeable that in the Hippolytan account of initiatory rites there are only two acts in which the neophytes are said to be 'sealed;' and in both cases the act is performed by the bishop. In the former instance the sealing *follows* the exorcism of evil spirits and *precedes* the baptism. In the latter instance which completes the series of initiatory rites we have the counterpart.

The human vessel is first closed against the powers of evil, then baptized into Christ and made partaker in his messianic anointing, and finally sealed as though to enclose the precious gift just received. Thus the transference of ownership from Satan to God is effected; and 'he who has been sealed' (unto the day of redemption) can join himself to the true Israel of God. All that is profoundly scriptural both in its sequence and in its unity. Yet in this formal document each element in the complex whole has its own distinctive character. 'Sealing', first and last, belongs to the bishop who fulfills a part which in scripture is assigned to angels. In that respect the *Traditio Apostolica* is true to its name; and yet the extension of this eschatological 'sealing' to every phase and aspect of the initiatory rites is, from another point of view, equally scriptural in character. For if Christian initiation is a single *mysterion* it corresponds, *as a whole*, to the one *mysterion* which is the Christ (Colossians 2²) and also to that wholeness and unity which is the true destiny of every person created in the divine image. Such restored wholeness, indeed, is an important aspect of salvation as understood in the New Testament.

Borrowing a word coined by J. C. Smuts in *Holism and Evolution* we may say that in the revealed religion of the scriptures there is a 'holistic' tendency which has never ceased to operate in the Christian dispensation, notwithstanding the devastating counter-tendency of evil in all its forms. The extension of the 'seal' terminology from its original scriptural significance to other parts and aspects of the baptismal mystery is one manifestation of this holistic tendency. Moreover, one might perhaps go so far as to say that this extension from the part to the whole is actually implicit in the principal biblical forms of 'seal' imagery. Although the mark of the sealing is localized upon the body of the sealed person, yet the whole person is thereby affected in respect of status. Once more, attention must be drawn to the fact that a dualism which differentiates 'inward experience' from its outward sign as a distinct or separate reality is alien from the typically biblical way of thinking. The sealed person belongs to the deity as his servant and worshipper. Further, the seal indicates that in his attitude of faith and obedience the sealed person is subject to the divine 'good pleasure' (*eudokia*) and thereby rendered secure. The seal is in itself the outward manifestation of this entire situation in all its aspects. This summary description would correspond equally to Abraham as treated in Romans 4 and to the elect of New Israel in the Apocalypse.

The above description also indicates that 'sealing' completes a process which began in the subject's due response of faith. The connexion of 'completion' with sealing, however, occurs in a number of Pauline forms. In 2 Corinthians 1²¹, ²² the gift of the

Spirit 'in our hearts' (cp. Galatians 4^{6}) is the last event in a series. It is the consequence of a sealing, which in turn is preceded by an anointing. Thus the seal secures the *final* effect of a process, just as in the quite different imagery of Romans 15^{28}. The peculiarity of Romans 4 is that the imagery can be understood in two ways. For the sealed person embodies a covenant through the response of his faith to the promises of God. The seal, once more, concludes a process as in the case of a written document. The Mosaic covenant was embodied in a document; but the new covenant follows the earlier precedent. For Jesus, like Abraham, embodied the covenant in his own person; and so the apostle had characteristically extended this idea to the church in earlier epistles. The Corinthian Christians are living witnesses to the genuineness of his claim to be an apostle (1 Corinthians 9^{2}). They are an embodied 'epistle of commendation' written by the Spirit in 'hearts of flesh'. For this is what we may venture to call the 'incarnational' character of 'the new covenant' (2 Corinthians 3^{1-6}).

In Ephesians 5^{26} the imagery of a bridal bath is employed to describe the initiation of the church by her divine bridegroom who 'gave himself up for her to consecrate her by cleansing her in the bath of baptism as she utters her confession' (Moffatt's translation). This statement clearly corresponds to the primitive method of adult baptism which is described in detail in the *Apostolic Tradition* of Hippolytus. The candidate gave a threefold assent to an interrogatory statement of the creed which was divided into three parts. After each credal question and act of assent the candidate was submerged beneath the baptismal waters. Thus the threefold confession of faith was interlaced into the threefold baptismal identification with the Christ so confessed. Such a rite might fitly be described as a dramatic embodiment of the baptismal covenant in a person. Moreover, its Hippolytan form (early in the third century) appears to correspond closely with the form presupposed in the Epistle to the Ephesians. But further, in the Hippolytan form the baptism so described is followed by the rites of anointing and sealing to which we have previously referred. The episcopal sealing comes after two baptismal events, one embodying the candidate's faith and the other anointing him 'in the Name'. If this sequence is compared with Ephesians 1^{13} we find an interesting parallel. The sentence runs thus:

'In whom also having believed ye were sealed with the Holy Spirit of the promise, which is the earnest of our inheritance....'

'Having believed', in the Greek, is a single word in the 'baptismal' aorist tense. It is the word which in Romans 13^{11} stands for the baptismal event (ch. I, § II, referred to in this appendix, above, p. 193). Thus it looks as if in Ephesians 1^{13} the sealing with the Spirit follows after that baptismal act which embodies the candidate's confession of faith. If this were the case the rite presupposed in Ephesians would be even more clearly parallel to that described by Hippolytus. Moreover, it is a characteristic feature of this epistle that it resumes details which have appeared in earlier Pauline epistles. It looks as if Ephesians 1^{13} is such a summary allusion to 2 Corinthians $1^{21, 22}$, where the middle item of the Hippolytan sequence, that is the 'anointing', is in the position in which we should expect to find it on the supposition that the *Traditio Apostolica* is true to its title. This exposition assumes that verse 22 refers to the initiation of both the apostolic missionaries and their converts at Corinth, first because the phrase 'us with you' requires this, and secondly because 'the earnest of the Spirit' belongs to all fully initiated Christians (2 Cor. 5^{5}, Eph. 1^{13}; cp. the synonymous expression in Rom. 8^{23}). Lastly, the three words, 'anointed', 'sealed', 'gave' are baptismal aorists as in Ephesians 1^{13} and 4^{30}, where 'sealing' and 'earnest' refer to the initiation of Gentile converts.

When we add to the above considerations the evidence offered in chapter II for a fourfold pattern of initiation in Justin's *Dialogue* and its connexion with St Paul as well as its correspondence with Tertullian's *de baptismo* we can see how amply justified was an earlier statement of mine that the phraseology of 'the seal', 'the ordinary name for confirmation in the Eastern Church today', has 'an unbroken ancestry reaching back into the New Testament' (*Confirmation To-day*, p. 7). A verbal tradition is not broken either by the silence of some writers or by alternative uses of the word in question. Since the introduction of railways the English word 'train' has referred continuously to traffic drawn by steam-engines, notwithstanding the fact that the word can also refer to a 'train' of thought, or to the 'train' of a wedding dress, or to a military baggage 'train', whatever be its method of locomotion.

INDEX

The numbering of biblical chapters and verses follows RV, except where, in (i) (*a*), a different numeration may be indicated by the letters G(LXX) or H(Hebrew text); a number in brackets is that of LXX. The letters *n* or *nn* indicate the footnotes of this volume.

(i) REFERENCES

(ii) PERSONS

(iii) SUBJECTS